— <u>Kaqnew Station</u> — Radio
transmitting, put Ethiopia
@ the top of US interests
in the HORN & indeed all
of Africa, p. 99.

The Lion of Judah in the
New World

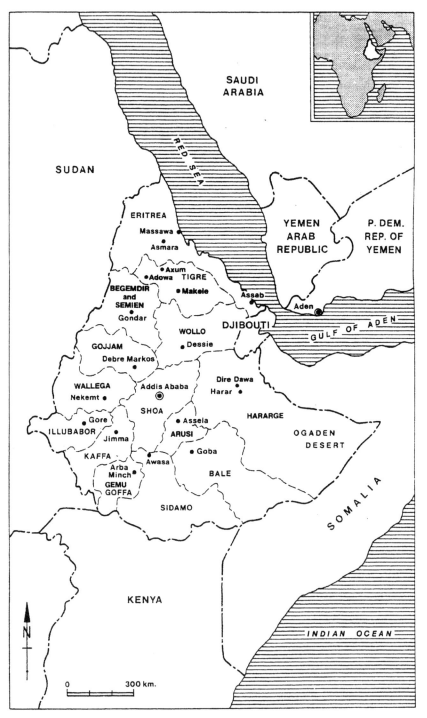

Administrative Divisions of Ethiopia, 1974 (Vestal, *Ethiopia: A Post-Cold War African State*, 1999)

The Lion of Judah in the New World

Emperor Haile Selassie of Ethiopia and the Shaping of Americans' Attitudes toward Africa

THEODORE M. VESTAL

 PRAEGER

AN IMPRINT OF ABC-CLIO, LLC
Santa Barbara, California • Denver, Colorado • Oxford, England

Library of Congress Cataloging-in-Publication Data

Vestal, Theodore M.
   The lion of Judah in the new world : Emperor Haile Selassie of Ethiopia and the shaping of Americans' attitudes toward Africa / Theodore M. Vestal.
       p. cm.
   Includes bibliographical references and index.
   ISBN 978-0-313-38620-6 (hard copy : alk. paper) — ISBN 978-0-313-38621-3 (ebook)   1. Haile Selassie I, Emperor of Ethiopia, 1892–1975—Influence. 2. Haile Selassie I, Emperor of Ethiopia, 1892–1975—Travel—United States. 3. Visits of state—United States—History—20th century.   4. Africa—Foreign public opinion, American.   5. Ethiopia—Relations—United States.   6. United States—Relations—Ethiopia.   7. Public opinion—United States.   I. Title.

   DT387.7.V47   2011
   963'.06092—dc22   2010047141

ISBN: 978-0-313-38620-6
EISBN: 978-0-313-38621-3

15   14   13   12   11   1   2   3   4   5

This book is also available on the World Wide Web as an eBook.
Visit www.abc-clio.com for details.

Praeger
An Imprint of ABC-CLIO, LLC

ABC-CLIO, LLC
130 Cremona Drive, P.O. Box 1911
Santa Barbara, California 93116-1911

This book is printed on acid-free paper (∞)

Manufactured in the United States of America

Portions of the text adapted from Theodore M. Vestal's article: "An American's View of the Horn of Africa from World War II to the Present," *Horn of Africa*, XXV 2007, (71–89). Used by permission.

To the Americans and Ethiopians who worked for a better
Ethiopia during the years of Haile Selassie

Contents

Photo essay follows p. 104.

Preface

Haile Selassie, the Emperor of Ethiopia, was an iconic figure of the 20th century, who came to embody the majesty of the African continent and its people in the minds of many Americans. Starting at least with his coronation as Ethiopia's King of Kings in 1930, and continuing through the velvet revolution that overthrew him in 1974, the emperor was a well-known celebrity in the United States. In the years following World War II, Haile Selassie cultivated his nation's friendship with the United States, and starting in 1954 he came to Washington on six state visits, the most of any reigning foreign head of state up until that time, and also traveled to many other destinations in North America.

His fame as an international celebrity was well earned. He won it the old fashioned way: by significant accomplishments. Wartime always produces new heroes, and before and during World War II, Haile Selassie was elevated into high visibility by being among the first to stand up to the European dictators, who shortly would wreak such worldwide havoc, and subsequently to champion an international order to prevent similar malevolence from threatening weaker nations again. At the League of Nations, the little king created, in image and in word, a composition of rich emotional eloquence. The Haile Selassie we see in the old newsreels is the one who registered on the national conscience and created a place for himself in the American heart that remained thereafter.

The emperor's visits to the United States generated rapt attention from the media, and the wily monarch manipulated that coverage to further the programs and causes that he believed in. Number one on his list of priorities was himself. Having briefly lost power during the Italian occupation of Abyssinia, he wanted to stay in power and never relinquish it again. To do this, he needed military might that was sufficient to put down rebellion at home and to defend Ethiopia against outside aggression. Economic development of his country also would help him remain on the throne—enough to satisfy progressives who clamored for change but not too much to antagonize feudal lords and the Ethiopian Church, who preferred the status quo. Further, Haile Selassie was intent on maintaining his nation's sovereignty and the boundaries of greater Ethiopia that he and his imperial predecessors had worked hard to establish. He was obsessed with collective security, thought the United Nations the best perpetuator of the idea, demanded an end to colonialism, especially in Africa, and promoted Pan-Africanism and African unity. The stone-faced ruler sought to project his image as an elder statesman and leader of Africa whose moderating voice would be heard and respected throughout the continent. At the same time, during the height of the Cold War, he wanted to be an active player in the nonaligned movement, a bravura act of tightrope walking, given U.S. bases in his country and treaties with the United States in his diplomatic portfolio. By royal ritual and performance, Haile Selassie hoped to persuade his foreign audiences that the king was a great person, one of illustrious lineage and with impressive actual and symbolic powers, especially in his heading of an ancient country of the Christian faith. To realize more fully these aspirations, the emperor needed the good will of the American people and the bankrolling of his causes by the U.S. government. Thus his frequent state visits were rationalized as needed personal diplomacy with the U.S. president in what he perceived as crisis after crisis involving Ethiopia's security—and as an excuse to extend his own power.

The American response to his visits was far greater than the emperor could have envisioned. The U.S. Department of State staged rituals with spectacular moments where diplomacy and entertainment converged before adoring crowds. Celebrity works on emotions, and the pseudoevents starring the Ethiopian king of kings provided an ecstatic merging of magic and reality that left an indelible imprint on Americans' emotional memory. Possessing exactly the right combination of gravitas and mystery, the emperor played upon the mystic chords of memory of his audiences. If kingship is created entirely by the way other people react to a ruler, the little king had willing subjects in the throngs that cheered him along the urban boulevards and rural routes of the country where "nice customs curtseyed to great kings."[1] And the memory stuck. Years later, a sighting of the patriarchal Haile Selassie on television, a casual reference, could call to remembrance, however fleetingly, the solemn monarch who so long and prominently made valued contributions to postwar life.

Critics, looking back from the 21st century, aware of the construction and manipulation of images by a celebrity-bound society, might see the state visits of the emperor as essentially the institutionalization of Haile Selassie's publicity stunts. There might be an element of truth to that judgment, but that does not detract from the mysterious quality of the monarch that so beguiled Americans. For many, Haile Selassie became a metaphor for Africa—that is, the understanding and experiencing one kind of thing in terms of another. His longevity and participation in world affairs maintained that metaphor far beyond his best years on the diplomatic circuit. Over time, we put our own gloss on our metaphors, and the emperor came to stand for what Americans wanted Africans to be: calm, regal, suave, strong, and silent—concepts important to Americans. The truth or falsity of such a metaphor is less significant than the perception and inferences that follow from it and the actions that are sanctioned by it. "We define our reality in terms of metaphors and then proceed to act on the basis of metaphors."[2] America's action was to store the memory of Haile Selassie, the traditions, his humanity and achievements, in the subconscious as a positive image of an African.

In present-day Ethiopia, few know just how popular their monarch was in the New World. It is perhaps difficult to understand how a ruler so reviled in his homeland for more than 35 years by successor governments could have been such an international celebrity and be so royally received abroad. Haile Selassie was a major actor on the world stage, and because of that, Ethiopia enjoyed prestige and respect throughout the world that has been absent in later years. In the 1950s and 1960s, in the nation of what once was, Ethiopia was like Terry Malloy, the protagonist of the 1954 motion picture *On the Waterfront*. As portrayed by actor Marlon Brando, one could believe that the prize-fighter Malloy could have been a contender for the title. He chose some wrong fights and had bad advice from his managers, and ended up as a dockworker instead of a champion. Ethiopia could have been a contender among the nations of the world, but it also chose wrong fights, and the post-royal managers were awful. The proud nation was knocked down and has remained on the canvas ever since. Although the country has many devoted fans who are hoping that Ethiopia will rise and become a contender, and hold its rightful place in main events in the Africa arena, the body politic has suffered some severe damage. Deficits of democracy, human rights abuses, and some harmful decisions by its people and its leaders have taken the ancient land in other directions. The country has yet to live up to its great potential that was touted widely during the emperor's time. Instead of becoming the breadbasket of Africa, Ethiopia became a famine-ravished basket case. The result is that the image of Ethiopia in the minds of many people worldwide became that of a wasteland peopled by starving children with bloated stomachs—a far cry from the image of a heroic caped and bearded emperor striding down the aisle of the League of Nations with imperial dignity, deep in grief, proud and resolute in expression—the image prevalent until Haile Selassie's death.

This book tells the dynamic story of how the emperor, the ruler of a developing country, strongly helped shape Americans' perceptions of and attitudes toward the entire continent of Africa and its people. By documenting the travels of Haile Selassie to North America and the reaction of government officials and the general public to his visits, this book will explore the following:

- Why Haile Selassie enjoyed such celebrity in the United States.
- How the emperor became the single-most important figure in influencing U.S. attitudes toward Africa.
- How the emperor's state visits reflected U.S. foreign policy toward Ethiopia and Africa over a period of two decades.

The book will include a brief biography of Haile Selassie, illuminating his era that extended from World War I through the Cold War. The tensions, contradictions, and unanswered questions raised during Haile Selassie's life are highlighted in significant episodes that demonstrate just how widespread the emperor's influence reached in North America. The work also describes how visits by celebrity foreign heads of state were majestically managed and reported when they were still rare and newsworthy events.

This book is not a paean to the emperor. There are many of those, some being well-written encomiums to the monarch. The emperor, being human, had his foibles, and these appear in the narrative. Likewise, he was deserving of praise for some of his actions, and this is recorded where appropriate. It should be noted that the Crown Council of Ethiopia, under the sterling leadership of Prince Ermias Sahle Selassie Haile Selassie, the emperor's grandson, keeps the memory of the Lion of Judah alive through various media. And of course, Rasta-farian authors write hymns of praise to the emperor they glorify.

On the other hand, this book is not a derogation of the little king. There are many of those written primarily by members of Ethiopian ethnic groups who viewed Haile Selassie as an Amhara imperialist who inflicted grievous wrongs upon their people. The evils of his rule and the analogy of the emperor's lack of clothes certainly were well known and have been recurrently recorded. The demise of the diminu-tive sovereign heralded open season for animadversions on the royal family, and there has been no shortage of vehement venting of spleen about hoary trespasses against the kith and kin of nations, nationali-ties, and people. For enlightened readers, it is a tricky matter of finding a proper perspective in which to balance the descriptions of a demonic despot administering large doses of cruelty with the accounts of the mythic recipient of beautiful, calculate diplomacy and lofty, lyrical lan-guage of praise.

Currently, when the United States has elected its first president whose father was from Africa, and when the troubled lands of Africa may well receive special attention in U.S. foreign policy, it is impor-tant to understand the background, the positive subconscious images or metaphors that are stored in American memory and that were rel-evant in this precedent-shattering election. The images of Africa and of Africans that the American people developed during Haile Selassie's prominence will no doubt be referred to by historians, psychologists, and sociologists—as well as the media—as having played a part in the election of Barack Obama as president in 2008. This book attempts to fill in blank spaces in recording when, how, and why the emperor made his mark on the American conscience. It is a true account of the world as we experienced it, what e. e. cummings called "a recent foot-print in the sand of was,"[3] and of the legacy of that experience today. It is an American's view of an Ethiopian's influence on Americans, and for that reason it was written primarily for an American audience. The author hopes Ethiopians will find it intriguing too.

* * *

There were so many wonderful people who encouraged me and gave good counsel in the preparation of this book, that to list them all would exceed my space limitations in a preface. Suffice it to say that all their assistance and benevolences were most appreciated. My work on this book was supported by generous grants from the Oklahoma

Humanities Council and Oklahoma State University. The OSU Department of Political Science and School of International Studies provided
vital funds for travel. My colleague Conrad Evans and other splendid
veterans of the Point Four program in the Oklahoma Ethiopia Society have assisted in myriad ways. Shlomo Bachrach's marvelous East
Africa Forum on the Web has kept me informed about the present,
past, and future of Ethiopia and the Horn. The International Conference of Ethiopian Studies in sessions at Hamburg and Trondheim provided me with fora to present papers that eventually became chapters
in this book. I thank the University of Hamburg, and especially Professor Siegbert Uhlig, for naming me the Hiob Ludolf Endowed Professor
of Current Issues of Ethiopian Studies in 2005 and providing me with
pleasant surroundings and stalwart colleagues at its Institute for Asian
and African Studies. My public lecture delivered under the Institute's
auspices developed into an outline of this book. Also at Hamburg, my
colleagues at the *Encyclopaedia Aethiopica* and the students in my semi-
nar on "Law and Politics of the Ethio-Eritrean Area" provided stimu-
lating ideas that made their way into my writing. Both Elias Wondimu,
publisher and editorial director of the *International Journal of Ethiopian
Studies,* and Dr. Said S. Samatar, editor of *Horn of Africa,* kindly published my articles and offered most useful suggestions for improving
them. Dr. Teffera Betru, one of the finest PhD graduates of OSU, served
as my excellent translator of Kebede Michael's detailed Amharic book,
His Majesty in America, about the emperor's first state visit in 1954.
The executive dynamos of the Junior Statesman Foundation, Richard
and Karen Prosser, allowed me to teach in the foundation's summer
schools and provided me opportunities to testify before a congressional committee and to do research in the libraries of Georgetown, Yale,
and Princeton. The Ethiopian-American Historical and Cultural Society and its founder Assefa Adefris invited me to speak and participate
in several of their conferences in Washington, DC, where I met Ethiopians and Ethiopianists who shared their wisdom about the topic of
my book. My scholarly friends, Professor Negussay Ayele and Berihun
Assfaw, provided me with little-known information about the emperor.
The all-star lineup of Ethiopian scholars and writers who honored me
by asking me to critically read prepublication manuscript versions of
their books, from which I learned so very much that was helpful in
my writing, included Ambassador Zaude Hailemariam and Professors
Danial Kendie, Paulos Milkias, Shumet Sishagne, Getachew Metaferia, Messay Kebede, and Daniel Teferra. My friends in the Ethiopia
and Eritrea Returned Peace Corps volunteers have been a wonderful

source of information—especially in their outstanding newsletter *The Herald*, edited by that nonpareil wordsmith Barry Hillenbrand. A special tip of the hat goes to the knowledgeable librarians, archivists, and audiovisual specialists of the National Archives and Records Administration and the presidential libraries of Dwight D. Eisenhower, John F. Kennedy, Lyndon B. Johnson, and Richard M. Nixon; the Library of Congress; and the university libraries of Boston University; Georgetown; Harvard; Oklahoma State University, Stillwater; Princeton; St. Andrews; University of Texas; University of Tulsa; Yale; and, most especially, the reference librarians of Oklahoma State University, Tulsa. Michael Millman, senior editor at ABC CLIO, was a patient supporter of my book from the proposal stage onward, and without his assistance and encouragement, this project would never have come to completion. Closer to home, I thank my granddaughter Julianne Thomson, a graduate student in archeology at Oxford, for editing work; my son Edward Vestal, in Singapore, who scoured U.S. military libraries to get me information on the air forces of Ethiopia and Somalia; and my wife Pat, who keeps fine arts at the center of our lives and encourages the pursuit of excellence.

CHAPTER 1

A Lion in the Streets

The petite, sepia man, resplendent in a regal uniform, looked up at the snowfall of ticker tape and confetti in the canyon of Broadway. From his vantage point in an open limousine, the black-bearded African monarch, with the face of an aesthete, Emperor Haile Selassie—Instrument and Power of the Trinity, Elect of God, Conquering Lion of the Tribe of Judah, and King of Kings of Ethiopia—was the center of attention of a cheering crowd of a million New Yorkers. Why was the little emperor, the personification of an ancient people, receiving such a tumultuous welcome in the New World? Who was this ruler from the dark continent, so little known in America, the honoree of a ticker-tape parade, New York City's most spectacular welcome to distinguished visitors? Why was this man, 7,000 miles from home, the subject of such adulation?

A large outpouring of noontime crowds was seeing, for the first time, a supremely dignified African leader and his handsome entourage of Ethiopians. Every foot of curbing was occupied by applauding and cheering humanity. In a city with a vast experience in welcoming celebrities, it took nearly an hour to cover the mile-long motorcade route. Haile Selassie was the first sub-Saharan African head of state to ride the magic mile up Broadway through the shower of paper and confetti in the canyon of heroes. The emperor had opened the gate to the Broadway parade for African leaders, and, five months later, President William V. S. Tubman of Liberia would be the second in a long line of developing nations' heads of state to be so honored.

As the 10-car motorcade made its way up Broadway from Battery Park to City Hall, the ticker tape and other shredded paper was so thick that the emperor could barely be seen. The tumult brought a rare public smile to the face of the monarch, who usually maintained an almost sphinx-like dignity. Beaming from his open car, he stretched wide and high as he waved and doffed his red-trimmed field marshal's cap at the sidewalk throngs and the audiences in the skyscrapers' windows above. Spectators snapped photographs of the king of kings. Pretty girls blew him kisses. Many usually blasé Manhattanites delayed lunch to see the iconic ruler. From churches, ceremoniously garbed clergy stepped out on the sidewalks to see and honor this titular leader of the Coptic faith.[1]

The emperor had reason to be happy. The year was 1954, and a series of events had made Haile Selassie secure in the rule of his homeland and the recipient of accolades on the world scene—a very different situation than had been the case only a few months before. He had just come from Washington, DC, where President Dwight Eisenhower had been his host at a White House dinner, the high point of the emperor's first state visit to the United States. A strong believer in the effectiveness of personal diplomacy, Haile Selassie had met with Eisenhower and his aides to put finishing touches on a military agreement that had been signed the month before and to request more bilateral economic assistance for his country. The meeting had lasted little more than an hour, but it was to shape U.S. foreign policy toward Africa generally and toward Ethiopia specifically for the two decades that followed.

In the limousine, Haile Selassie rode beside Richard C. Patterson, chairman of the city's Committee on Public Events, who remained with him throughout the official ceremonies. Also in the car were John Simmons, State Department chief of protocol, and Major General Arthur C. Trudeau, who as presidential military aide to the emperor, had Ethiopian troops under his command in Ethiopia—representatives of the State Department and the U.S. military that were to play vital roles in all of the emperor's official relations with the United States for the rest of his life.

Haile Selassie enjoyed his close-up view of the downtown canyon. He seemed especially impressed with the Woolworth Building and talked animatedly about it to the others in his car as they drove by—after all, the 57-story, 650-foot high Woolworth Building, the Cathedral of Commerce, had been the tallest in the world from 1913 until 1930, the year of Haile Selassie's coronation. The emperor kept looking back at it as he spoke.

The parade had gotten off to a late start at 10 minutes after noon from lower Manhattan's Bowling Green, the oldest public park in the city. One of the Ethiopians in the official party joked that the tardy procession was on Ethiopian time. In the motorcade rode the emperor's youngest son, the handsome, Cambridge-educated, 24-year-old Prince Sahle Selassie, who was noted for flying his own airplane, driving an American car, and collecting jazz records; the emperor's stylish granddaughter, Princess Seble, who was 19 and a student at Oxford University in Great Britain; and several of Haile Selassie's ministers of state and other members of his official touring party.

Marching with the motor caravan were thousands in uniform—detachments from all branches of the military as well as from police, fire, and sanitation departments, and their bands, passing through the canyon of buildings, past Wall Street, the capital of American wealth. Prince Sahle noted there would be tons of litter to clean up, and the young prince contributed to the debris when his hat blew off his head—but as he later wrote to President Eisenhower, "luckily the photographers did not see."[2]

At the end of the ride, Haile Selassie stepped up to a platform on the city hall steps, where Patterson introduced him to Mayor Robert F. Wagner, who gave his formal and ceremonial welcome. The emperor responded in Amharic, the official language of Ethiopia, with warm words of thanks and appreciation, translated by the Oxford-educated chief of protocol of the Ministry of Foreign Affairs, Endalkachew Mekonnen. Haile Selassie then surprised and pleased the mayor and a large audience by presenting three gifts from his African domain to the City of New York—two highly polished elephant tusks, capped with gold and mounted on a base of rare woods, two glinting silver-dipped spears, and a red leather warrior's shield of intricate gold design. In return, the mayor gave the emperor the city's medal of honor and a scroll.

The royal party then drove to the Waldorf-Astoria Hotel, their residence during the New York visit, where the mayor gave a formal luncheon in Haile Selassie's honor. The emperor and Mayor Wagner again made addresses, and the United Nations Secretary General Dag Hammarskjöld also spoke. Formal toasts were drunk to the emperor, who responded with a toast to the City of New York. After the luncheon, Haile Selassie and his party stood in a receiving line to meet the more than 500 guests.

At four o'clock the emperor went to the United Nations headquarters on the East River. Secretary General Hammarskjöld escorted him on a tour of the general assembly hall, the security council chamber, and other significant offices and facilities. An informal reception was held for the emperor in the secretary general's office on the 38th floor. This was followed by a formal UN dinner, attended by delegates of, at the time, the 60 member nations and high officials of the UN, in an atmosphere far different from the emperor's last address to the delegates of an international peacekeeping body, almost two decades earlier.[3]

Then, as Haile Selassie wrote in his autobiography, "We were present at the 16th general assembly of the League of Nations (in Geneva) on June 30, 1936, to explain the fascist invasion of Our country and the atrocities perpetrated on the people."[4] He was the first head of state to appear before the assembly, and the only one who would ever address it. As the lonely figure of the emperor climbed the high stairs and approached the podium in the white assembly hall, Italian journalists in the gallery made such a racket of boos and catcalls that they had to be removed from the hall. Emperor Haile Selassie, an exile from his own country, which was occupied by the fascists of Benito Mussolini, had come to the League of Nations to make a final appeal for sanctions against Italy. The emperor, although fluent in French, spoke in Amharic. With calm dignity, the emperor prophetically said, "It is us today, it will be you tomorrow." He then made his historic appeal on behalf of collective security: "Apart from the kingdom of the Lord there is not on this earth any nation that is superior to any other. Should it happen that a strong Government finds it may, with impunity, destroy a weak people, then the hour strikes for that weak people to appeal to the League of Nations to give its judgment in all freedom. God and history will remember your judgment."[5]

The League's judgment was to do nothing meaningful—a nonaction well remembered throughout the world. But Haile Selassie, the epitome of composure in adversity, had won his place in history. A generation of Americans was to grow up remembering Ethiopia's betrayal at the League, and the brave, black-cloaked Ethiopian ruler who asked the League to live up to its covenant. Many of the Allies' propaganda films of World War II included scenes of the emperor's address at Geneva, the tragic landmark of the League's sordid last days, and in the postwar era, most textbooks on international relations or international organizations included the text of the emperor's speech. Americans saw the images and read the words over and over again, and remembered. In one of his darkest hours, Haile Selassie had become an international celebrity.

Thus, it was a poignant homecoming at the United Nations in 1954, when the emperor responded to a toast by Secretary General Hammarskjöld with these words:

It is a significant moment for me when after eighteen years I again find myself in a center where are concentrated the passionate hopes of the thousands of millions of human beings who so desperately long for the assurance of peace. The years of that interval somber as they were and sacred as they remain to the memory of millions of innocent victims hold forth for us bright hope of the future. The League of Nations failed, and failed basically because of its inability to prevent aggression against my country. But neither the depth of that failure nor the intervening catastrophe could dull the perception of the need and the search for peace through collective security.

Saying that the last two decades had justified, in Ethiopia's case, her own conviction that the UN ideals will triumph, Haile Selassie reminded the delegates that his country was liberated during that period, and that it "has finally seen the rectification . . . of injustice and the vindication of the right of brothers to be reunited."[6]

The emperor could speak to the UN delegates with moral suasion. His nation would rank high on any list of strong supporters of the ideals of the United Nations. Ethiopia had signed the Declaration of the United Nations on January 1, 1941, and had been among the 50 states that had formally adopted the UN charter in San Francisco on June 26, 1945. Further, the emperor had sent approximately 1,200 Ethiopian soldiers to join the UN forces in the Korean War in 1950, and they had shown their mettle in combat. The formal events at the UN honoring Haile Selassie were auspicious and appropriate. The little emperor had earned his place center stage on the world's proscenium and was enjoying every minute of it.

* * *

Perhaps it was the best of all times for Haile Selassie to come to the United States. Nine years after the end of World War II, the emperor's speech before the League of Nations still was the defining, positive image of Ethiopia for most Americans. The emperor's persona and familiar name added to his stature. His stalwart military bearing and dress were the epitome of dignity. Haile Selassie's solemn demeanor and magnetic dark eyes complemented his titled, mythological descent from Solomon and Sheba, and his rule of a nation of Christians was another positive factor in his reception. The exotic, catchy ring of his name made it easy to remember, and the emperor even was the subject in the lyrics of a parody of a popular song, "Shanty in an Old Shanty Town," by Johnny Long, who averred, "I'd be just as sassy as Haile Selassie, if I were a King wouldn't mean a thing!" Some who cheered him could remember that in the early 1930s, a common American expression was, "Well! If that's so, then I'm Haile Selassie."

In 1954, most Americans knew little about the dark continent. Indeed, an American international banker who knew Ethiopia and his homeland well thought "there are few countries about which Americans know less."[7] The dominant colors of maps of Africa were the colonial-designating pinks for Great Britain and blues for France. Even the U.S. State Department deferred responsibility and blame for events in Africa, and especially in sub-Saharan Africa, to the colonial empires that had scrambled to claim lands there in the late 19th and early 20th centuries and still tenaciously held on to their possessions in the face of increasingly strengthening independence movements. In World War II, Allied landings and eventual victories in North Africa sparked American interest in the Maghreb, but the focus soon shifted to the more familiar terrain of Europe as General Dwight Eisenhower led his armies first into Italy and then into France. The American image of Africa was shaped more by Hollywood motion pictures that portrayed Africans stereotypically as savages, by church slide shows of Christian missionaries showing assorted tribal people in need of redemption, and by the romanticized writing of Ernest Hemmingway about big game, white hunters, and the snows of Kilimanjaro.

The attractive, largely British-educated royal party that accompanied the emperor was a far cry from the Africans portrayed in Hollywood motion pictures at that time. Ethiopians generally are a handsome people, with large eyes, high cheekbones, and a proud, self-assured demeanor stemming from their unique history of not having kowtowed to colonial masters. Haile Selassie's good-looking entourage, genetically a mix of Arab and African peoples, made a favorable impression wherever they traveled throughout the United States. The itinerary of the royal party that included acclaimed visits to racially segregated states was a timely counterpoint to the U.S. Supreme Court's decision in *Brown v. Board of Education,* mandating an end to segregated public schools, handed down only a few days before the emperor's arrival in America.[8]

With the Cold War heating up, the emperor was a proven ally against communist aggression. Ethiopia's Kagnew Battalion had served alongside U.S. troops in the Korean police action. In the UN, Ethiopia usually voted with the United States and against Eastern Bloc interests. Haile Selassie's timely signing of military agreements with the United States just before his state visit placed Ethiopia on the right side in the bipolar world developing around NATO and Warsaw Pact countries.

In 1954, Africa was on the brink of emerging from the shackles of colonialism, and in contrast to the uncertainty surrounding the future of French and British colonies, Ethiopia, as an independent nation, appeared stable. Neighboring Sudan was just electing a Sudanese prime minister for the first time, while, according to Ethiopian tradition, the Emperor Haile Selassie represented the 225th ruler of his line. The chaos created in British-controlled Kenya by the Mau Mau uprising was in sharp contrast to the tranquility of the highlands of Ethiopia.

The stability of Ethiopia was backed by a large American presence, especially in the Point Four programs, a close relationship between Trans World Airlines and the fledgling Ethiopian Airlines that provided links between the nation's capital and isolated towns in the highlands and the U.S. military's operating a communications center or listening post near Asmara, in the north of the country.

In his visit to the capital of wealth, the emperor was seeking investments in his country by American business. The development of Ethiopia's natural resources, possibly including oil reserves and uranium, a blue-chip mineral at that time, sounded promising.

Members of the royal party accompanying the emperor on the state visit changed in various destinations. The entourage that traveled together most often during the tour included Prince Sahle Selassie; Princess Seble Desta; Wolde Giorgis Wolde Yohannes, minister of justice and minister of the pen (next to the emperor, the most powerful man in the Ethiopian government, who had been called "the real ruler of Ethiopia" and the "Eminence Grise"); two future prime ministers: Aklilu Habte Wold, minister of foreign affairs (who had signed the United Nations charter for Ethiopia in San Francisco in 1945) and Endalkachew Mekonnen, the Oxford-educated chief of protocol of the Ministry of Foreign Affairs, who did most of the interpreting for the emperor during the American tour; aide de camp to the emperor, Colonel Makonnen Deneke, a bald giant of a man thought by some Americans to be Haile Selassie's personal bodyguard; John H. Spencer, an American who for many years had served as advisor to the emperor and to the Ethiopian Ministry of Foreign Affairs and who wrote the emperor's numerous

speeches and toasts given during the tour of North America;[9] other
Ethiopian officials and the emperor's personal aides;[10] Ambassador Simonson and officers from the U.S. Department of State;[11] and the vice
president of Trans World Airlines (TWA), Thomas K. Taylor.

* * *

The country that Haile Selassie ruled over was a mythical, mountainous land of contrasts, which was little known in the United States.
Ethiopia sat as the centerpiece of the Horn of Africa, the elbow-like
peninsula that juts out from the east side of the continent toward the
Saudi peninsula. The region was a meeting place of the earth's tectonic
forces, a bridge between Africa and Asia, and a crossroads of civiliza-
tions and races. The Red Sea provided a slender separation between the
Horn of Africa and the Middle East. At its narrowest, in the straits of the
Bab-el-Mandeb, meaning "Gate of Tears" in Arabic, where the Red Sea
flowed into the Indian Ocean, the waterway separated Africa and Western Asia by a distance of less than 20 miles. People and goods flowed
easily back and forth across this transcontinental bridge, making the
Horn a yeasty mixing bowl of cultures and trade from earliest times.

Most of the region is mountainous due to faults resulting from the
Great Rift Valley, a giant breach in the crust of the earth where the
African continent slowly splits into two parts. The Great Rift Valley ex-
tends 3,000 miles from Syria in Southwest Asia to Mozambique, south
of the equator. From its Asian beginnings, the Great Rift runs southward through the Dead Sea, the Gulf of Aqaba, the Red Sea, and comes
ashore in eastern Ethiopia, where it meets the East African Rift and
the Aden Ridge in the Afar or the Danakil Depression. The junction of
these three rifts, the Afar Triple Junction, provides a spectacular divid-
ing line of sheer cliffs in Ethiopia's geography. The rift cuts southwest
through Ethiopia, bifurcating the country's eastern plateau of Harar
from the central plateau, the fertile highlands that extend from Asmara
in the North to Addis Ababa and Jimma in the south. The rift valley in
Ethiopia is marked by the Awash River and a group of large lakes in
the southwest. There, the Great Rift exits Ethiopia before continuing
on to Kenya and then farther south.

The rift slices Ethiopia's vast mountain massif, the nation's dominant
physical characteristic. These compact groups of steep mountains and
big plateaus are studded with what Ethiopians call *ambas*, flat-topped
hills whose badly eroded, barren sides slope down almost vertically.
The *ambas* are surrounded by green meadows and lush vegetation of

the highlands that comprise much of the country. Dense forests cover some areas with eucalyptus, firs, jacaranda, junipers, and acacia in abundance. Big game abounds where humans have not encroached on their natural habitats.

It is in these grandly beautiful highlands that rise on average more than 7,000 feet from the torrid plains that enclose them that most Ethiopians have traditionally lived. Even though Ethiopia lies near the equator, the highlands' altitude-induced climate is temperate and invigorating. The light at this altitude provides spectacular contrasts in the shades of pastel reds, creams, and pinks that bejewel this land of "enigmatic beauty."[12] There usually is a haze that softens the colors and contours, and as an artist describes it, "the sunlight is brilliant, yet cool and soft."[13]

In this part of the roof of Africa, the highest weathered peaks are in the Simien Mountains of northwestern Ethiopia, where Mount Ras Dashan reaches an elevation just under 15,000 feet and many others exceed 13,000 feet, creating grand canyons of breathtaking splendor, some rivaling the Grand Canyon of the Colorado in size. Arising in the highlands near Lake Tana, the Abay, or Blue Nile, considered by many to be a holy river, "winds like a mainspring through the land," carving one of the deepest and widest canyons in the world.[14] This Blue Nile Gorge makes its way on into the Sudan, where, at Khartoum, the Blue Nile joins the longer White Nile, coming from Uganda, to form the mighty Nile River that carries the water and silt that bring life to Egypt's dry sands.

The Ethiopian highlands descend in a huge escarpment to the Red Sea and the Indian Ocean, along the way making a transition from the lush vegetation of the plateaus of Ethiopia to brown scrub and barren desert. At the foot of the escarpment in northeastern Ethiopia lies the Afar Depression, a formidable landscape that includes the Danakil Desert, one of the hottest places year-round anywhere on earth, where temperatures reach 120 degrees. There, in the gateway to hell, active volcanoes create new earth near the lowest point in Africa, Lake Asal, which is 510 feet below sea level.

In 1954, the area of Ethiopia, 471,371 square miles, was slightly larger than Texas, Oklahoma, and New Mexico combined. The estimated population was only 19.5 million, so overpopulation was not a problem. In normal times, without the scourges of drought and famine, the land could support the people. The highlands enjoyed a mild climate, fertile soil, and an industrious peasantry. Its people thought of it as a heaven-blessed land of plenty, although statistically it was one of the poorest countries on earth. Foreign observers recognized Ethiopia's agricultural potential and thought it capable of being the breadbasket of the Middle East. Highland farmers traditionally grew two crops a year in verdant fields that some Americans thought resembled the best agricultural lands of California's Central Valley. Large livestock herds flourished in several regions. Abundant rain came in two waves: the little rains of March and April, and the big rains in the summer months. Over 90 percent of the people were subsistence agriculturists who still tilled small plots of land with plows drawn by two oxen. Their fields fanned out from small clusters of round, thatched roof houses called *tukuls,* which had thorn enclosures to keep animals penned in. Better-off peasants invested in corrugated-tin-roofed houses, a sign of modernization. Throughout the country, Ethiopian Orthodox churches, monks, nuns, and priests were seen, testimony to the deeply spiritual living faith that permeated the land.

As Ethiopianist Edward Ullendorff observed, Ethiopia embraced "a complex of ethnic elements composed of a veritable mosaic of races, tribes, and linguistic groups."[15] The people comprise more than 100 ethnic groups, each speaking a dialect of one of more than 70 languages. A national census was not taken in Ethiopia until 30 years after the emperor's first visit to the United States in 1954, so the demographics of the nation before that time were at best educated guesses. Consensus estimates held that the Oromo and the Amhara were the largest ethnic groups, with each accounting for about one-third of the population. The Oromo were widely dispersed over large sections of the country from the southern deserts to the western and northern highlands. The Amhara, concentrated in the central highlands, dominated government and economic life during the reign of Haile Selassie. The Tigrayans inhabited Eritrea and the northern highlands of Tigray province and may have composed roughly 15 percent of the population. Smaller ethnic groups included the Gurage, the hard working business class; the Somali people who dwelt in the deserts of the east and southeast, touching the borders of Somalia and Kenya; and the Omotic, or Nilotic peoples in the lowlands of the southwest along the border with Sudan. These people were in constant interaction through trade, warfare, religious activities, migration, and intermarriage. The country was multireligious too. In the 1950s it was thought that a majority of the people was Orthodox Christian (especially the Amhara and Tigrayans), that about 40 percent were Muslim, and the rest were animist or from smaller sects.

The land of these people was ancient , where humans and their ancestors had dwelt for millennia. It was in the river valleys of the Afar region of Ethiopia that paleontologists were to recover the fossilized skeletal remains of the earliest known human ancestors. Lucy, or *Dinkenesh* ("you are wonderful" in Amharic), sometimes called the missing link between modern humans and ape-like ancestors, was a petite, 3.2 million-year-old *Australopithecus afarensis,* whose skeleton was found in 1974. Lucy and her kin stood upright, lived in groups, and adapted to living in open spaces rather than in forests.[16] In 2007, Lucy, or rather her bones, began an exhibition tour to museums throughout the United States, making her the most famous Ethiopian visitor since Haile Selassie. But Lucy was a latecomer compared to her tree-loving predecessor, Ardi, a female of the species *Ardipithecus ramidus,* who lived in a woodland Danakil, 4.4 to 5.2 million years ago. Ardi, the oldest known hominid fossil, was discovered in 1992 but was not officially recognized in the scientific community until October 2009, when the journal *Science* published its encomium. From the general body plans of these hominids would evolve the body plan of the genus *Homo,* who, from an African genesis, would inherit the earth.

For those who might distrust the veracity of paleontologist evidence, Orthodox Ethiopian Church believers have their own genesis of the origins of man in their homeland. In the holy Ethiopian community of Lalibela is the grave of Adam. The whereabouts of the tomb of the Biblical Eve, however, remain a mystery. Ethiopia's holy literature even has the recipe used in making the first man: "God took a grain of dust, a drop of water, and a puff of wind, and a bit of warmth and formed Adam." Further, a pearl was placed in the belly of Adam that was passed on in the act of begetting to Solomon and on from generation to generation to the dynastic rulers of Ethiopia.[17]

Whatever their origins, by the time of the late Stone Age, *Homo sapiens* were roaming back and forth across the Red Sea, mixing and mingling people of Africa and Asia. Some spoke related languages of the Afro-Asiatic language families including Omotic, Cushitic, and Semitic, all of which continue to be used in Ethiopia today.[18] Some linguists postulate that Semitic-speaking migrants from southwest Arabia settled in present day Ethiopia, bringing with them a written script called Sabaean and monumental stone architecture. Other linguists maintain the flow went the other way, from Africa to Arabia.[19] By the first millennium B.C.E., the nascent Semitic-speakers fused with Cushitic- and Omotic-speaking inhabitants to produce a culture known as pre-Axumite. From its major trading center, the Red Sea port city of Adulis, the pre-Axumites established economic ties with nearby Africans, Asians to the east, and Europeans from the north.

From this root, the Axumite state, one of the most powerful in ancient Africa, emerged in the highlands of southern Eritrea, Tigray, and Wollo at approximately the beginning of the Christian era. The Axumite Kingdom flourished from the fourth through sixth centuries C.E. and controlled the Red Sea coastline, southern Sudan, and southwest Arabia, in what is now Yemen. The Axumites exported gold, rhinoceros horn, ivory, incense, and obsidian to the Greeks and Egyptians, the Roman Empire, Arabia, and India. The people created a civilization with a body of written records in Ge'ez, the ancestral language that would evolve in the Middle Ages into Amharic, Tigrinya, and other Semitic languages of Ethiopia. Ge'ez was written in an indigenous Ethiopic script still used today.[20] The Axumites gave their king the title *negus nagast* (king of kings), a designation that would endure in the highlands through the 20th century. Over a 300 year period they minted coins in gold, silver, and copper, a practice unique in ancient Africa. In their capital city, Axum, they devised an original architectural style that featured stone palaces, public buildings, and, most notably, carved stone stelae as monuments to past rulers. Some of these stelae, rising more than 100 feet in height, were among the largest of the ancient world.[21]

Christianity came to Axum around 330 C.E., when Ezana, the greatest Axumite king, was converted by two shipwrecked Syrian monks. King Ezana proclaimed Christianity the state religion, and it remained so well into the 20th century. In the ensuing centuries, that faith evolved into the Monophysite Ethiopian Orthodox Church, which was to play a defining role in the country's history. The Church validated the legitimacy of the emperors and was in turn protected by them.

Another enduring legacy of the Axumites is the Solomonic legend, the story of the journey of the Queen of Sheba from Axum to the court of King Solomon in ancient Israel. According to the national epic, the lineage of Axumite kings originated with Menelik I, the offspring of the union between the Queen of Sheba, known as Makeda in Ethiopia, and Solomon the wise. Royal legitimacy thereafter was derived from descent in a line of Solomonic kings. According to the legend, young Menelik took the Ark of the Covenant from the Temple in Jerusalem "in the blink of an eye" and brought it to Axum when he returned to Ethiopia. The faithful of Ethiopia believe the Ark has remained in Ethiopia ever since, providing the people a unique spiritual privilege and designating their land as the new Zion, the place of God's dwelling.[22]

The Axumite Kingdom went into eclipse during the sixth century when Sassanian Persians, the last pre-Islamic Persian Empire, occupied Yemen and attacked Byzantine Egypt. The Persians so disrupted the Axumite networks of trade in the Red Sea area that the kingdom gave up its maritime ambitions and withdrew into the interior of northern Ethiopia. With its rugged topography as a deterrent to would-be attackers, and as a limiting factor to its people's interactions with the rest of the world, Ethiopians retreated to centuries of isolation on their central plateau. The descendants of the Axumites split into two major linguistic groups of related but distinctive Semitic languages, the Amhara and the Tigray. In the complex identity of Ethiopian people, the speakers of these languages morphed into ethnic groups that have vied for hegemony of the highlands throughout modern Ethiopian history.

In the seventh century, adherents of a new faith from across the Red Sea sought refuge in Ethiopia. In 615 C.E., in the earliest days of Islam, 70 Muslims fleeing persecution by the Kurayshites in Mecca came to Axum. The Christian Axumite emperor Armah gave sanctuary to the party. This benevolence on the part of the Ethiopian ruler so touched the Prophet Muhammad that he issued a hadith abjuring jihad against Abyssinia and proclaimed that "Abyssinia is a land of justice in which no one is oppressed." Their sojourn in Ethiopia greatly impressed these early Muslim migrants and influenced the future development of their new faith. For although Mecca, the rock of Islam, was only 250 miles away, the adherents of Islam in seeking to convert or conquer the land the Arabs called El Habesha stayed out of the highlands for the most part and populated the surrounding lowlands. Thus the benevolence of the Axumite emperor Armah brought about centuries of relatively peaceful coexistence between the two faiths.

Around the 10th century, the Axumite Empire gave way to a new line of rulers, the Zagwe dynasty. It was during the reign of the most famous of the Zagwe rulers, King Lalibela (1190–1225), that the Ethiopian Church reached its peak of splendor. In the north-central village now known as Lalibela, artisans hewed 11 incredible churches out of solid rock. The churches, which rank with the major wonders of the world, are still used as sites of worship today. Legends claim that the artisans, who worked 12 hours a day cutting each church (in one piece) out of the rocks, were assisted by angels who labored during the 12 hours of the night.[23]

Sacred literature also flourished during the Middle Ages in Ethiopia. Writing in the indigenous Semitic language of Ge'ez, the language said to have been used by God when he spoke to Adam and Eve, Ethiopian priests compiled the Fetha Negast, or Laws of the Kings, the Kebra Negast, or Glory of the Kings (which tells the legendary story of Solomon and Sheba and of the transfer of the Ark of the Covenant to Ethiopia), and the royal chronicles (which recorded and described the reigns of individual kings). There are no other indigenous documents from which so much may be learned about the Ethiopian way of life and thought. The literature's main theme is that Ethiopians are the new chosen people of God—the new Israel—as demonstrated by the Ark of the Covenant being in Axum.[24]

Although Ethiopian Christians maintained close relations with Egypt and traveled frequently to Jerusalem on pilgrimages, Europeans of the Middle Ages knew little about the African country considered a "Christian island surrounded by an Islamic sea."[25] For Europeans, Ethiopia, one of the only Christian state outside of Europe, was a fabled land believed to be ruled by a wealthy sovereign called Prester John. The monarchs of Europe were interested in finding such a powerful Christian emperor who might aid the crusading powers against Islam.[26]

Europeans, or at least the Portuguese, were soon to know much more about Ethiopia. During the Age of Discovery, Portugal developed a keen interest in Africa, and her sailors explored the continent's shorelines. In 1497, Vasco da Gama boldly sailed around the Cape of Good Hope, and a short time later, Portuguese envoys were dispatched to Ethiopia to investigate a united Christian front against Turkish expansion in the Red Sea area. The Portuguese spent 16 productive years in Ethiopia learning about the descendants of Sheba and leaving a European imprint on the architecture of the land and other aspects of the culture. But the era of good feeling was brought to an end when frustrated Portuguese diplomats left in 1526 without obtaining an alliance.[27] The closing of the Portuguese embassy set the stage for the first successful invasion of the Ethiopian highlands by an outside conqueror.

The Muslim religious and military leader Ahmad ibn Ibrihim al Ghazi, known in Ethiopia as Gragn, reigned in the area of present day Somalia. With access to Gulf of Aden ports, Gragn engaged in a lively arms trade and amassed a mighty arsenal of imported weapons. After the Portuguese left, Gragn rallied ethnically diverse Muslims possessing superior firepower in a jihad intended to break Ethiopia's Christian power and to spread Islam. His armies overran most of the country

wreaking havoc—razing churches and monasteries, burning manuscripts, taking prisoners, and collecting booty throughout the highlands.[28] In one of the country's darkest hours, Ethiopians regrouped
and prayed for relief in the face of the invaders' scourge.

Relief came in the form of 400 Portuguese musketeers who landed
at Massawa in 1543, scaled the escarpment, and joined the fray. Mus-
keteer sharpshooters killed Gragn, whose death destroyed the unity
of the Muslims. The defeated invaders retreated to eastern Ethiopia,
where they constructed a walled capital at Harar, which has remained
a center of Islamic culture ever since.[29] It took centuries for Ethiopia to
recover from the material and moral losses of the invasion, and even
today, Ethiopians remember the bitter war against Gragn.

In the war-ravaged Ethiopian highlands, the Portuguese resumed
efforts to convert the country to Roman Catholicism. They succeeded
in converting two Ethiopian emperors, but the people refused to abandon their orthodox faith. Overzealous proselytization by Jesuit priests
wrecked Portuguese relations with their hosts, and in 1632, King Fasiladas expelled the Jesuits and forbade Roman Catholics in the land.[30]

The conflicts in the highlands during the 16th century opened the
way for the great migrations of the Oromo, the most populous ethnic
group in present-day Ethiopia. A Cushitic-speaking, pastoral people,
they moved northwards from the far south of Ethiopia to occupy much
of the center and north of the country.[31] The Oromo intermingled with
local populations, descendants of the Axumites, mainly the Tigrayans
in the north and the Amhara farther south. In the 18th century, the influence of the central government of Ethiopia declined, and Oromo
regional rulers and kings enjoyed greater autonomy and rose to prominence in the feudal state.[32]

Another architectural marvel was created in Gondar, the city that
became the nation's capital during the reign of Emperor Fasiladas in
1636. Fine castles, churches, and other buildings combining Moorish,
Portuguese, Ottoman, and Mogul architectural styles that endure to
this day were built during the two centuries that Gondar served as the
country's political, economic, and cultural capital.[33] By the middle of
the 18th century, however, the centralizing power of the monarchy in
Gondar had declined. Infighting between a succession of weak emperors and feudal lords loosed disunity and civil wars that ravaged the
country for decades. Various provinces became independent of each
other, and fighting broke out between different regional rulers. This
era was known as the Mesafint, or the period of the judges. Emperors
became figureheads, controlled by warlords.[34]

In the mid-19th century, Emperor Tewodros (Theodore), one of the most remarkable African rulers of his era, unified, for the first time, much of what is now central Ethiopia. He sought to reunite the country and modernize it and restore the glories of past Ethiopian empires. By force of arms, he brought various break-away provinces under his power. His success in making reforms throughout the land earned him the enmity of the Church and many feudal nobles. At the same time Tewodros unintentionally created a brouhaha with the British over what he felt was a royal snub by Queen Victoria, who did not reply to his letter proposing an alliance between the two countries. He chained and imprisoned the British consul and other foreigners at his court. In response, Queen Victoria sent Sir Robert Napier, commander in chief of the Bombay Army, to rescue them in 1867.[35]

Napier's British expedition to Abyssinia landed at Zula in Eritrea with an Anglo-Indian force of over 62,000 men and 36,000 animals, including 44 elephants and 5,735 camels, all shipped for the occasion. For the second time in Ethiopian history, foreign invaders successfully scaled the country's mountain citadel and attacked in the rugged highlands. The swashbuckling Red Coats traveled more than 400 miles from the Red Sea to Tewodros' supposedly impregnable mountain fortress at Magdala. Tewodros seemed confident that his brave warriors would prevail against his numerically superior attackers because he had a secret weapon—a great cannon, built with the help of his European prisoners, that would turn the tide of battle.

When the two armies clashed on April 10, 1868, the Ethiopians eschewed their strategic fortification and bravely charged again and again down the mountain directly into the slaughtering fire of massed British artillery and infantry. Almost all of Tewodros' men were massacred or slipped away from battle. When the Ethiopians first fired their great cannon, it exploded and cracked. The British then bombarded the fortress, and a storming party assaulted the citadel. Rather than fall into enemy hands, Tewodros committed suicide as British gunners stormed the last gate. The victorious British and Indian troops looted the fortress and shipped vast amounts of booty, much of it religious artifacts, to Great Britain. The British had no interest at that time in occupying or colonizing Ethiopia, so the expeditionary force did not stay long. Having accomplished his mission of freeing the European captives, Napier marched his troops back to the coast and sailed for home.[36]

Reporting the Napier expedition for the *New York Herald Tribune* was young Henry Morton Stanley, probably one of the first Americans to visit Ethiopia. Stanley's reports were the first to reach New York and

London, earning him such fame as a correspondent that he later was given the opportunity to find the missionary and explorer Dr. David Livingstone (who was not really lost) in 1871—presumably the biggest newspaper scoop of the 19th century. Stanley subsequently devoted part of a book titled *Coomassie and Magdala* to his adventure in Ethiopia.[37]

Napier's brief campaign in Abyssinia left the headless empire in chaos. Further civil wars ensued, and important nobles struggled to rule. The noble who benefited most from the British expedition was Yohannes of Tigray, whose territory Napier's troops had crossed coming and going from the Red Sea to Magdala. As a reward for his neutrality, the British bestowed a large gift of arms on Yohannes. He was crowned Emperor Yohannes IV in 1871, and with superior firepower he dominated the central highlands, expanded the empire's borders, and defeated foreign invaders emboldened by Napier's victory. Well-armed Egyptian forces were soundly beaten in 1875 and 1876, and Italians seeking to expand a colony in Eritrea met a similar fate a decade later. In 1888–1889 Mahdists, or Dervishes, from the Sudan (the ones who had beaten the British general Charles "Chinese" Gordon at Khartoum) invaded the highlands but were defeated by the Ethiopians at the battle of Metemma. This was a costly engagement, however. Yohannes was killed in March 1889 on the battlefield by a Dervish sniper, one of the last crowned heads in the world to die on the field of battle.[38]

The King of Shoa, Menelik II, became emperor upon the death of Yohannes. Menelik, like his predecessor, began his rule with a large cache of imported arms. Being aware of the dangers of the scramble for Africa by European nations seeking new colonies—Italy had even scrambled into the northern region of Ethiopia in 1882, establishing a colony they called Eritrea and into neighboring Somaliland—Menelik sought protective ties with foreign powers. A disputed clause of a treaty of perpetual peace and friendship with Italy, however, led to hostilities in 1895. Expansionist leaders of the recently unified Kingdom of Italy dreamed of a second Roman Empire stretching from the Alps to the equator, and it was assumed that a show of military might would quickly bring barbarian lands and riches into an Africa Orientale Italiana. From their colonial base in Eritrea, Italian forces marched into Ethiopia and occupied much of northern Tigray before being driven back.

On March 1, 1896, the Italian dream of conquest was turned into a nightmare in the mountain passes and valleys near the northern Ethiopian city of Adwa. There, Menelik massed contingents of Ethiopian warriors from throughout the empire and inflicted a resounding defeat on the Italian colonial army. The Battle of Adwa put Ethiopia on the map of the modern world, and European powers hastened to establish diplomatic missions in Addis Ababa, Menelik's new capital in the central highlands.[39] News of the battle awakened Pan-African consciousness in most of Africa, and in the United States, it inspired Marcus Garvey's Back to Africa movement.

During the last quarter of the 19th century, Menelik conducted his own scramble for outlying areas around the highlands. His conquests brought long-isolated regions under the central control of a reunited empire. The map of Greater Ethiopia as known in the 20th century was filled in by the success of Menelik's expeditions. Not only did he change the map of Ethiopia, Menelik also altered the landscape by importing thousands of Australian eucalyptus trees that gave Addis Ababa a distinctive look and aroma.[40]

It was during Menelik's reign that official contact between Ethiopia and the United States began. In 1903 President Theodore Roosevelt commissioned diplomat Robert Skinner to lead a mission to the court of the emperor of Ethiopia.[41] Skinner successfully negotiated a treaty regulating commercial relations between the two countries. Menelik was so pleased with the proceedings that he sent gifts including two lion cubs, a hyena, and two elephants' tusks to Roosevelt.

Menelik took Ethiopia into the 20th century, a more powerful and united country than he had found it upon his succession to the throne. He continued the work of his two predecessors in attempting to modernize the country, but the brunt of that burden soon fell to his successor, then known as Tafari Makonnen, who came to Menelik's court as a youngster to learn the ways of ruling in a feudal society.

CHAPTER 2

From Sly Fox to King of Kings

Since his preemperor days in the 1920s as Ras Tafari Makonnen, the image of the man who came to be known as Haile Selassie had flashed like a comet in the Western media and hence in the American conscience in brief multiyear intervals. He was born on July 23, 1892 in the village of Ejersa Goro in Harar Province, in eastern Ethiopia, a kingdom where an ancient feudal system was very much intact. His father, Ras Makonnen Woldemikael, was governor of Harar and a cousin and confidant of the nation's ruler, Emperor Menelik II, and the grandson of King Sahle Selassie, who had ruled Shoa, one of the preeminent provinces, from 1813 to 1847. The illustrious Ras Makonnen, a brilliant horseman, played a leading role as a general in the Battle of Adwa, was a close friend of the French poet Arthur Rimbaud (who lived in Harar and carried out his business there), and, in 1902, attended the coronation of King Edward VII in England. In his later years, he was a trusted diplomat and de facto foreign minister.

Young Tafari was educated in Harar by Orthodox priests and a French Capuchin monk before moving to Addis Ababa, the nation's capital, where he studied at the Menelik II School for nobles. Tafari was on a fast track to be one of the country's highest ranking nobles, but his ascent suffered a major setback when his father died suddenly of typhus in 1906. In the following years, Tafari proved to be a survivor in the midst of court intrigue and dynastic dirty tricks. He overcame major roadblocks to be named successively Lij, Dejazmatch, and

Ras (royal titles that denoted increasing responsibilities) and served as governor of Harar and Kaffa provinces. He proved adept at diplomacy and emerged as a leader of progressive reformers. In 1911, Tafari married another royal, Woizero Menen Asfaw, granddaughter of King Michael of Wollo, a major highlands province. During World War I, the future emperor supported the British though his country's rulers at that time were convinced the Germans would win.

When Emperor Menelik's health began to fail in 1909, a power struggle ensued between rival factions of would-be successors. To restore calm, Menelik named his grandson Lij Iyasu Michael as his imperial successor. Although Iyasu was never crowned emperor, he was the supreme ruler from 1911 to 1916. During that time, his erratic behavior did not endear him to the nobility, the church hierarchy, or the people. Iyasu showed blatant disrespect for government elders and Christian traditions and was a notorious womanizer. Worst of all, it was rumored that he had secretly converted to Islam. After Menelik's death, the aristocrats turned against Iyasu, who was declared an apostate by the archbishop of the Ethiopian Church and removed from office. Tafari, supported by both progressive and conservative factions of the nobility, was suddenly in center stage of a new power arrangement. In 1916, Abuna Matteos, head of the Coptic Church in Ethiopia, proclaimed the late Emperor Menelik's daughter, Zauditu, empress, the first woman to ascend the throne since the Queen of Sheba, and the progressive Ras Tafari, all of 24-years old, was proclaimed heir to the throne and regent and was the de facto ruler of the Empire.[1] Immediately after Tafari was installed as crown prince, he sent a letter to "His Excellency Doctor Woodrow Wilson, President of the United States" on January 12, 1917, and assured President Wilson that the friendship between the two countries "will expand and endure in the future."[2]

During his regency, Tafari developed a policy of cautious modernization. The first ruler of his country, at least since Axumite times, to speak a European language, French, Tafari was in charge of foreign affairs and matters connected with foreigners. He employed White Russian officers to train his military, and in 1917, the regent established an Imperial Bodyguard, a modern force composed largely of Ethiopians who had served with the British in Kenya or with the Italians in Libya. A short time later, the Bodyguard received training from a Belgian military mission. At the end of World War I, Tafari dispatched diplomatic missions to the victorious Allies in Europe and to the United States congratulating them upon their military triumph.[3]

To gain international recognition for his nation, the regent formally applied to join the League of Nations in 1919, but Ethiopia's admission initially was rejected because of concerns about its slavery, slave trade, and arms trade. Italy and Great Britain led the opposition, implying that independent Ethiopia was not yet civilized enough to join an international organization of free nations. Britain demanded a League campaign against pockets of slavery that continued to exist in Africa, one of which was in Ethiopia. In reply, Tafari pointed out that his government was making progress in ending slavery and the slave trade.[4] On September 28, 1923, Ethiopia finally was admitted to the League by unanimous vote but on the condition that Ethiopia strictly apply existing conventions prohibiting slavery. Although an old-guard noble grumbled "we are now under the evil eye of the foreigner,"[5] the Ethiopian public rejoiced, according to the crown prince, because "the people thought that the Covenant of the League would protect Ethiopia from attack."[6] This overly optimistic presumption about the League's ability to preserve world peace would not long endure, but Tafari's accomplishment in gaining League membership and its popular acceptance by the public despite vocal opposition at home and abroad illustrate what an effective politician he was. Time and again in his rise to power, the ras-regent was to outsmart, outmaneuver, and outwait the xenophobic, isolationist conservatives who stood in his way. His political skills earned the young ras the name "the sly fox of Harar."

In 1922, the sly fox had become a flying fox when Tafari made a dramatic break from long-standing tradition by traveling abroad—the first time an Ethiopian emperor or heir to the throne had left his country. Then, the regent had crossed the Red Sea to the British protectorate of Aden (present-day Yemen), where he had his first ride in an airplane at a Royal Air Force air show. Thereafter, Tafari delighted in flying all over the world. He established the Ethiopian Air Force in 1929 and built rudimentary airports in Addis Ababa and in eight other towns.

In 1924 the young regent broke into world headlines by undertaking a well-publicized four-and-a-half month tour of Europe, Egypt, and the holy sites in Jerusalem "to see the prosperity" of their countries, "the good fortune and riches of their people, the beauty of their cities, and the wisdom and knowledge of their scholars." More practically, Ras Tafari hoped to observe some aspects of European civilization that Ethiopia might copy and benefit from and to find a sea-port,[7] or at least a free port on the coast of one of the neighboring colonial territories. The latter idea was an illusion of grandeur, given the cast of wily, tight-fisted colonial leaders he would be dealing with.

Many Ethiopian noblemen were not impressed by the crown prince's stated goals for his trip and opposed the overseas tour. The regent, however, already had demonstrated his adaptability in forging new paths and overcoming, dodging, or otherwise getting around the opposition of Ethiopia's feudal aristocracy, and he went ahead with his travel plans.

Before beginning his 1924 tour, Ras Tafari issued new and comprehensive laws about arms[8] and slavery,[9] a clever public relations ploy assuring a positive start to his mission in the eyes of the press. The media lavished its attention on the charismatic young nobleman and his entourage from an exotic, storied land. How could they do otherwise to an official party whose men wore the traditional white shawls, called *shammas,* jodhpurs, black velvet cloaks, and great green pith helmets and who included in their traveling menagerie six lions and four zebras that were given as gifts to heads of state and zoos along the way? Wherever he went, the press and public were fascinated by Ras Tafari's appearance. European newspapers referred to him as "the thoughtful Prince" with an extraordinarily "handsome face, a fine hawkish nose, and large, gleaming eyes... "agreeable, intelligent, and appreciative of courtesy, a person of strikingly refined appearance." He was described as having "the appearance of a deity receiving homage... serenely unmoved by the pomp of his welcome." The regent's refined features were contrasted to those of others in his party that were described as "burly and fierce looking" by reporters unaccustomed to writing about visiting Africans.

The Ethiopian royal party made Paris the hub of their grand tour of Europe that, in addition to France, included visits to Belgium, Luxembourg, Sweden (by way of Amsterdam and Hamburg), Italy, Great Britain, Switzerland (to visit the Geneva headquarters of the League of Nations), and Greece. In addition to personal head of state diplomacy, the ras-regent and his courtiers enjoyed visiting major tourist attractions, partaking of nightlife, and shopping. Among Ras Tafari's most notable purchases were two automobiles, a stock of fine wines, and £1,000 worth of goods from Harrod's. More important to the crown prince were his visits to schools, universities, social service centers, and hospitals.[10] Cambridge University awarded Ras Tafari an honorary doctor of law degree in recognition of his plans to establish schools to train young Ethiopians in the paths of service. The university vice-chancellor, using the hyperbole common on such occasions, praised the regent as possessing "knowledge exceeding that of orientals and Egyptians" and as one who explored "ancient and modern knowledge" and studied "all the ancient Christian traditions" as well as modern science. The Cambridge degree was the first of many honorary doctorates that the emperor would receive in his later world travels.

The crown prince was received with pomp and circumstance at all stops on his itinerary but especially by the flourishing royalty in Cairo, Brussels, Luxembourg, Stockholm, Rome, London, and Athens. Belgium's King Albert I and Queen Elisabeth may well have described to their young guest the ticker-tape parade welcoming them to New York City in 1919, the first royalty so honored. Although Ras Tafari was disappointed by what he perceived to be a lack of proper respect for his party and by a "lack of warmth" by British leaders,[11] the regent recognized the success of his tour as an international public relations coup. Under pressure from the British establishment, King George V bestowed upon Ras Tafari the Grand Cross of the Order of Bath, the highest honor available for visiting royalty. As another gesture of good will, the English king returned to Ethiopia one of two imperial crowns belonging to Emperor Tewodros, brought to Britain in 1868 by the Napier expedition, arguably the 19th century's most swashbuckling armed excursions into Africa by a colonial power. Overlooked in the diplomatic niceties and excitement about the King of England's returning some of the loot purloined by Lord Napier was the fact that a better crown of Theodore and other royal trappings from Ethiopia remained in British museums. Nevertheless, Ras Tafari accepted the action of King George as a mark of friendship and expressed his "profoundly sincere gratitude"[12]—adding to the gracious stature of the crown prince in the eyes of the public. Indeed, the regent's tour was sometimes compared to that of Peter the Great to Western Europe two centuries earlier.

Amidst the pomp and splendor of official state ceremonies in the summer heat of Europe, the regent's requests for a seaport received a chilly reception. In Paris, London, and Rome, political leaders politely listened to Haile Selassie discuss the sources of the Nile, but they avoided or dismissed out of hand the crown prince's proposals for access to the sea that would be acceptable to the Ethiopians.

In Rome, Ras Tafari had an audience with Pope Pius XI and met the new fascist premier of Italy, Benito Mussolini, who gave him a "hearty slap on the back and the verbal promise of financial aid."[13] The ras-regent thought Mussolini physically impressive and "theatrical."[14] The subsequent interaction of these two international actors would not be so cordial.

Other than the crown of Theodore and his Cambridge degree, the ras-regent did not have much from his grand tour to show his detractors

back home, but he had learned an important lesson in the public relations benefit of good press coverage. The international media had
made Ras Tafari a popular hero by the time he returned to adoring
crowds in Addis Ababa. According to first hand observers, "He was
given a really extraordinary welcome."[15] Empress Zauditu praised Ras
Tafari for enduring what she called "the turbulence of the sea and the
heat of the sun" for the prosperity of the country and the good fortune
of the people.

The crown prince returned to a capital seething with intrigue. Various factions of the aristocracy sought to discredit Ras Tafari or to re-
move him from power. Some of the regent's governmental colleagues
considered his trip an expensive failure with no diplomatic gains to
show for it. Such critics did not see the value of royal travel in encouraging Ethiopian society to become aware of the rest of the world as
well as to adopt foreign inventions.[16] For the next six years, the crown
prince fought for his political life, most notably in the "palace conspiracy," and survived the struggle—again demonstrating his superlative skills as a master politician in a feudal setting. By 1928 he had
gained such power that the empress was forced by the military to pro-
claim him "His Majesty King Tafari Makonnen, Heir to the throne of
Ethiopia and Regent Plenipotentiary," a new royal title. As king, Tafari
successfully suppressed rebels and challenges to his throne. When Empress Zauditu died unexpectedly in April 1930, the stage was set for
the coronation of the 37-year-old Tafari as the new emperor.[17]

Set the stage was exactly what the heir to the throne did. Determined
to impress foreign guests that Ethiopia was an up-to-date, civilized
nation, King Tafari personally supervised preparations for practically
all aspects of the coronation. He directed the installation of triumphal
arches and newly paved roads with street lights, sidewalks, and electric and telephone lines to dress up Addis Ababa for the 10-day round
of ceremonies, feasting, and dancing. Invitations to this coming-out-
party for a rejuvenated and vital Ethiopia were sent to seven monarchs
and six presidents (including President Herbert Hoover of the United
States)[18] who designated appropriate envoys to represent them, including nobility (the Duke of Gloucester for Britain, the Prince of Udine for
Italy, and Marshal Franchet d'Esperey for France), colonial governors,
and high-ranking military leaders. Ambassador Herman Murray Ja-
coby and Brigadier General W. W. Harts represented the United States
and were treated with marked courtesy. Invitations also went out to
important Ethiopians and foreign residents of the country and to the
international press corps.[19] Most of the guests who were invited, some

700 of them, came to the celebration. Beribboned and beplumed royal visitors attended the coronation ceremony that Tafari had modeled on the 1902 Coronation of King Edward VII in London (that Tafari's father, Ras Makonnen, had attended). What they witnessed was one of the first demonstrations of African nationalism. There was confusion over the country's name, however. In the 1930s, the nation was widely known to the world as "Abyssinia," but the inhabitants preferred the historical "Ethiopia," which eventually prevailed in the media.

Early in the morning of November 2, 1930, in Saint George's Cathedral, Abuna Kyril, the head of the Ethiopian church, anointed the head of King Tafari Makonnen with seven differently scented ointments of ancient prescription and placed on it the jewel-studded, golden, triple crown of Ethiopia, proclaiming him "His Imperial Majesty Haile Selassie I, Conquering Lion of the Tribe of Judah, Elect of God, King of Kings and Emperor of Ethiopia" (titles chosen by Tafari for the occasion). His coronation, with its chanting of ancient solemn words, was, in a very special sense, a sacramental act for him, the sacred relationship that now would define his existence. Beneath the immemorial rounded ceiling of Saint George's Cathedral, the king of kings sat on his throne. Then the emperor joined his newly coroneted Empress for a grand tour of the cathedral. They were escorted by bishops and priests and other high dignitaries carrying palm branches and chanting, "Blessed be the king of Israel." The guests had gamely sat through a 90-minute mass in Ge'ez, the ancient Ethiopian liturgical language. Journalist Irene Ravensdale described Haile Selassie in his purple and gold coronation robes as looking exactly like a processional statue from Seville. Colored photographs in *National Geographic*'s expansive 70-page coverage of the coronation confirmed her impression. The royal celebrations were also extensively reported in the *Illustrated London News* and other British publications of the day.

When the king-emperor emerged from the cathedral, a military band struck up the newly composed national anthem, a fanfare of a thousand trumpets sounded, and a 101-gun salute boomed across the capital. Ethiopia's great men made formal obeisance to the new monarch prior to Haile Selassie and Empress Menen's riding the two miles from the cathedral to the royal palace in a state coach before the adoring masses.[20] That evening a great dinner was held in the Imperial Palace, followed by a fireworks display and a military parade at Jan Hoy Meda, the Royal Field, with the capital's vast race track. Many of those in attendance received lavish gifts. The newly crowned emperor even sent a gold-encased Bible to an American bishop who had not attended the coronation but who had dedicated a prayer to the emperor on the day of the coronation.

The coronation made the Addis Ababa regime credible to Europeans, whose presence was evidence for Ethiopians that the world recognized their nation's sovereignty and independence. The emperor's acceptance by royal families of Europe impressed Ethiopians, while, at the same time, Haile Selassie sought to impress European guests that Ethiopia was an up-to-date, civilized nation. In this he was successful, for foreign guests were impressed with the Ethiopians' mounting "excellent ceremonies, full of decorum, pomp and circumstance, and superb hospitality."[21]

One European, however, cast a distasteful eye on the events. The young Evelyn Waugh reporting "the Coronation of the Emperor Haile Selassie" as a special correspondent for *The Times* thought the spruced-up Addis Ababa was a Potemkin village, although "the true state of affairs inevitably appeared from time to time. Addis Ababa was little more than a ramshackle town, a shabby, dirty, dusty place, with lepers and eunuchs and slaves. It had a palace with two rows of lions in the drive, one hotel, a railway station, a post-office, two cinemas, a radio transmitting station, a few plaster-covered Indian shops, and a collection of mud, wattle, and corrugated-iron huts."[22] It was all a clever deception to persuade world opinion that Ethiopia was a civilized nation, according to Waugh, and the coronation was the final move in a long and well-planned strategy to pull the wool over the eyes by Haile Selassie. Waugh's strategy, on the other hand, was to profit from his adventures in Abyssinia, and this he did by publishing a travel book, *Remote People,*[23] in 1931 and, later, his satirical novels, *Black Mischief*[24] and *Scoop.*[25]

In the Caribbean, the coronation marked the beginning of a new persuasion. In Jamaica, where Marcus Garvey's return to Africa movement was by then well established, the islanders saw the coronation as no less than the realization of the biblical prophecy that "Kings would come out of Africa." They rejected traditional European missionary-based Christianity and created a new religion of their own. The new Rastafarians accorded the emperor the rank of divinity, the Messiah of African redemption.[26]

Riding the crest of the world's attention to the coronation, Haile Selassie was voted *Time* magazine's Man of the Year in 1930, and the emperor began a long and proactive reign that had, as one raison d'être, the task of convincing the world that improvements were being made in Ethiopia. Continuing the unfinished work of his predecessors

Tewodros, Yohannes, and Menelik, the new emperor sought to build a modern nation-state out of the mosaic of races, religions, tribes, and linguistic groups. Haile Selassie was noted for his capacity for hard work, a capacious memory, and a mastery of detail. The emperor also had a remarkable ability to adapt himself to changing circumstances.[27] He vowed to safeguard the nation's independence and to rule as an absolute monarch. He backed up his authority with "modern national organizations of coercion."[28]

As his first major act as emperor, Haile Selassie issued a constitution in July 1931, ushering in a new era for his country. Although the document was a glorified apologia for the divine right of kings, or at least the Ethiopian one, for the outside world, the constitution was evidence of Ethiopia's progress under its new emperor. There was a two-house legislature, but the same constitution declared the emperor's person to be sacred and his power indisputable. The formal signing of the new constitution was almost as spectacular an event as the coronation. Rases and other members of the Ethiopian nobility were required to come to Addis Ababa to witness the signing of the historic document, and they were instructed to bring their robes and coronets.[29] The Rases were sworn in as the first senators of the empire in the new upper house of parliament. The event was marked with lavish entertainment and great banquets.

The purported sacred, omnipotent emperor surrounded himself with astute foreign advisors and continued to outmaneuver any would-be opponents to his reign—including the one-time ruler Lij Iyasu, who reappeared and was promptly imprisoned in gold chains in a remote mountain village, where he remained the rest of his life. Haile Selassie arranged strategic marriages for his children and named relatives and allies to govern the provinces. Life seemed to be going as planned for Ethiopia's ruler, but the heady glow of the accolades of the coronation and the emperor's new clothes were to be short lived. Perhaps Haile Selassie had been too successful in calling attention to the riches of his nation. The strutting leader of a European colonial power with a grudge against Ethiopia cast a covetous eye on the kingdom in the Horn and set about to conquer it by force of arms. Fascist Italy had taken envious notice of the Abyssinian phenomenon.

CHAPTER 3

Mussolini and the Legacy of Adwa

By the time Haile Selassie became emperor, a fascist government, led by Benito Mussolini, was firmly in place in Italy, seething with a resurgence of imperial ambitions and determination to avenge an unforgotten humiliation by Ethiopia at the close of the 19th century. On March 1, 1896, the Ethiopian emperor Menilek II had inflicted a resounding defeat on an Italian colonial army at the Battle of Adwa, perhaps the greatest victory of an African over a European force since the time of Hannibal. A French observer at the time commented that the world would have to find a place for Ethiopia, the African continent's only independent state.[1]

Indeed, the defeat of the Italians assured Ethiopian independence during the age of European empire-building and the scramble for Africa in the 19th and early 20th centuries.[2] Italian feelings of inferiority festered in subsequent years. The country's humiliation left a scar on the Italian psyche, the Adwa complex. Jingoistic Italians sought "a capable and wide revenge" for the only defeat inflicted on a European power in the heyday of imperialism. When Mussolini came to power in 1922, Adwa still was not avenged, a task many expected him to fulfill.[3]

By 1934 the Italians had colonies on generally desolate real estate in Tripolitania and Cyrenaica (in present day Libya) and in Eritrea to the north and in Italian Somaliland to the east of Ethiopia. The Italians used Eritrean *askari,* colonial troops under Italian officers, to defeat

Arab nationalists in Libya during the 1920s and early 1930s, and they would not hesitate to bring Libyan soldiers to fight in the Horn of Africa. In 1935, Italy mobilized its ground forces. With war looming, troopships brought enthusiastic Italians conscripts to Eritrea and Somaliland to take part in a civilizing mission. The fascist's proximity to the lush highlands of Ethiopia whetted their appetite for an expanded colonial empire, where a surplus Italian population could be settled and attention diverted from failed domestic policies. Mussolini, ever mindful of his image in the world's press, looked for a legitimizing reason to attack Ethiopia.

When Mussolini, the Roman Wolf, was prepared to launch an offensive from his two redoubts in the Horn, he drummed up a casus belli at an oasis in a disputed boundary area between Ethiopia and Italian Somaliland. The December 1934 Welwel incident, a low-level military engagement that cost more Ethiopian than Italian lives, produced unreasonable fascist demands for apologies and reparations.[4] The Ethiopians took the matter to the League of Nations, which worked to avoid hostilities.[5] Mussolini's brash warmongering was in marked contrast to the gracious Emperor Haile Selassie's appeals for peace.[6]

The fascist's aggression outraged and galvanized blacks throughout the world. As the American historian John Hope Franklin noted, Ethiopia was seen by Africans in Africa and in the diaspora as "the sole remaining pride of Africans and Negros in all parts of the world."[7] Twenty-thousand African Americans demonstrated in New York in the summer of 1935 in support of the Ethiopian cause. Haile Selassie, however, was denied an entry visa to the United States to prevent him from taking his case directly to the American public and garnering support. On August 24, 1935, the U.S. Congress passed a Neutrality Act that placed an embargo on the supply of arms to Ethiopia or Italy, which actually punished Ethiopia, because Italy was already well armed. The United States also abstained from imposing an oil embargo on fascist Italy, which might have had a more practical effect on the fascists.

In 1936, Ethiopia requested the United States to uphold the Kellog-Briand Pact, a multinational treaty that prohibited the use of war as "an instrument of national policy."[8] The U.S. government refused the request and refrained from supporting Ethiopia, an obvious victim of aggression. The Kellog-Briand Pact established international norms stating that the threat or use of military force in contravention of international law, as well as the territorial acquisitions resulting from it, were unlawful. Unfortunately for the world of the 1930s, Italy, Germany, and Japan had not ratified the treaty and did not feel bound by its provisions.

The League ultimately appeased Italy at the expense of Ethiopia,[9] however, and Britain and France, intent on keeping the Italians from aligning with Nazi Germany, were persuaded to give the aggrieved Mussolini a free hand in Ethiopia. So emboldened, he struck.

At dawn on October 3, 1935, one hundred thousand Italian troops commanded by General Emilio de Bono crossed the Eritrean frontier in a three-pronged attack. A cocky, strutting Mussolini announced his declaration of war from the balcony of the Palazzo Venezia in Rome. The superior firepower of the Italians' planes, tanks, armored cars, and artillery—and the use of the mustard gas, described by the emperor with the French term *yperite*, against barefoot Ethiopian soldiers, some armed with swords and shields—quickly turned the tide of battle.[10] The Ethiopians put up a good fight, but within six months, they were overwhelmed.[11] De Bono captured Adwa and, shortly thereafter, Axum, which he entered riding a white horse. The Battle of Maychew on March 31, 1936 was decisive. Haile Selassie and the remnants of his army retreated to Addis Ababa on the last day of April.[12] There, a council of royal advisors debated whether Haile Selassie should retreat to a new, remote capital and lead armed resistance against the Italians or whether he should leave the country and continue to present Ethiopia's cause before the League of Nations and in Europe. The council voted 21 to 3 in favor of the emperor departing. On the third of May, the emperor, his family, and a small entourage fled Ethiopia, taking the train to the French colonial port of Djibouti, where they sailed on the British cruiser HMS *Enterprise* for life in exile. They stopped in Jerusalem, where the royal family had a residence and the Ethiopian Orthodox Church maintained a monastery near the Church of the Holy Sepulcher.

Two days later, Marshal Pietro Badoglio led Italian troops into Addis Ababa. In Rome on the evening of May 9, Mussolini declared Ethiopia an Italian province and proclaimed King Vittorio Emmanuele III emperor of Ethiopia before a cheering crowd of almost half a million at the Palazo Venezia. Aglow in victory, the Italian people celebrated, and Mussolini and his fascists enjoyed the height of their popularity.[13]

Haile Selassie and his party continued onward through the "Italian-infested *Mare Mediterranean*" to Gibraltar on another cruiser, the HMS *Capetown*. Eventually they arrived on June 3 in Southampton on the Orient Line Steamer *Orford*.[14] The British Government did not give the emperor an official welcome, and he was clearly an unofficial guest in the country. Hundreds of antifascists, however, chose to make their presence felt by thronging the docks upon Haile Selassie's arrival in

England. In London's Waterloo Station, he received a tumultuous welcome, and friendly crowds cheered and paid their respects at the various places he visited.[15]

Later in the month the emperor made his memorable but futile last appeal for collective security at the League in Geneva.[16] The speech stung the world's conscience, and the emperor of Ethiopia was toasted and hailed around the world by antifascists. *Time* magazine again named him Man of the Year, the second time he had been so honored in six years.

After Haile Selassie's speech at the League, societies dedicated to the support of Ethiopia were founded in Great Britain, the United States, Holland, and a number of other democratic countries. British suffragette Sylvia Pankhurst's pro-Ethiopian weekly the *New Times* and *Ethiopian News* was widely read in Great Britain and quoted in African publications. Throughout Africa, the war inspired Pan-African awareness, and Jomo Kenyatta, of Kenya, and other Africans in Britain founded the International African Friends of Abyssinia. In the United States, the *Voice of Ethiopia* that had a large readership among African Americans was started by an Ethiopian medical doctor, Melaku Bayen.[17] Most of the nations of the world recognized Italy's claim over Ethiopian sovereignty, but the United States, the Soviet Union, Mexico, New Zealand, and Haiti refused to recognize the fascist conquest.

Although the Italians had proclaimed a new fascist empire, Ethiopia was hardly conquered and pacified. Many parts of the countryside remained outside Italian control and would remain so for the duration of the occupation. Major urban areas were occupied by Italian troops, but rural areas were restive and were the scene of guerrilla actions.

During his exile in Great Britain from 1936 through 1940, Haile Selassie kept his crown in a bank vault and made his home in London and in Bath, where he purchased Fairfield House. He complained of being financially strapped, but he turned down the Texas Centennial Exhibition's offer of $100,000 for a two-week appearance in Dallas.[18] From Britain, the emperor continued to counter Italian propaganda as to the state of Ethiopian resistance and the legality of the occupation. He spent much of his time handwriting his autobiography in Amharic.

Many Britons were outraged by the betrayal of Ethiopia by the League of Nations in the mid-1930s, but nevertheless, the government was reluctant to give the emperor recognition. Indeed, some British colonial officers had "a great deal of sympathy for the Italian settlers and administrators."[19] With most European leaders still in a colonial powers mindset, Haile Selassie turned his attention to the United States, a country that he had long trusted for having neither imperial ambitions nor territorial designs on African lands. His determination to broadcast a Christmas day 1936 radio message to the American people on the BBC demonstrated the seriousness of his predilection.[20] On the way to the studios, the emperor's taxi was in an accident, and Haile Selassie fractured his knee. Nevertheless, he delivered the speech as expected. He ended his broadcast with "People of America! I wish you a merry Christmas. I plead with you to remember in your prayers all those weak and endangered peoples who look to the flags of the free nations with confidence, hoping to discern the star which will announce their peace and future security."

Life looked bleak and at its nadir for the little king, who had been stripped of his throne and forced into exile. Haile Selassie could ponder Mussolini's occupation of his homeland in light of Whittier's axiom that all revenge is a crime, but there was no court of international law to punish the Italians for their revenge of Adwa. How could the deposed ruler survive in such circumstances? Was the short-lived reign of Ethiopia's king of kings to end so ingloriously? Was there any chance that he might attempt to regain his throne?

CHAPTER 4

Liberation under the Shadow of Britain

The official British attitude of indifference toward Ethiopia changed when Italy declared war on Great Britain on June 10, 1940, and the British allowed the emperor to fly to the Sudan to take part in the liberation campaign to free the Italian colonies. A fortnight after the declaration of war, Haile Selassie flew in a Sunderland flying boat over France and landed at Malta, Alexandria, Luxor, and Wadi Halfa before arriving by train in Khartoum. In the men's room at the airport in Alexandria, he donned his uniform as emperor and commander of the Ethiopian army. In the emperor's new clothes, Haile Selassie spent much time patiently waiting for the British commanders to organize fighting forces combining Ethiopian guerrillas with British officers and noncommissioned offers (NCOs). The emperor was half-affectionately called the "little man" by the British while biding his time for half a year in Sudan.[1] In the face of this inaction and frustration, he remained "dignified, mild, and courteous."[2] On July 8, Haile Selassie issued a proclamation, to the people of Ethiopia, declaring that "from today, Great Britain grants us the aid of her incomparable military might, to win back our entire independence." The aid was slow in arriving, but finally the British and their allies were prepared for action on the Sudanese-Ethiopian border.

In the early years of World War II, the battered Allies needed a success on the battlefield to boost their spirits, and they got one in East Africa in early 1941—with significant help from Haile Selassie and

Ethiopian guerrilla forces. On January 23, 1941, the emperor, accompanied by Major Orde Wingate, crossed from Sudan into Ethiopia at the head of the Gideon Force, a small, eclectic brigade of British and Ethiopian troops, accompanied by 15,000 camels laden with arms and ammunition. Joining forces in Gojam with the Patriots, as the guerrillas inside Ethiopia were called, this 300-man Ethio-British force formed the center of a three-pronged advance, with a British and British-Indian army in the north forcing its way from Sudan into Eritrea, and a British and South African army in the south advancing from Kenya into Italian Somalia. The Italians, attacked from all sides by Ethiopian and Allied forces, and harassed internally by the Patriot army, collapsed. Gideon Force, operating in some of the geographically most difficult terrain, brought renown to Wingate and his unorthodox tactics. Wingate was later to gain even greater fame during World War II in Burma with other irregulars, the Chindits. Allied victories enabled Haile Selassie to triumphantly reenter Addis Ababa and reclaim his throne on May 5, 1941, five years to the day after the Italian had taken the city. President Franklin Roosevelt was among the first world leaders to congratulate the emperor upon his return to power.

The Allied offensive swept the Italians out of Ethiopia and the Horn within a matter of months—the first victory of the Allies in World War II. Ironically, the British, in accepting the surrender of Italian forces in Addis Ababa, were a party to the first act in the decolonization of the European empires that was to take place over the next 35 years.

Following the liberation of Ethiopia, the country was placed unilaterally under British military administration, an Occupied Enemy Territory Administration run from Nairobi, a center of colonial and white-settler rule. Haile Selassie sought to consolidate his rule, often frustrated by the short reins allowed him by the British, who were still fighting a war in Africa. The virtual total curtailment of national sovereignty by the British military administration was accepted by the emperor because he had effectively no way to object.

Haile Selassie had reason to be wary of British intentions. During the Occupied Enemy Territory Administration, some British officials sought to partition Ethiopia. In the north there were plans to unite parts of Tigray with the adjacent highlands of Eritrea to form a new state under British protection. In the southeast the British government proposed incorporating the already British-occupied Ogaden with the British-occupied Somalia, to create a Greater Somalia, under British trusteeship. British officials also for a time envisaged the partition of Eritrea, with the western portion annexed to the then Anglo-Egyptian Sudan.[3]

While the emperor chafed under British military control of his kingdom and the former Africa Orientale Italiana, he continued a charm
offensive aimed at America, by then in the war, and especially President Franklin Roosevelt. In letters to the president, Haile Selassie
kept Roosevelt apprised of his continuing problems with the British
and sought American financial and military assistance and advisors.
Roosevelt replied to a 1942 letter with heartening words:

> It is a source of much satisfaction to me and to the people of the
> United States that your country, which fought so courageously
> against a ruthless enemy, has regained its independence and self-
> government. The steadfast friendship of the American people and
> their sympathy with you in your period of trial will continue to be
> manifest during the days of reconstruction now facing your country.[4]

Solace of sorts came to Haile Selassie in late 1942 when the United
States opened a lend-lease center in Eritrea and increasingly played
a more important role in Ethiopia. The opening of relations with the
United States enabled the Ethiopian government to begin to free itself
from dependence on Great Britain. The emperor received moral support from the United States, a limited amount of technical assistance,
and promises of more substantial aid. This ultimately led to the signing of a mutual aid agreement between the United States and Ethiopia
on August 9, 1943. The agreement, "planned in Washington, agreed to
by Washington, and condoned by London," was a watershed in Ethiopian diplomatic, social, and economic history.[5]

The new role of the United States as the paramount economic power
in the Horn and the Middle East generated friction with Great Britain. The Allies' concern with defeating the Axis powers loomed larger,
however, than American rhetorical anticolonialism or British imperial
ambitions. As Wm. Roger Louis described it, the "historic antagonism
between Britain and the United States continued to exist along with
the spirit of cooperation engendered by the war."[6]

Ethiopia and the United States reestablished diplomatic relations in
1943, and Ethiopia, for the first time, sent a resident minister to Washington, DC. The following year Haile Selassie, in recognition of American support for Ethiopia, gave the United States full title to a handsome
10-acre compound near the edge of town to replace the old legation
in downtown Addis Ababa. The emperor frequently used diplomatic
connections there and in Washington to underscore Ethiopia's commitment to the war effort and to the fledgling United Nations.

Emboldened by the American presence, the Ethiopian government demanded termination of its 1942 agreement with Britain that had set up the benighted Occupied Enemy Territory Administration. Concord between London and Washington set the stage for a new agreement in Ethiopia and deprived the emperor of diplomatic leverage with which to play the two powers against each other. The ensuing Anglo-Ethiopian Agreement of 1944, which provided the Ethiopian government with much greater leeway to manage its internal affairs, was considered generally a triumph for Ethiopia.[7] Any British colonial aspirations about Ethiopia were abandoned with the end of World War II and with the coming to power of a new Labour government in Britain, which had different ideas about empire.

Haile Selassie enjoyed a closer relationship to the United States and began to drop hints that he would like to meet President Roosevelt. His wish came true when FDR went to the Yalta Conference in February 1945. On his return voyage from the Black Sea resort meeting with Churchill and Stalin in the Soviet Union, the president, on board the heavy cruiser USS *Quincy,* stopped at Great Bitter Lake off the Egyptian coast. There, on February 13 and 14, he held successive one-hour port-side chats with the three kings—King Farouk of Egypt, King Ibn Saud of Saudi Arabia, and the king of kings, Emperor Haile Selassie (on ornate, Persian rugs just beyond the second eight-inch gun turret). The USS *Quincy* was a poignant wartime meeting site for heads of states. The original heavy cruiser USS *Quincy* had been sunk by the Japanese Navy in the Solomon Islands in 1942. A successor cruiser with the same name was built in Quincy, Massachusetts, and commissioned in December 1943. By the time of the meeting in Bitter Lake, the *Quincy* had already taken part in several campaigns in the European theater and was to continue on to the Pacific, where it would establish a distinguished record in fighting the Japanese.

Getting the emperor to the rendezvous turned out to be a comedy of manners. A U.S. Air Force DC-3 was sent to Addis Ababa to fly Haile Selassie to Cairo—unbeknown to the emperor's British handlers. The noise of the plane's 5:00 A.M. takeoff rudely awakened Robert Howe, the British minister in Addis Ababa, whose permission was supposed to be granted for such a departure. While grumbling about American secrecy, Howe hurriedly cabled news of the Bitter Lake meeting to Churchill, who not to be outdone diplomatically by Roosevelt, flew from Athens to meet Haile Selassie before he left Cairo. Their first face-to-face meeting was short but not sweet. It was described as "cold and perfunctory...more symbolic than substantive." The emperor did cadge a Rolls Royce to add to his royal fleet of automobiles from the prime minister, however, and a major thoroughfare in Addis Ababa was named "Churchill Road."[8]

In contrast, the early evening meeting between Roosevelt and Haile Selassie had been "exceptionally cordial and agreeable," and official photographs show the emperor smiling broadly at the haggard American leader who was to live only two months longer. Roosevelt died of a massive cerebral hemorrhage on April 12, only days before the organizational conference of the United Nations opened on April 25, 1945. Roosevelt invited Haile Selassie to visit the United States, an offer that the emperor would harbor for almost a decade. The Ethiopians presented Roosevelt with a four-inch solid gold globe, with the continents incised on it and a six-point supplicant memorandum (asking for financial assistance and for U.S. backing for Ethiopian territorial claims, which included the return of Eritrea to Ethiopia), which the United States, in due course, satisfied.[9] Perhaps what is more important, the emperor had met his first American president, and the efficacy of his preferred style of face-to-face diplomacy had been affirmed—at least in his own mind.

Haile Selassie later honored Roosevelt by ordering in 1947 the Roosevelt Memorial Issue of Ethiopian postage stamps in commemoration of the second anniversary of the death of FDR. The late stamp-collecting president might well have enjoyed the set that included pictures of Roosevelt and Haile Selassie's meeting on the USS *Quincy*.[10]

Relations with the United States remained cordial during the Truman administration. In 1941 Ethiopia had become a member of the United Nations, and in July 1945, the U.S. Air Force transported the Ethiopian delegation, led by Prime Minister Makonnen Endalkachew, from Cairo to attend the San Francisco founding conference of the United Nations. The continuing amity of the two nations was demonstrated in 1949 when they jointly elevated their diplomatic missions to the ambassadorial level, a harbinger of increasing contacts between the two countries.

A new Ethiopian national currency came into being in 1945, backed by America's providing the silver needed to mint 50-cent coins, whose intrinsic value ensured popular acceptance of the new paper money.

The most significant American private-sector undertaking in Ethiopia also began in 1945 when John Spencer, an American advisor to the emperor, contacted Transcontinental and Western Airlines (TWA) in San Francisco about the possibility of helping to establish and then manage Ethiopian Air Lines (EAL), the country's first national airline.

Later in the year, TWA and Ethiopia signed a contract that was to endure until 1975. Beginning with DC-3s, EAL developed into one of the best equipped and most successful airlines in the developing world. Over the years EAL went through several generations of predominantly American-made aircraft. Even today, all of its wide-body fleet is Boeing.[11]

Another American corporation, Sinclair Oil Company, began operations in Ethiopia in the 1940s. The emperor personally watched the beginning of the company's explorations in the Ogaden in 1949,[12] but the results did not produce much of substance. Sinclair's early efforts, however, paved the way for yet another U.S. firm, Tenneco, to discover reserves of natural gas and noncommercial crude oil in Ethiopia almost 30 years later.

In 1951, the Imperial Highway Authority (IHA) was established with loans from the U.S.-sponsored International Bank for Reconstruction and Development. The IHA bought millions of dollars of American-made road building supplies and equipment to restore old roads and build new ones. The United States provided personnel to direct and supervise the program that required challenging feats of engineering.

Among the most significant accomplishments of the Truman administration was the start of the Point Four Program that provided U.S. technical assistance to developing countries. The Point Four Program was announced by Truman in his presidential inaugural address on January 20, 1949, in what many thought was the finest speech he had ever made, and took its name from the fourth foreign policy objective mentioned in the speech. Truman called for a bold new program for making the benefits of American science and industrial progress available to underdeveloped countries. The president noted that half the people in the world were living in conditions close to misery and that for the first time in history the knowledge and skill were available to relieve such suffering. Truman's "Fair Deal" Plan for the World, as the *Washington Post* described it, emphasized the distribution of knowledge rather than money.[13]

Haile Selassie played a role in furthering the Point Four idea when he invited the president of an American college, Dr. Henry G. Bennett of Oklahoma A&M, to come to Ethiopia to explore the possibility of establishing an agricultural college there. The two men held productive meetings, and upon his return to the U.S., Bennett talked with President Truman and Senator Robert S. Kerr (D-OK) about his visit to Ethiopia and his philosophy of educational aid to developing countries. Truman was so impressed by Bennett's report that in November 1950, he appointed him the first head of the Technical Cooperation Administration to implement the president's fledgling Point Four technical assistance program.[14]

Because of Bennett's 1950 trip to Ethiopia and his friendship with Emperor Haile Selassie, Ethiopia was the first country to request technical assistance under the Point Four Program. On June 16, 1951, one of the first Point Four general agreements was signed by Ethiopia and the United States, initiating a number of economic development projects that would include the development of an Imperial College of Agriculture modeled after the American land-grant system; agricultural research, extension and technical schools; crop and livestock protection programs; teacher training; vocational trade schools; health programs; nurse education; malaria eradication; mapping and national archives; and a Blue Nile basin survey. Point Four also assisted the Imperial Ethiopian Government (IEG) in programs of regional development, national airlines training, and public administration. Three months after the Point Four Program agreement was signed, the two countries negotiated a Treaty of Amity and Economic Relations. This was the beginning of an American foreign aid program that was to become the largest in Africa, buoyed by Point Four's successor organizations the International Cooperation Administration and the Agency for International Development.[15]

As the Truman administration came to an end, Ethiopia was emerging as the major client state of the United States in Africa. Increased U.S. involvement in Ethiopia, both governmental and private, occurred as the Cold War was heating up and the world's security and economic maps were being redrawn. In January 1952, U.S. Ambassador to Ethiopia J. Rives Childs reported to the State Department that "the people of Ethiopia were aware that Ethiopia had alone among countries in her geographic and economic position met her obligations under the charter of the United Nations, and is alone among them in meeting those obligations to the full extent of military sacrifice and commitment."[16] What would this awareness bode for the nascent U.S. programs getting under way throughout the country? What would the new relationship between Ethiopia and the United States bring for both countries and for the Horn of Africa?

CHAPTER 5

The Treasure of Kagnew

During World War II, the United States had its eyes on a special prize in the highlands of the Horn. A U.S. Army feasibility study identified the former site of an Italian naval radio station, Radio Marina, located outside the Eritrean town of Asmara, as an extraordinary site for a communications base. Situated near the equator at an altitude 7,600 feet above sea level, "far from the North and South magnetic poles, the Aurora Borealis, and magnetic storms, and in a zone where there was limited seasonal variation between sunrise and sunset," Radio Marina offered exactly what the U.S. War Department was looking for as "a fixed radio station."[1] The station's locale was in a relatively quiet electronic environment with suitable topographic features and climate characteristics that required fewer radio frequency changes.[2] All of these features contributed to the "anomalous propagation of radio signals" by which broadcasts from amplitude modulation, or AM stations, could be received from as far away as Finland, Australia, and Brazil.

In May 1943, soldiers of the U.S. Army Signal Corps began refurbishing existing buildings, and, by December, communications and receiver sets were in place. A staff of four officers and 50 enlisted men operated Radio Marina, or Asmara Barracks, as it officially was called.[3] During the next two years, Asmara Barracks developed into a significant link in the U.S. military's worldwide communications network. From Eritrea, radio signals were relayed to the Middle East, Europe, North Africa, and the Pacific theater, with specific circuits maintained to

New Delhi, Tehran, and Washington, DC. The base also served as an intelligence-gathering outpost. In October 1943, coded Nazi radiograms about German defenses in the Westwal and the Siegried Line were sent from Berlin to Tokyo and intercepted by Asmara Barracks. These messages were passed on to General Dwight D. Eisenhower's headquarters and used in preparing strategy for the conquest of Germany.[4]

After the end of World War II, operations at the barracks were cut back. Soldiers stationed there complained about the post being "the most remote in the Army." To get there, GIs had to travel to Dhahran in Saudi Arabia and from there catch a ride on a once-a-week C-47 flight to the base. When the Korean War began in June 1950, however, the base again became vital to American communications. Circuits were activated to Europe, the Middle East, and the Philippines, and increased U.S. military involvement worldwide necessitated the expansion of Radio Marina. If electric and magnetic disturbances upset communications in the higher latitudes of Europe, the base could serve the members of the newly created North Atlantic Treaty Organization (NATO). It soon became clear to U.S. policy makers that the maintenance of the communications station in Eritrea was of strategic importance. The Pentagon grew nervous about the imminent British evacuation from Eritrea and increasingly came to appreciate that only Ethiopian sovereignty there would guarantee U.S. control over what had become a strategically important signals facility and a convenient supply and oil depot in the nearby Eritrean Red Sea port of Massawa.[5]

United States-Ethiopian military ties grew stronger at the outbreak of the Korean War. To show Ethiopia's appreciation for the United States' support on the Eritrean and Ogaden issues in 1950, Emperor Haile Selassie sent a contingent of 1,200 troops from the Imperial Bodyguard to join the United Nations peacekeeping mission. An American ship transported the troops to Korea early in 1951. Ethiopia was the one non-NATO nation in Africa to contribute a contingent to the UN forces in Korea.[6]

The Ethiopian Expeditionary Force to Korea, or Kagnew Battalion, as the unit was known, proved in combat alongside American troops that they were very effective soldiers. The Kagnew Battalion fought in 253 battles in which not one of the Ethiopian troops was captured, and their heroism was chronicled in the book *Pork Chop Hill*.[7] Before the most intense fighting ended in 1953, three Ethiopian battalions, totaling 5,000 men, had rotated to Korea, where they fought with distinction.

The Amharic word *Kagnew*, meaning "to bring order out of chaos," first gained significance in Ethiopian history during the Battle of Adwa in 1896, when a riderless horse named Kagnew galloped towards the attacking Italians, heartening the Ethiopians into repulsing them. According to Ethiopian legend, it was Saint George, the dragon slayer and patron saint of arms, who rode unseen by mortals upon Kagnew in that charge. The name Kagnew, still associated with arms, would soon take on a new meaning for Americans and a notorious one for some Ethiopians.

ETHIOPIAN-ERITREAN UNION

Haile Selassie's foreign policy in late 1940s was mainly concerned with the question of the future of Eritrea, the integration of which was considered a matter of major economic as well as strategic importance. Eritrea's Red Sea ports of Massawa and Assab would be attractive links to the commerce of landlocked Ethiopia. Above all to Ethiopia, Eritrea represented the historic route of Italian invasion. When the British military mission withdrew from Eritrea in early 1951, Washington applied pressure on the emperor to seek hegemony over the former colony to assure that a friendly host would continue to welcome the American presence at Radio Marina.[8]

Among Eritreans, various factions had disparate designs for the future of the territory. The largest political party in the country, the Unionist Party, and most Christians of the highlands wanted unity with Ethiopia. The political opposition and Muslims of the northwest wanted an independent Eritrea.[9] For its part, the government of Italy demanded restitution of Eritrea, the oldest Italian colony and home of 37,000 Italians (in contrast to Somalia, where there were only 5,000 Italians). The Italian argument was countered by fear of putting Ethiopia between two pincers of Italians in both Somaliland and Eritrea. In Britain, Labour's Foreign Secretary Ernest Bevin did not want to reestablish "Italian rule with British bayonets." Another possibility would have been a UN trusteeship under which Italy, Ethiopia, or some other nation might supervise over a period of years the transition of Eritrea from colonial status to self-government. The powers of an administering state would include full legislative, administrative, and judicial authority and, in certain cases, the right to treat the former colony as if it was part of the administering state. Finally, the future of Eritrea was passed to the United Nations.[10]

Britain wanted to keep anticolonial Ethiopia out of the UN Trusteeship Council and thus did not opt for Ethiopian trusteeship of Eritrea. At the height of negotiations about the disputed future of Eritrea, the British denounced Haile Selassie as "the greatest intriguer of all time intriguers."[11] Ethiopian participation in the Korean War, however, convinced U.S. officials that all Eritrea should be federated with Ethiopia.[12] Such a federation would expedite American plans to further develop Radio Marina as a strategic listening station and secure other military installations of import to the defense of the Near East in an Eritrea united with a war-tested, anticommunist ally.

The disposal of the territory was finally decided by the UN, and in September 1952, Eritrea officially became "an autonomous state federated with Ethiopia" under the Ethiopian crown. A decade later, Eritrea was absorbed into Ethiopia as just another province. An American, Don Paradis, legal advisor to the Ethiopian prime minister, drafted the proclamation reuniting Ethiopia with Eritrea. Many Eritreans, who under the British administration had learned respect for parliamentary democracy, pluralist elections, the rule of law, and the protection of human rights, were disappointed in their fate in being forced into an authoritarian monarchy.

After the federal solution for Eritrea was completed, Ethiopia began to pressure the United States for a military alliance. For its part, Ethiopia played the we-are-a-good-ally-and-true card while asking for military aid. Ethiopians were aware that their nation had "alone among countries in her geographical and economic position met her obligations under the UN charter" and was "alone among them in meeting those obligations to the full extent of military sacrifice and commitment."[13] In the event of a world conflict, Ethiopia would be on the side of the United States, and, therefore, it was important for it "to be in a position to assume its external obligations in that respect and it was particularly important for internal security." In insisting on a suitable quid pro quo for the Radio Marina base, Ethiopian Minister of Foreign Affairs Abete-Wold Aklilou warned the Americans, "Many European bees will want an equal right to sip the Ethiopian honey." To buy entitlement to the Ethiopian hive, suitable compensation for the leasing of Radio Marina would be the rights to procure arms and have the United States provide a formal military training mission.[14] Haile Selassie wanted a permanent U.S. military mission of about 50 personnel, not one that would come to Ethiopia for a brief period to show the Ethiopians simply "how to insert cartridges in rifles."[15]

The Radio Marina acreage near Asmara had become prime real estate and a high-value bargaining chip in U.S.-Ethiopian relations. Six years of frustration and rejection by the United States finally came to an end on May 22, 1953, when diplomats signed a Mutual Defense

Assistance Agreement (MDAA) and a Defense Installations Agreement (DIA).[16] Emperor Haile Selassie personally facilitated the signing of what U.S. Secretary of State John Foster Dulles viewed as very favorable base rights agreements The two treaties were to serve as the foundation for U.S.-Ethiopian military relations for the next quarter of a century. The treaties had required nine months of sometimes acrimonious negotiations to reach a satisfactory agreement on the substantive contents. A tacit quid pro quo, arms-for-base-rights exchange had been enacted. In return for the Americans' guaranteed access to Ethiopian military bases and the preservation of a special position at Radio Marina, known after the signing of the agreement as Kagnew Station, Ethiopia agreed to a longer-term lease of 25 years for Kagnew and to much lower rental than those being negotiated by the United States at that time in Libya and Saudi Arabia. Washington would grant Ethiopia up to $5 million of military assistance and provide military training for three Ethiopian Army divisions of 6,000 soldiers for Ethiopia's internal security. Ethiopia also had requested that the United States agree to defend Kagnew from possible attack, but the Americans turned down the proposal.[17] Ethiopia profited enormously from the arms aid, the training mission that was called the Military Assistance and Advisory Group (MAAG), and rentals and expenditures produced by the base agreement. On the other hand, some Ethiopians were never comfortable with the presence of a military base of a foreign power within the country's borders. With its operations shrouded in secrecy, Kagnew actually had little to do with Ethiopia or Africa. The suspicions and xenophobic railings of some of the local populace were to becloud Ethiopians' public perception of Kagnew Station throughout its existence.

The United States may have been compelled to act by pressures from the developing Cold War. U.S. State Department spokespeople rationalized the treaties by pointing out that (1) Ethiopia was not a member of a bloc such as the then problematic Arab Bloc or Colonial Powers; (2) in Korea, Ethiopia had demonstrated that it was on "our side" and was a strong supporter of collective security; (3) "colored troops" (African Americans) were of great value in the propaganda war; and (4) Haile Selassie would gladly join any alliance of nations opposed to communism.[18] In truth, the United States simply wanted to pay rent for Radio Marina and limit its military involvement in Ethiopia.

To give a royal imprimatur to the military agreements, the emperor attended the name-changing ceremony at the new Kagnew Station. Dressed in a military uniform with cape and pith helmet, Haile Selassie reviewed a U.S. honor guard. The emperor told a U.S. colonel accompanying him on the tour that the mess hall "was much too fine for any common soldier and should be reserved for officers."[19] The colonel's reply is not recorded.

The ratification of the treaties gave new impetus to Haile Selassie's ambition to visit the United States. The emperor had a "standing enchantment with the United States," and he was determined to visit North America.[20] He also harbored the belief that diplomacy was primarily to be conducted between heads of state. The little king was a strong believer in personal diplomacy—the idea of having direct and frank discussions with those he was seeking to persuade. That's why he often engaged world leaders in a one-on-one conversation, to diminish any fear of his country's intentions and to seek common ground for reducing tensions and promoting peace. The emperor wanted to establish a personal relationship and to break down any barriers of mistrust that divided their countries. When Dwight Eisenhower, whom Haile Selassie admired for his role as commander of allied forces, became president in 1953, the emperor pressed for a state visit.[21] In doing this, the emperor signaled that he was sure of the stability of his nation and the safety of his throne—sureties that he had not enjoyed only a short time before.

The times were propitious for such a journey by the emperor. Haile Selassie had signed the Anglo-Ethiopian Agreement of 1954 that completed the restoration of Ethiopia's internationally recognized pre-1935 frontiers, a goal the emperor had pursued since the end of World War II. His nation had gained access to the sea when Eritrea, became "an autonomous state federated with Ethiopia" under the Ethiopian crown. In short, the emperor had brought his country to the position of military and political leadership in a continent which, with the exceptions of Egypt, Liberia, and South Africa, was still under colonial rule.[22]

Haile Selassie had a willing helper in his effort to get an invitation for a state visit to Washington. The new American ambassador-designate to Ethiopia, the Reverend Joseph Simonson, an ambitious Lutheran minister, cabled U.S. Secretary of State John Foster Dulles for authorization to extend an invitation to the emperor, an action that would not only be of general benefit to Ethiopian-American relations but would start off the new ambassador's mission under exceptionally favorable circumstances.[23] According to John Spencer, Dulles sought to prevent the emperor's visit.[24] But using all the political and diplomatic capital at his disposal, Haile Selassie insisted, and the new U.S. ambassador's intervention prevailed.

In October 1953, Secretary Dulles wrote a memo to Eisenhower urging that the emperor be invited for a state visit in 1954. "The United

States has no more genuine friend than Haile Selassie," Dulles wrote.[25] "He has sent troops to Korea and has been most cooperative in our economic and military aid programs." Dulles also cited the emperor's role in accelerating the signing of the military agreements. "We are often accused of placating our potential opponents. Here is an opportunity to reward a constant friend." A visit from Haile Selassie "would be popular in America and would give the Administration a ready-made and non-controversial opportunity to make a genuine gesture with respect to the Negro population." This was especially pertinent since no African head of state had been received in Washington since President Edwin Barclay of Liberia had visited Roosevelt in 1943.

Five days after receiving the Dulles memo, Eisenhower approved Haile Selassie's visit in April or May 1954.[26] A short time later, the emperor wrote to the president, accepting the invitation and expressing regret that Empress Menen's ill health would preclude her accompanying him.[27]

On May 18, 1954, the emperor and his entourage received a traditional send-off from the Addis Ababa airport, complete with an honor guard of the Imperial Army, the royal family, ministers, and diplomatic corps present. They flew in a U.S. Army DC-6 to Khartoum and Tripoli, where they landed at Wheelus Air Force Base, a U.S. installation, and finally, to Orley Field in Paris. On the flight to Paris, "while Haile Selassie was sitting in the co-pilot's seat, the outer port-side engine suddenly failed. The Emperor's staff froze in quiet terror, but Haile Selassie remained up front, amused by their consternation."[28] In France the royal party continued on to Le Havre, where they boarded the SS *United States* for a transatlantic voyage to New York.

The SS *United States,* the product of the finest American engineering, was bigger than a battleship at 59,000 tons, 17 stories high, and 990 feet long. It was the fastest ocean liner of its day and on its maiden voyage in 1952 shaved 10 hours off of the record of the *Queen Mary*. The Big U, as it was called, had an average speed of 35 knots or 40 miles per hour. When it first sped by the *Queen Mary*, the Captain cabled his British counterpart: "Sorry Old Girl." Replied the *Queen Mary*'s captain, "Your girls are faster than our girls."[29]

The Ethiopian royals enjoyed the speedy three-and-a half-day crossing that introduced them to air-conditioned state rooms and to steaks cooked in five minutes in a microwave oven.[30] Each day the emperor enjoyed an hour's massage from the ship's masseur, who was so proficient in his work that he was offered a position in Ethiopia as Haile Selasie's personal masseur. A fan of the afternoon movies, the monarch enjoyed several, including the film tragedy *Julius Caesar,* starring Marlon Brando.[31] Haile Selassie might have enjoyed seeing the entire assassination scene, because after he attended the first production of Shakespeare's *Julius Caesar* in Addis Ababa in 1952, censors had required that the stabbing of Caesar take place behind a thin curtain with lights dimmed.[32] Performances of *Androcles and the Lion* by George Bernard Shaw also fell under close scrutiny by Ethiopian censors. The Lion of Judah was sensitive to what lions said.

An African American hairstylist gave Princess Seble a "swirl curl" of her very "fine" hair that drew acclaim shipboard. The last day at sea was marred by the ship's stewards declaring that the $1,100 in gratuities distributed by Haile Selassie was "inadequate," although the rest of the party had taken care of their own tips.[33] Nevertheless, the emperor sailed into American waters fully energized and ready to realize his long held ambition of going to the United States and practicing his special band of personal diplomacy. Unknown, however, was how the leader of a poor, sub-Saharan African nation would be received in the most powerful nation in the world—where racial segregation still existed in many guises throughout the country.

CHAPTER 6

A Very Royal First State Visit, 1954

President Eisenhower's plane, the *Columbine II,* a Lockheed C-69 Constellation, the heaviest and fastest transport plane of its time, made a perfect landing at 4:00 P.M. at Washington's National Airport. As the pilot, Lt. Col. William Draper, taxied to the VIP terminal, an honor guard of companies from all four of the U.S. military branches was brought to attention. After the Super Constellation came to a halt, Emperor Haile Selassie I of Ethiopia stepped briskly from the plane. The "Elect of God, King of Kings, Conquering Lion of the Tribe of Judah, Branch of the Tree of Solomon, and Implement of the Trinity" had arrived in Washington on his first state visit to the United States on May 26, 1954. The 61- year-old emperor, who stood five-feet four-inches tall, was dressed in a field marshal's olive dress uniform with brilliant scarlet touches adorned with nine rows of campaign ribbons (including the U.S. Legion of Merit). He carried a very long leather swagger stick. His Imperial Majesty (or "HIM," as protocol required the emperor to be called) was greeted by Vice President Richard Nixon and Admiral Arthur W. Radford, chairman of the joint chiefs of staff. A 21-gun salute thundered throughout the airport and echoed among the flats along the Potomac River. The emperor snapped to a smart salute and held it for nearly five minutes while a military band played the *Star Spangled Banner* and the Ethiopian national anthem, *Mazmur.* Then, Haile Selassie, joined by Nixon, Radford, and a cadre of high-ranking officers, stepped off in a quick march to review the honor guard.[1]

The military honors concluded, the emperor, whose "bushy hair was flecked with grey," turned to his interpreter, Endalkachew Mekonnen, the Oxford-educated chief of protocol of the Ethiopian Ministry of Foreign Affairs, to ask, "Where is President Eisenhower?" Endalkachew replied that, according to the U.S. State Department, it was customary for the president to wait at the White House for a formal state arrival ceremony while the vice president or secretary of state welcomed visiting heads of state at the airport. The emperor obviously preferred Ethiopian protocol where he personally greeted visiting rulers upon their arrival at the Addis Ababa airport. The emperor's disappointment in not being met by the president was palpable to his entourage but lost to the admiring throng at the airport. To further offend the emperor, Nixon did not board the big, open limousine with Haile Selassie for the ride from National Airport to the White House but rode in a different vehicle in the motorcade.[2]

This was not the welcome that the emperor had expected. After all, HIM had been greeted in a regal way upon his arrival the day before in New York City. Even though protocol required the emperor's entry into New York be made unostentatiously, Haile Selassie received a noisy harbor welcome as his sleek liner the SS *United States* moved up the bay with an escort of police launches.[3] The first greeting came serendipitously from a CBS reporter. Thousands of television watchers of *The Morning Show* at 7:45 A.M. had a live interview with Haile Selassie as he stood at the rail, viewing for the first time the famous Lower New York skyline from the upper harbor. There were no television cameras aboard the vessel, but CBS hired a tugboat to steam parallel to the liner as she proceeded toward the pier. The tugboat carried a TV camera with a long-range lens, and a CBS reporter interviewed the emperor beside the rail with a portable mike and an amplifier that gave a two-way audio feed to the picture on the television screen. At one point, Walter Cronkite, speaking from the CBS studio, asked Haile Selassie if he would wave to the television audience. The emperor good-naturedly complied and went to deck on the starboard side just as the liner entered the upper harbor. The tugboat swung into position in perfect timing and suddenly Haile Selassie was on the air. HIM heard the cue on the amplifier and gave a vigorous wave and smile to the camera on the tugboat.

A short time later, Haile Selassie formally received a welcoming delegation of State Department officials, the mayor's reception committee, and the press in his suite. He obligingly went to the ship's sport deck to pose for photographers and in a lounge below, HIM received reporters with friendly dignity, exchanging casual remarks with them in English. The U.S. Coast Guard had taken reporters into the harbor on a cutter so they could sail into New York aboard the liner with Haile Selassie.

In his first interview in America, the emperor emphasized two themes that would characterize his visit: international collective security and U.S. investment in Ethiopia. Haile Selassie noted that "Ethiopia has done everything within her means to oppose aggression everywhere. She was the only state in the Near East and in the Middle East to send troops to resist aggression in Korea"[4] The emperor asserted that a strong Ethiopia stands in the "delicately poised" Middle East for collective security and the "high ideas which the United States as well exemplifies...Ethiopia remains more profoundly convinced than ever that her appeal was right and that God is now vouchsafing unto her recompense for all her sufferings." The emperor said he was not personally seeking financial aid from the United States, "however, my countrymen would be greatly pleased to see more American business enterprises and capital in Ethiopia."

When asked the purpose of his visit, the emperor explained, "President Eisenhower, for whom I have held the greatest admiration for many years, has extended an invitation to me to visit this great country. My visit is, consequently, in response to this invitation and to my own desire personally to become acquainted with the great and friendly American people."[5] The emperor was most polite to members of the press and went out of his way to accommodate African American reporters. Although personal interviews were rare, Haile Selassie granted one to the young *Afro-American* reporter, James Hicks.

After the press had left, the royal party disembarked and was escorted through an honor guard of firemen carrying 17 American flags, who lined the gangplank. The emperor was subjected again to a phalanx of paparazzi and then led to a limousine with an escort of motorcycle police and a security guard for a fast ride to the Waldorf-Astoria Hotel, where Ambassador Simonson was host at a luncheon. The national flag of Ethiopia—three broad horizontal stripes of, from top to bottom, green, yellow, and red—was flying in honor of HIM. This was the first time the Ethiopian flag was ever flown at the hotel, which had ordered it two months earlier upon learning that the emperor would be a guest.

The emperor, Prince Sahle, and Princess Seble were housed in the Presidential Suite, a nine-room suite that on other occasions was the pied-à-terre of the Duke and Duchess of Windsor, on the 28th floor of the Towers at the Waldorf. Other members of the official party refused to stay in any rooms at the Waldorf higher than that floor—resulting in the hotel's staff having to rearrange accommodations previously made for most of them.[6] The nonroyalty ended up scattered over five lower floors. According to the *New Yorker*, the royal party was by no means outsize, by either royal or Waldorf standards, but it was well-luggaged, with 110 pieces.

As soon as the royal party was settled at the hotel, Princess Seble, who was a striking figure wearing a gray tailored suit, a white cloche hat with an egret wing, and jade earrings, went immediately to Saks Fifth Avenue, where in less than an hour and a half, she purchased "two evening dresses, a silk suit, a pair of shoes, a hat, a pair of gloves, and a handbag."[7] Later in the afternoon, the emperor, having changed from his uniform to a gray business suit, white shirt and figured neck-tie, made a trip around Manhattan on a special sightseeing tugboat, *Dalzellaird,* as the guest of Leland Stanford, executive vice-president of the Sinclair Oil Company.[8] Upon his disembarkation at Pier 1, HIM received the gift of a Chrysler limousine from Sinclair Oil.

Haile Selassie's stay challenged a Waldorf tradition. Whenever a distinguished foreign visitor arrived, it was the hotel's practice to have the guest served by a waiter who spoke the visitor's native tongue. None of the waiters at the Waldorf spoke Amharic. Not that it mattered to the emperor, whose French and creditable English would suffice; it was just that the Waldorf hated to fail at anything. In the end, the emperor was assigned a waiter who spoke French.[9]

Unfortunately, another resident of the Waldorf Towers, Cole Porter, the witty songwriter and lyricist, who lived in a nine-room memorabilia-filled apartment, was away in California at the time of the Emperor's stay. Had the two met by chance, Haile Selassie might have thanked Porter for dropping the line "You're Mussolini" from the song lyrics of "You're the Top," when his musical *Anything Goes* returned to New York after a 1935 London production. The line about the fascist dictator was not in Porter's original 1934 New York production but had been written by P. G. Wodehouse and inserted in the song's refrain in London. "Haile Selassie" did not rhyme with any of Porter's superlatives in the song.

On the day after the royals' arrival, Mayor Wagner paid a courtesy call at the hotel. The emperor greeted the mayor in a business suit but graciously, if rather wearily, changed to his field marshal's uniform upon the insistence of the newspaper photographers present.[10] At 2:30 P.M., Haile Selassie departed for Washington, DC, in President

Eisenhower's personal plane, the *Columbine*.[11] The president had named his plane after the state flower of Colorado, his wife Mamie's adopted home state. Eisenhower's *Columbine II* was the first to use the call sign *Air Force One* that denoted the president was aboard.

With such royal treatment already showered upon HIM in New York City, was there any doubt that President Eisenhower should have been at the airport to personally receive the emperor? According to Spencer, Haile Selassie had a long memory, and incidents that seemed of relatively minor importance stuck in his mind. The emperor would remember what he considered a personal slight, but such thoughts faded as the head of state's seven-limousine motorcade made its way across the Potomac to the cheers of thousands of capital residents augmented by District of Columbia and federal government employees, who were dismissed early for the occasion. Not since the summer of 1939 when Britain's king and queen came to the United States had the District of Columbia greeted an emperor. The weather was magnificent, as only a spring day in Washington can be, and police estimated a crowd of more than 30,000 who lined Pennsylvania and Constitution Avenues. Lampposts sprouted Ethiopia's tri-color flag, the District's flag, and the stars and stripes. In addition, small hand flags had been distributed. Eight hundred police and 2,300 members of the armed forces patrolled the parade route. After a quick stop at the District of Columbia Building, where he was presented with the key to city before a crowd of 5,000, the Emperor proceeded in an open black Cadillac to the East Executive Drive of the White House. There, President and Mrs. Eisenhower, waiting on the White House steps when the motorcade arrived, gave the emperor and his family members a warm welcome. As Haile Selassie stepped from his limousine, Eisenhower told him, "For Mrs. Eisenhower and me, it is a rare privilege to have you as our guest in this house."[12] When the emperor was introduced to Mrs. Eisenhower, he clicked his heels and bowed in a courtly fashion as he took her extended hand. Princess Seble carried a huge bouquet of red roses that had been given to her at the District Building ceremony lending a colorful touch to the White House greetings.

"The American people," the chief executive said, "are honored to have you on their shores so they may salute one who has established a reputation as a defender of freedom and a supporter of progress." Haile Selassie responded in heavily accented English: "This is a moment to which I have looked forward with the keenest anticipation. For years it has been my fondest hope to be able in person to convey to the President and the people of the United States the expression of the profound admiration which I and my people have for your great Nation."[13]

Ike and Mamie walked out on the North Portico and saw Haile Selassie into his limousine as he was leaving the White House. A huge box wrapped in silver foil and tied with a large white bow was placed in one of the cars, a gift from the President and Mrs. Eisenhower to Haile Selassie and Empress Menen. In the box was the Gazelle Bowl of splendid Steuben glass. Eisenhower established a tradition by that act in making Steuben glass the official White House gift presented to visiting diplomats, royalty, and American heroes.

Haile Selassie gave Eisenhower a personally inscribed photograph in a silver frame, an engraved silver and gold cigarette chest, an attractive wool rug which was woven in the palace, and a 27-inch by 33-inch pictorial map of Ethiopia. To Mamie, the emperor's gifts included a silk rug, a gold evening bag, and ornately embroidered material. Empress Menen, in absentia, gave Mamie a gold mesh bracelet that had been made in the palace and an autographed photo of the empress in a silver frame.

At a white-tie White House dinner, President Eisenhower spoke of Haile Selassie as a man "who has established a reputation as a defender of freedom and a supporter of progress." The emperor thanked the president and the American people for "your friendship and assistance which encouraged and aided us in resuming our march on the road of progress from which we had been detained by the imperatives of war. That assistance is today, in yet more varied forms, strongly impelling us forward on the path of progressive development."[14]

The state dinner was relatively small by White House standards, with only 26 government officials and their wives plus the royal party. In attendance were Chief Justice Earl Warren, Speaker of the House Joseph W. Martin, Ralph Bunche of the United Nations, Ambassador to the UN Henry Cabot Lodge, cabinet secretaries, and members of congress. Although Mrs. Eisenhower staged the event according to strict military protocol, there was something of a family aspect about the party, formal and official though it was. The décor of the White House was polished and pruned for the banquet. The president and the emperor sat in throne-like chairs at the head of a U-shaped table. Mrs. Eisenhower chose a silver-gilt service for the occasion, and the dining room was festooned with yellow roses, irises, and snapdragons. The marine band played throughout the dinner, and later, entertainment was provided by Metropolitan Opera coloratura soprano Patrice

Munsel.[15] After dinner, Haile Selassie remained at the White House as an overnight guest.

On May 27, the *Washington Post* in an editorial, "Lion of Judah," noted that "in the parade of foreign leaders visiting this capital it is seldom that Washington has the chance to play host to a man of the unique distinction of Emperor Haile Selassie of Ethiopia."[16] That morning, the uniquely distinctive guest was transferred from the White House across Pennsylvania Avenue to Blair House, the official state guest house of the president. The royals were then driven to Mount Vernon where the emperor inscribed the visitor's book in Amharic: "In memory of the visit to the memorial of the famous George Washington. Haile Selassie I, 1954." HIM laid a wreath on Washington's tomb and shortly afterwards laid another wreath on the Tomb of the Unknown Soldier at Arlington National Cemetery. Haile Selassie's appearance at the cemetery created a stir among the crowd of tourists as 21-gun salutes boomed out upon HIM's arrival and departure. Honor guards from the army and marines added flair to the ceremony. Back in Washington, the emperor had a lunch meeting at the Statler Hotel with the capital press and photographers corps. In the afternoon, the Ethiopian Ambassador Yilma Deressa gave a reception and official dinner for Haile Selassie at the Mayflower Hotel, attended by some 2,500 guests. In the main ballroom, a 50-foot banquet table laden with food was banked with five-foot high flower decorations. A fountain spouted scotch and soda. The emperor chatted with Secretary Dulles and Foreign Operations Administrator Harold Stassen, but he did not partake of the feast. Four official dinners and two luncheons in two-and-a-half days were too much, even for a Lion.[17] The official day concluded with a dinner in honor of HIM given by Secretary of State and Mrs. Dulles at Anderson House, the Beaux Arts mansion at DuPont Circle where other visiting royalty had been feted in the past.[18]

The last full day of the royal party in Washington began with a morning visit to the National Cathedral, where special worship services were held in honor of Haile Selassie. Prior to giving a short address at the cathedral, the emperor made an unscheduled presentation, thrusting into the hands of the Right Reverend Angus Dunn, Bishop of Washington, a richly decorated Bible and a solid gold Coptic cross. This was the second cross HIM had given the cathedral. In 1931 the emperor had made a gift of a silver and gold cross as a symbol of Ethiopian Christianity, given in appreciation for prayers read on the occasion of his coronation in 1930. The first gift cross was carried in the procession on the occasion of Haile Selassie's visit to the cathedral. As titular head of the Ethiopian Orthodox Church, HIM sat in the chancel. After the religious service, the emperor planted a peace rose in the bishop's rose garden.

The royal party paid a brief visit to the supreme court building, where Chief Justice Warren and Associate Justices Stanley Reed, Felix Frankfurter, Tom Clark, and Robert Jackson donned their black robes to welcome them in the chief's chambers.[19]

Then the royals went to the neighboring Library of Congress, where there was a special exhibit of books, documents, and photographs highlighting Ethiopian culture, history, and recent advances in education and health facilities. The exhibit was the first of its kind in the United States. At the Library, the ruler received prolonged applause, a spontaneous gesture of affection from the visitors present. When a photographer's flash bulb exploded, Haile Selassie jumped about three feet, according to a bystander. Secret Service agents promptly prohibited any more flash photography. Most of the Emperor's 1954 visit was captured in black and white, most often by still photographers. The technology was to change, and, in the decade that followed, state visitors were, more often than not, caught in living color on tape or film.

At 12:30 P.M. in the Capitol, Haile Selassie addressed a joint session of Congress. It was the beginning of a holiday weekend, so only about half of the congressional membership was present. Sitting immediately behind HIM at the rostrum were Vice President Nixon and Speaker Martin, who introduced the emperor. The joint chiefs of staff, headed by Chairman Admiral Radford, four members of the cabinet, the chief justice and three associate justices of the supreme court, and a full representation of the diplomatic corps were on the House floor. A whole row of House seats was empty, and page boys and other legislative employees were sent in to occupy them. The galleries were crowded, however, as HIM took his position on a red-carpeted platform behind the podium in the House of Representatives. Many who could not find gallery seats were forced to stand in the aisles. Haile Selassie was received warmly and was given a standing ovation at the beginning and at the end of his address. Dressed in a dark civilian suit, Haile Selassie read the first 200 words of his half-hour address in labored English and then switched to Amharic. His listeners were given copies of the text in English.[20] He thanked Congress for lend-lease assistance during the war and for mutual security aid and technical help since then. HIM recalled that Ethiopians who fell alongside Americans and other UN troops in Korea had fought and died "in defense of that principle" of collective security. He declared that collective security was a universal principle "or it is no principle at all."

> No state large or small can refuse the call of another for aid against aggression…I call upon the world for determination fearlessly to apply and to accept, as you and as we have accepted them, the sacrifices of collective security. That is why we, like you, have sent troops halfway around the world to Korea.[21]

Speeches by heads of state were still newsworthy in the 1950s, and the full text of Haile Selasie's address was published the next day in the *New York Times*.[22]

After the congressional address, the emperor went to a lunch at the International Bank for Reconstruction and Development, hosted by the bank's president, Eugene R. Black. Later, at a special afternoon convocation, Haile Selassie received an honorary doctor of laws degree from Howard University. Before an audience estimated at 10,000, university president Mordecai Johnson conferred the degree on Haile Selassie. In accepting the honor, HIM made his first public statement about African Americans. Said the emperor:

> It is certain that the United States would not have reached its present world stature were it not, in part, for the enormous labors of Africans whose great descendants are here represented on this occasion. Events in recent days, here in the United States, have brilliantly confirmed before the world the contribution you have made to the principle that all men are brothers and equal in the sight of God.[23]

It was appropriate that Howard should be the first American university to bestow an honorary degree on the emperor. Howard and Ethiopia enjoyed a special relationship dating back to 1934, when several of the university's distinguished academics, including Dr. Ralph Bunche, established the Ethiopian Research Council that has disseminated information about contemporary Ethiopian and African affairs ever since.

In the evening, the emperor was host of a state dinner for President and Mrs. Eisenhower at the Ethiopian Embassy on Kalorama Road. There, HIM bestowed the Grand Cordon of the Order of the Star of Ethiopia on President Eisenhower and five other top officials who were associated with Ethiopia: Admiral Radford; Harold Stassen; Mordecai

Johnson; Assistant Secretary of State for Near Eastern, South Asian, and African Affairs Henry Byroade; and Ambassador Simonson. On September 10, 1948, when Eisenhower was president of Columbia University, Haile Selassie had conferred another singular honor, the Order of Solomon, on him "in recognition of his worthy leadership in World War II." Ethiopian Ambassador Ras Imru Haile Selassie had visited Eisenhower's New York office to present him, on behalf of the emperor, with a certificate and a handsome gold star medal.

On Friday morning, Haile Selassie, accompanied by Minister of Foreign Affairs Aklilu, and a secretary interpreter, met Eisenhower at the White House. From the Department of State, Stassen and Simmons, chief of protocol, sat in on the meeting.[24] The leaders had already exchanged profuse greetings, so the emperor quickly moved to the business at hand. He made it clear that Ethiopia would welcome the expansion of private investment in the country, and there were excellent opportunities for Americans whose money would be welcomed in the country. The emperor mentioned that new ports in Eritrea needed development and "some ships to stand guard." He also hoped that Ethiopian Airlines would be expanded with U.S. aid.

The president said friendly consideration would be given to all of these matters. Eisenhower said he was complimented by Haile Selassie's visit to the United States and that he looked forward to a future relationship of friendship. The president stressed that "the United States did not want to dominate any country but to work with them as independent sovereign nations on a friendly basis." The United States was willing to continue work in programs of social and economic progress in Ethiopia.[25] Furthermore, Eisenhower stated that the United States believed in the future importance of Ethiopia— particularly in Africa—as an area of stability. The U.S. government "may not be able to do all that it would like because what the United States does has to be considered in terms of our many other global commitments." At the conclusion of the meeting, HIM left a memo with the president that contained proposals for (1) loans for improvements of ports, highways, and aviation for Ethiopia's expanding economy; (2) encouragement of American private investment in Ethiopia; (3) assistance in education; and (4) military aid in fulfillment of the U.S.-Ethiopian agreement of May 1953.[26]

The meeting apparently ended amiably, but soon its ramifications affected both sides. According to a nonplussed John Spencer, the emperor had "suddenly decided to seek, without previous preparation or notice, new measures of military and technical aid."[27] Spencer thought this move "constituted an abuse of hospitality on a visit designed as a goodwill mission." This was an instance, according to Spencer, of HIM's "superficial approach to foreign affairs without deep appreciation of the substantive and technical issues, or of the obstacles involved." The end result was not only a failure of his impulsive initiative, but offense on the part of state department officials. Assistant Secretary Byroade tried to dispose of the military requests by informing the emperor that Ethiopia was of no strategic interest to the United States, thereby contradicting his assertions of the previous year that there were few nations in the world with whom the United States "had such close and friendly ties as with Ethiopia," a nation "essential to the defense of the Free World." Byroade's warning was largely ignored by Haile Selassie, who apparently held out hope that he would receive a favorable response from his hosts until the last day of his visit.[28] He would send Foreign Minister Aklilu and his advisor Spencer back to Washington to attempt to work out details with the State Department while HIM continued his state visit.

What Haile Selassie had demonstrated was that he was indeed the supreme ruler and did not have to clear his actions or requests with anyone else. This was in stark contrast to the cautious approaches his American presidential hosts had to pursue in their face-to-face diplomacy. Like the emperor, Eisenhower had great faith in the power of personal diplomacy. Eisenhower liked face-to-face meetings, where differences could be discussed frankly and openly, as had been the way he had dealt with Churchill and Montgomery during World War II. What Haile Selassie did not know was that Eisenhower's presidential meetings with foreign leaders had not ordinarily been for the transaction of business—that was left to the secretary of state and the professionals. Such meetings were rather for the purpose of generating goodwill—what came to be called high-level massage. Perhaps the emperor was aware that Eisenhower believed that foreign aid was the best possible way for the United States to spend its money abroad, far more important than military aid. Ike had been an early and strong advocate of the Marshall Plan, and he wanted to extend similar aid to third world countries as well. Eisenhower had a caveat about foreign aid, however. He would use it to help the cause of democracy in the third world at the expense of defense expenditures, but not at the expense of a balanced budget.

Following the White House meeting, the emperor and his party boarded a train bound for Princeton, New Jersey, and were seen off at Union Station by President Eisenhower. Unbeknownst to Haile

Selassie at the time, he had met three future presidents during the festivities in Washington: Senators John Kennedy and Lyndon Johnson and Vice President Richard Nixon.

The royal party paid a two-and-a-half hour visit to Princeton University. At Princeton Junction, university officials met the Emperor's train and accompanied him on the short automobile ride to the campus. "The slight, bearded monarch," as *The Daily Princetonian* described him, visited the grounds of the Institute for Advanced Study and the modest home of Albert Einstein, then a professor at Princeton, before inspecting the campus. He toured the Graduate School, Nassau Hall, and the Firestone Library, where he viewed Ethiopian manuscripts from the Garrett Collection of Near East and Oriental literature and signed the Library's guest book. The signature immediately above the Emperor's was that of the Shah of Iran, Mohammed Phalevi. Approximately 200 faculty members and wives shook hands with HIM at a reception in the Library's Faculty Lounge. A surprise guest at the reception was U.S. Senator H. Alexander Smith (R-NJ and Princeton '01).[29]

By that time, a group of 400 students had assembled and waited for HIM as he crossed from the gray stone library to the University Chapel. The Tigers gave the Lion of Judah a rousing cheer that elicited a smile from the emperor. Escorted by John K. Simmons ('13 Princeton), state department chief of protocol, Haile Selassie saw the Rittenhouse Orrery, one of the university's oldest instruments for the teaching of science, in Peyton Hall. Devised to represent the motions of the planets about the sun, orreries were regarded as essential teaching equipment of 18th-century lecturers on natural philosophy. The emperor, "Instrument and Power of the Trinity," had a strong fascination for science and asked his faculty tour guide many questions in French. When HIM and his party left Princeton, assembled students and townspeople accorded him a round of applause. The royal party, accompanied by a state police escort, drove in automobiles to New York City and their abode at the Waldorf Astoria.[30]

Early Sunday morning, Haile Selassie, in a dark blue business suit and a stylish felt, attended a solemn doxology service at the Hellenic Cathedral of the Trinity, the Greek Orthodox Church, on East 74th Street. There, HIM received a blessing from Archbishop Michael of the Greek Orthodox Church of North and South America, who called him "chief of a renowned and venerable people." The emperor presented the Archbishop with a hand-hammered gold processional cross of Ethiopian design for the cathedral. During the service, which was attended by 400 persons, Haile Selassie stood alone in front of the altar. Outside the cathedral, a Boy Scout honor guard presented HIM with a set of bookends from the Manhattan Council of the Boy Scouts of America.

After the service, the royal party traveled 90 miles north of the city to Hyde Park, the home of Franklin Roosevelt on the Hudson River, where they were the guests of Eleanor Roosevelt, the president's widow. Mrs. Roosevelt and her son, FDR Jr., greeted him and conversed in French. In solemn silence, the emperor placed a wreath on FDR's grave. After a luncheon in honor of HIM, the former first lady took the royal party on a tour of the mansion and the grounds.[31]

Later in the afternoon, Haile Selassie, Defender of the Faith, went to his second church service of the day, receiving a tumultuous welcome on the way. The emperor attended a special service in his honor at the Abyssinian Baptist Church on West 138th Street, which was described as "the biggest affair for a foreign dignitary ever given in Harlem." A gleeful crowd of 25,000 people jammed the streets of the church block, and thousands more gathered along the route of the ruler's cavalcade, cheering and shouting as his car passed by. It was the most enthusiastic and spontaneous welcome he received in America. The motorcade's route down 7th Avenue was decked with banners and photos of Haile Selassie, while from 155th Street to 138th Street a cheering throng clapped, jumped, and waved small green, yellow, and red Ethiopian flags. The mass of spectators pressed against police lines was rewarded by the little monarch poking his bearded head out of the car and waving his thanks. The Abyssinian Baptist Church had been founded in 1808 by Ethiopian traders who resented being segregated in other churches and in the 1950s was one of the largest Protestant churches in the United States.

After waving to the crowd, the emperor and his party were greeted at the church by the Reverend Dr. Adam Clayton Powell Jr., the pastor of the church and also a member of the U.S. House of Representatives, "in the name of the 700,000 Afro-Americans of New York City"—"men and women of every faith, belief and disbelief." Powell extolled HIM as "the symbol around which we place all our hopes, dreams, and prayers that one day the entire continent of Africa shall be as free as the country of Ethiopia." During the 30-minute service, the emperor was so moved by a 200-voice choir fervently singing "And He shall reign forever and ever" from the Hallelujah chorus of Handel's *Messiah* that he made a short, impromptu speech. Standing at the altar between vases of flowers, the titular head of the Ethiopian Orthodox Church told a cheering congregation of 3,000 Baptists, through an interpreter, that he and his country believed in collective security to halt aggression "wherever it arises and whenever necessary." Haile Selassie then presented the church with an Ethiopian-design gold processional cross inscribed on the back in commemoration of HIM's visit. This cross subsequently became the official symbol of the church and still stands on the pulpit. The emperor also gave Powell a large gold medallion which he proudly wore on a chain around his neck for the rest of his life. Throughout the service, worshippers shouted "Amen!" and applauded enthusiastically. This mood continued until the emperor departed as the organ played Elgar's "Pomp and Circumstance."

Outside, the unrestrained ovation continued. For a moment the monarch stood looking up at tenement window filled with people waving. The cheering got louder as he got into his car and drove east along 138th Street. Along his route, other thousands caught the spirit and yelled to HIM. News of the emperor's presence had spread throughout Harlem, and crowds gathered along 7th Avenue as far south as 118th Street as the cars with American and Ethiopian flags, proceeded by a motorcycle escort, journeyed back to the Waldorf.

At the hotel, the monarch held an informal reception for 10 Ethiopian students who were studying in the United States. That evening the royals visited a Broadway movie house to see the then new and novel "Cinerama," a widescreen process that simultaneously projected images from three synchronized 35-mm projectors onto a huge, deeply curved screen. Then they went to Radio City Music Hall to watch the Rockettes and the stage show.[32]

The next morning, the small monarch took a few turns on the observation deck of the Empire State Building, the tallest building in the world at the time, but the visibility was not good. The emperor gave his memorable high blessing to a pregnant Manhattanite also visiting the tower before making his descent.[33] After a private luncheon, the royal party was taken out to the ballpark and to the game—actually, two games, a doubleheader—between the New York Yankees and the Washington Senators. On the way, to the chagrin of HIM's State Department escorts, his limousine was stuck in a traffic jam for several minutes on the Triborough Bridge waiting for a smaller motorcade bringing President Eisenhower from LaGuardia Airport to a Columbia University–related event in the City. The emperor was unaccustomed to such delays. In Ethiopia, when Haile Selassie drove down the streets in his Rolls Royce, people stopped their cars, get out, and prostrated themselves in honor of their monarch. After the brief interlude on the bridge and a proper introduction to heavy holiday traffic, the royal procession made its way to the Bronx and Yankee Stadium, where 30,000 fans were on hand for the game.

The emperor, seeing his first baseball game, was greeted by cheers and applause when he took his seat in a box near the Yankee dugout. He enjoyed himself, posing repeatedly for photographs with Yankee manager Casey Stengel, who presented HIM with an autographed baseball, and chatting with Yankee infielder Bobby Brown, who had served as a physician in the Korean War. The bearded ruler received his largest ovation when he playfully took a batboy's glove and, standing in his box, waved his gloved hand to the cheering crowd. Haile Selassie showed himself to be a master diplomat by maintaining strict neutrality. HIM explained that both Washington and New York City had been so hospitable to him that he could not take sides in any fierce competition between them. In the first inning when Stengel argued too aggressively with umpire John Stevens and was tossed out of the game, Haile Selassie observed diplomatically that "each man was probably only trying to help his own side." Before leaving the stadium at the end of seventh inning, the emperor held an impromptu news conference. In the Yankee home club box, asked by reporters how he liked the game, he replied through an interpreter. "It was not at all difficult for me to follow." It may have helped that Major General Trudeau had answered the emperor's questions throughout the game. Haile Selassie pointed out that his favorite game in Ethiopia was Gana, "a sort of combination of field hockey and baseball."[34] After the game, the emperor was the evening guest of Mr. and Mrs. John D. Rockefeller III at their home in Tarrytown.

On the following day, Tuesday, June 1, the emperor was honored with a ticker-tape parade down Broadway and a historic visit to the United Nations (see Chapter 1).

On the afternoon of June 2, Haile Selassie received an honorary doctor of laws degree from Columbia University. Dr. Grayson Kirk, president of the university, made the award. The citation honored HIM for his resistance to totalitarian invasion by fascism of his own country and to communism in Korea. The emperor paid tribute to Columbia on its 200th anniversary, on its contributions to development of the United States, and on the aid it is giving to Ethiopian students. Two grandsons of the emperor Merid Beyene and his brother Samson, attended Columbia. Haile Selassie presented Kirk with a copy of the New Testament, hand-lettered in Amharic, for the university.

Afterwards, at the Waldorf Hotel, the monarch awarded decorations to six distinguished New Yorkers: Mayor Wagner; Manhattan Borough President Hulan E. Jack; Richard C. Patterson; Congressman Powell; Walter White, president of the NAACP; and Bishop Robert C. Lawson of the Pentecostal Church. HIM also held a reception for 3,000 officials of the United Nations and the city. Earlier in the day, the emperor, escorted by Laurence Rockefeller, had visited Rockefeller Center, viewed the skyline from the 65th floor, saw color television for the first time, and attended the dress rehearsal of a television show in color.

In the evening, HIM was the private dinner guest of the Council on Foreign Relations. In brief remarks, the emperor said the United Nations principle of collective security offered a better guarantee of world peace than any system of power politics, alliances, or regional arrangements among the great powers. After dinner, the royals went to the movies to see *Dial M for Murder*, Alfred Hitchcock's film with Ray Milland and Grace Kelly. The show was over at 12:40 A.M., late hours for the early rising emperor.

Later the same morning, the royal party departed by air for Boston bringing to an end the state visit of the emperor. Only the events in Washington, DC, and New York City were official and the responsibility of the U.S. government. After Haile Selassie's departure from New York, the trip became entirely unofficial and private, with the chief responsibility under the aegis of the Imperial Government of Ethiopia.[35] Of course, the Lion of Judah, while in the New World, would enjoy state visits to the other great powers of North America, Canada and Mexico, but those excursions were of no official concern to the U.S. State Department. State, however, would shadow Haile Selassie whenever he was in the United States.

Haile Selassie finally had realized his long-held ambition to visit the United States. As the center of brilliant social and ceremonial functions, he had enjoyed himself and had affirmed his ability to charm a foreign public with his solemn charisma. He had practiced his particular style of personal diplomacy, made his pitch for more aid to the U.S. president, and still had hopes of receiving a positive response to his requests before he left the country. Meanwhile, having completed his dealing with official Washington and New York, HIM began a 7,000 mile, six-weeks tour of North America to see the country and to observe "industrial development and the life of the people in general." In doing so, HIM would see more of the United States in a short time than many Americans see in a lifetime. For a visiting foreign head of state, especially one from sub-Saharan Africa, to take in so much of the American scene in 1954 was truly astounding. He left New York City with the cheers and applause of the governmental and financial capitals of the nation ringing in his ears. The Haile Selassie show had enjoyed rave reviews on and off Broadway. But would it play in Peoria?

CHAPTER 7

The Spring of the Lion

When Haile Selassie went off on his grand tour of North America in the spring of 1954, he was traveling at a time when the weather in most places he visited was at its best. The Conquering Lion of the Tribe of Judah was 61 years-old and still sprightly. Several reporters commented on the emperor's looking younger than his years and his maintaining equanimity in the face of a flurry of activities and a busy schedule. He could still scamper up and down ladders into the innards of great dams and exuberantly climb around working roughnecks and roustabouts on oil drilling rigs. A grave, courteous man of frail figure but commanding presence, HIM carried himself with shoulders squared and bearded chin imperiously up tilted, and he could hold a smart military salute for five minutes without blinking while anthems played and cannons roared. The emperor was at his best while exploring the new world, and a look at the respect he garnered from Americans of all classes and walks of life demonstrates the efficacy of his personal public diplomacy. The skillful use of public relations was his forte.

The gait of the lion is relaxed until he is ready to charge. The charge is a series of great springs. So it was with Haile Selassie, who traveled relaxed until he sprang into the memories of Americans far more powerfully than he could know.

On June 3, 1954, Haile Selassie arrived in a specially chartered TWA Constellation at Boston's Logan Airport, where he was met by Mayor John B. Hynes. The two conversed in French and were whisked in an 11-car motorcade to what is now called the Old City Hall, where a crowd of about 1,000, including many of Boston's most prominent citizens, awaited them. Brilliant skies and cool breezes greeted the emperor, who was again dressed in his field marshal's uniform. The mayor welcomed HIM to "the oldest and best city in America." Haile Selassie signed the city hall guest book in Amharic and told his assembled admirers, "We have been tremendously impressed with the wealth of learning amassed around the city of Boston in institutions of unparalleled influence in cultural and scientific fields."[1]

The royal party then drove to the golden-domed statehouse. Reporters noticed a new addition to the parade of limos—a Cadillac convertible sporting a huge "Welcome to Boston" sign and filled with attractive ladies from the Del-Thomas modeling agency. The car was sponsored by a state legislator from a predominately African American district in the city and definitely drew the attention of male spectators. In the executive suite of the statehouse, the emperor met Governor Christian B. Herter, who would replace the ailing John Foster Dulles as Eisenhower's secretary of state in 1959. State employees who lined the corridor gave HIM an enthusiastic ovation as he made his way to the legislative chambers to address a joint session of the Massachusetts legislature. Haile Selassie moved with great dignity, apparently impervious of the crush of newsmen, photographers, and a heavy police guard. John Spencer had misplaced the short speech that he had prepared for HIM to deliver in English, so Haile Selassie went to the rostrum and improvised in Amharic in a low voice almost inaudible in the gallery. The translation also was low voiced. Despite the audio level, Spencer thought the emperor made a creditable oration.[2] The House adopted a resolution saluting "the career of service of Haile Selassie, a man who, standing before kings has always placed his trust in the common people." Leaving the capital, the emperor sped to the Harvard University campus across the Charles River in Cambridge. Householders waved from apartments and boaters from the water as the motorcade passed. Sunbathers along the river side stood up to cheer.

The emperor was greeted by a noontime crowd of several thousand Harvard students who formed a human aisle through which the motorcade passed. Haile Selassie parked his car in Harvard Yard and stood in his open Chrysler as the students applauded. The emperor sat down then stood up as the clapping continued. He then removed his officer's cap and bowed with aplomb to the cheering students. Harvard President Nathan M. Pusey welcomed HIM to the campus and accompanied him to Houghton Library where the monarch examined several tomes, including the first book published in Africa (in 1516), *Commentary on the Book of Prayer*, by David Abudraham.[3]

The king of kings concluded his visit to the hub of the universe with a late lunch at the Sheraton Plaza Hotel hosted by Hynes and Herter. He told the 300 diners that Boston was "undoubtedly the cultural capital of the United States." Prince Sahle was asked to say a few words, and in one of his rare public talks said that he was deeply moved by the reception being given his party in America. Before he left for the airport, the emperor was presented with a silver bowl, the traditional gift from Boston to visiting heads of state. Altogether the emperor had spent only six whirlwind hours in Boston, but he had impressed the Bostonians with his sincerity and his dignity.[4]

OH, CANADA!

The royal party left Boston for Ottawa at 4:00 P.M. on a four-engine Royal Canadian Air Force transport *North Star*. Only five years earlier, the *North Star*, a reengined C-54/DC-4, had been the first aircraft to fly nonstop across Canada, the 2,785 miles from Vancouver to Halifax. That feat had put the RCAF Air Transport Group on the map, a reputation further burnished during the Korean airlift in the early 1950s that was a contributing factor to bolstering UN forces during the fighting.

Precisely on schedule at 6:00 P.M., Haile Selassie was met at Ottawa's Rockcliffe Airport by Governor General Vincent Massey, Prime Minister Louis Saint Laurent, and the Canadian chiefs of staff, resplendent in dress uniforms and carrying their swords. The emperor passed a guard of honor from the army and air force on a red-carpeted dais while a 21-gun salute boomed. Haile Selassie later confided in Spencer that in the Americas, it was the Canadians who best knew how to treat royalty. Of course, HIM may have felt more at home in Canada, being able to speak French wherever he went. His trip to Canada was described by the emperor as "a long sought opportunity." Canadian media gave extensive coverage of Haile Selassie's state visit and the history of Ethiopia in both English and French. The press noted that the emperor wore a Sam Browne belt, a Commonwealth-specific detail that reporters in the United States failed to recognize.[5]

That evening, in honor of HIM, Massey was the host of a reception and state dinner attended by cabinet ministers and heads of diplomatic missions at his residency at Rideau Hall (Government House). Haile Selassie had completed a gourmand's trifecta in one day, having had breakfast in New York City, lunch in Boston, and dinner in Ottawa.

In remarks at the state dinner, the emperor commended the work of Canadians in the reconstruction and development of the educational system of Ethiopia.[6]

On the next morning (June 5), the affable Haile Selassie was dressed in a neatly cut grey suit with a dark blue polka-dot tie, topcoat, and homburg as he drove through the capital on his way to the gothic revival suite of buildings on The Hill, as the Parliament Hill is called colloquially. Despite rain and overcast skies, many Ottawans turned out to applaud the emperor. As he entered the parliament buildings, out over the foggy air wafted the national anthem of Ethiopia played by Robert Donnell, carillonneur. HIM marched slowly from the Senate to the Commons side, accompanied in stately procession, first by the Gentleman Usher of the Black Rod, and then by the Sergeant at Arms of the Commons. It was the apotheosis of regal pomp and circumstance, and the emperor gloried in it. When Haile Selassie took his seat in the diplomatic gallery to observe the Commons debate, the members pounded their desks in salutation. The king of kings sat impassively as the Speaker expressed Parliament's welcome. The public galleries were unusually crowded for a morning session. The *Ottawa Citizen* noted that upon entering the gallery, Haile Selassie "did more than any British king [could] do." Ever since the Commons had banned Prince Charles, no British monarch had ever set foot in the Commons.

The emperor wore reading glasses low on his nose as he read in French and English his address at the opening of Parliament "in recognition of Canada's valuable support to Ethiopia's claims to Eritrea at the time of the Paris Peace Conference."[7] He expressed his pleasure in being in Ottawa "in this centennial year." After leaving the diplomatic gallery, Haile Selassie held a press conference where he spoke softly in Amharic to a crowd of newsmen who jammed the parliamentary press gallery lounge. The little king was described as having Solomon-like qualities when he was asked whether there were any statesmen in the world today with the attributes of his wise forebear, Solomon. The ruler pondered the question for some time before replying. Then he softly said, "There are very many wise men in the world today. It is difficult to choose one; other wise men might not like it."[8]

In the afternoon, Massey held a reception attended by cabinet ministers and heads of diplomatic missions. In shaking hands with the dignitaries, Haile Selassie limply presented only a piece of his hand that one could not "crush or squeeze." This defensive mechanism, called "a trick of famous men" by the Canadian press, saved the hand of HIM to shake another day. The sangfroid perseverance of the emperor earned him the accolade of "probably the most informal monarch who ever visited Ottawa."[9] That evening, Massey escorted the emperor to Rockcliffe airport and bade him farewell as the monarch left the city and flew in a RCAF aircraft to Montreal.

There, the bearded monarch was the guest of the Montreal Metropolitan Commission, at a reception attended by 225 at the Windsor Hotel and at a dinner for 1,200 at Chalet de la Montaigne, situated on Mont-Royal with the most spectacular view of Montreal.[10] On June 5, the emperor received an honorary degree from McGill University at a special convocation.[11] Afterward, a luncheon was given for HIM by Gaspard Fauteux, the lieutenant governor of Quebec before the royal party was driven to the Port of Montreal through applauding crowds in the crowded street. The royals sailed down the Saint Lawrence River to Quebec City aboard the government ship *d'Iberville,* an icebreaker. Haile Selassie was the recipient of another honorary degree from Laval University in Quebec City, the oldest center of education in Canada and the first institution in North America to offer higher education in French. From there the emperor flew to Windsor, Ontario, where he spent the night.

WESTWARD, HO!

Early the next morning, the royal party drove North across Ambassador Bridge to Detroit, where they were met by top officials and dignitaries of the city. At a reception at the Detroit City Hall, Mayor Albert Cobo presented HIM with the key to the city and a medallion showing the beginning and growth of the Motor City. In a brief press conference, Haile Selassie lauded the Supreme Court's *Brown v. Board of Education* decision that "won the praise of the entire world." A crowd of 3,000 gathered outside City Hall and cheered as the slight, military-erect monarch departed. His motorcade drove to Ann Arbor, where, in a morning convocation HIM received an honorary degree of doctor of civil laws from the University of Michigan, the oldest land-grant state university in the country. The royals then enjoyed a luncheon with the university's regents and leading faculty members. Haile Selassie presented the university with an antique Amharic Bible for its rare books collection.[12]

From Ann Arbor, the royals flew to the state capital, Lansing, for a tour of an Oldsmobile automobile plant as guests of General Motors and then to a reception given by Michigan Governor G. Mennen Williams, which was attended by 80 state officials. HIM presented the governor with a gold medal and in return was given a ceramic plate with a map of Michigan on it and a bow tie (a sartorial trade mark of Governor "Soapy" Williams).

In the afternoon, at the Lansing Airport, the royal party boarded the special TWA Super Constellation, *Star of Bombay*, the aircraft that would be their air transport throughout the rest of their stay in the United States. The plane was especially equipped with the front made into a state room compartment for the royal family, with drapes shutting it off from the rest of the plane. Handsome, thick carpets and rugs were laid in the compartment. According to the pilot, Captain V. J. Statt, of Kansas City, "The royals stayed in the compartment by themselves." On the tarmac in Lansing, the engines of the red and white TWA plane came to life. The *Star of Bombay* sped down the runway, cut across the sun and pointed westward toward Chicago. As they approached the Windy City, Haile Selassie was impressed by the air view and asked the pilot to circle the city before landing. Captain Statt found the emperor to be very reserved and stately, and conducted himself "as you'd expect a monarch should. He asked questions about everything."[13]

The grave, courteous king, the first reigning emperor ever to visit Chicago, was greeted at Midway Airport by Mayor Martin H. Kennelly. The mayor described HIM as "a world figure who symbolizes lion-hearted courage and passionate resistance to aggression and enslavement." The emperor made the mayor a Grand Officer of the Order of the Star of Ethiopia, the award level apparently deemed appropriate for mayors and city leaders. The royal party then was driven, with a motorcycle escort, to the Drake Hotel on North Michigan Avenue, where they occupied 31 rooms. A cheering crowd of 25,000 lined the route from the airport along Michigan Avenue.[14] A young graduate student at the University of Chicago, Donald Levine, who later would be the dean of American Ethiopianists, had to move quickly to the route of the motorcade to catch a glimpse of the emperor speeding by.

At the crack of dawn the next morning, Haile Selassie started a whirlwind of activity, beginning with a visit to the mammoth Chicago union stockyards, where the little king gaped at the livestock and shook hands with a towering cowboy from Montana. This was followed by a tour of the Swift and Company packing plant. After a lunch with 1,000 civic leaders at the Sherman Hotel, the royal party took an afternoon Burlington train to Cicero, Illinois, where they inspected a railroad roundhouse and a steel mill, the South Works of U.S. Steel. Back in Chicago, HIM made an unscheduled stop to attend a worship service at the Parkway Baptist Church, where he briefly addressed a mainly African American congregation of 3,000. Ending a tightly scheduled, 24-hour stay in Chicago, the royals took an evening flight to Saint Paul.[15]

The *Star of Bombay* landed at the Twin Cities airport, and the emperor was greeted by the mayors of Saint Paul and Minneapolis. The small man of great composure and many titles looked drawn and weary as he inspected another honor guard and made his way to the Hotel Saint Paul. But the next morning he was full of energy, which was a good thing, because Ambassador Simonson had requested HIM to spend considerable time in Minnesota, his home state, and had scheduled a very full day of activities. The Defender of the Faith attended early devotions at Christ Lutheran Church on Capitol Hill, where Simonson had been the pastor. After a Scandinavian breakfast at the church, the emperor walked across the street to visit the state capitol and meet Governor C. Elmer Anderson. The royal's 13-car caravan led by Haile Selassie in a flashy red convertible then paraded through downtown Saint Paul and, accompanied by troops of the Minnesota National Guard and the highway patrol, crossed the Mississippi River to Minneapolis. They visited the state fair, the main campus and agricultural campus of the University of Minnesota, and a flour mill on their drive through the city.

The cavalcade drove southeast to Rochester, Minnesota, where the royal party saw the Mayo Clinic. Youngsters waving little Ethiopian flags greeted the emperor as he drove through small towns. The motorcade continued 90 miles south to make a brief stop at a typical Minnesota farm, where the fields were green with sprouted corn. After looking over beef cattle foraging in pasture, the royals were served crisp homemade cookies and lemonade by their hosts, the Doty family. The tour resumed with the entourage viewing wheat fields and fodder-filled silos jutting up from barnyards in southern Minnesota.[16] At Austin, Simonson's hometown, they donned white coats and inspected the Hormel Meat Packing Plant, home of Spam. Haile Selassie was interested in the meatpacking industry because, as he noted, Ethiopia had none. The response of the citizens of Austin to a royal visit was typical of the exuberance displayed by small towns in America in playing hosts to the distinguished Ethiopian guests. The local newspaper had a banner-sized headline, "Austin Entertains Royalty."[17] An editorial stated, "Austin today welcomed sincerely and with warm felicitations its distinguished guest, Emperor Haile Selassie. It also whets our community pride to note that Austin and the Midwest's metropolis, Chicago, shared an initial experience—the first time either community has had occasion to be host to an emperor." The content of the Austin editorial, the main points repeated in newspaper editorials through-out the country, recalled the events surrounding the Italian invasion of Ethiopia, Haile Selassie's attempts to modernize his nation, his efforts to rule as a constitutional rather than absolute monarch, and the status of Ethiopia as a nation friendly to the United States.

On the way back to Saint Paul, the emperor stopped at Northfield where he visited two liberal arts college, Saint Olaf, Simonson's alma mater, where he had tea with Clements Granshou, the college presi-dent, and Carleton College. En route, The royals made an impromptu stop at the town, Owatonna, which was celebrating its centennial. All males in the area were ordered to grow beards or face indignant pun-ishments. The celebrants refused to let the motorcade pass until they made a presentation to HIM in honor of his beard. They gave the em-peror a top hat, some wooden nickels, and a T-shirt. The little king was amused. Later, he sent the town a medal from Ethiopia.

At a press conference in Saint Paul, Haile Selassie told reporters he was favorably impressed with U.S. agriculture being so carefully planned and thought out. He found that America surpassed anything he knew or had read about the United States. In the evening, a civic state dinner honoring HIM was held in the University of Minnesota Memo-rial Union Ballroom. Dr. Charles W. Mayo, head of the Mayo Clinic and president of the American Association for the United Nations, pre-sided. Mayo introduced Simonson who introduced HIM to the over-flow crowd of diners. Among those attending was Carl Rowan, then a prize-winning reporter with the *Minneapolis Tribune,* who would later have a distinguished career in diplomacy. In his remarks, the monarch stressed that a recently negotiated commercial treaty and an American dollar-based currency in Ethiopia should encourage the investment of American capital in his country. The emperor added to the ever-growing ranks of the Order of the Star of Ethiopia by making Mayor Eric Hoyer a grand officer of the order.[18]

On the morning of June 10, the royal party flew to Spokane, Washing-ton, landing at Geiger Field. Washington's acting Governor Emmett T. Anderson was the official greeter and host of the inland empire. The entourage drove directly to the Grand Coulee Dam, where they ob-served the facilities with which the mighty Columbia River had been harnessed. They inspected the powerhouse and pumping plant, ac-companied by officials of the reclamation bureau. The emperor, who climbed down some long ladders during the tour, was especially inter-ested in the dam operations because he was "hoping to return to his na-tive Ethiopia with plans for development of water-power projects for that country." At the time, the United States was assisting in surveying the Blue Nile, a great potential power source.[19] After the tour, the party returned to the Davenport Hotel, where they spent the night.[20]

The emperor's flight to Seattle the next morning received a military jet escort into the airport, and HIM was greeted with the crash of a 21-gun salute upon deplaning. The royals visited a massive Boeing Aircraft plant, where 35,000 workers, including 5,000 engineers were employed. The visitors saw the prototype U.S. Air Force B-52 jet bomber, described as mighty, which was still a year away from being put in active service. Boeing was about to enter the infant jet airliner business, and the emperor was intrigued with the company's new designs. For decades thereafter, Ethiopian Airlines was one of Boeing's best customers. After lunch with the commanding officer of the Bremerton Naval Base, Admiral Homer N. Wallin, at his residency, and a tour of the base, the entourage went to the Puget Sound Naval Shipyard, where HIM was cheered by thousands who threw confetti in his path. The navy brass took Haile Selassie on an inspection of a destroyer. In the evening, the mayor of Seattle, Allan Pomeroy, gave a reception for the monarch at the swank Rainier Club, which was attended by 1,000 people. On the next day, the emperor made one of the few cancellations of a scheduled event when he decided not to make a trip to Mount Rainier in order to rest.[21] Haile Selassie and his entourage were serenaded by the Shrine Oriental Band at the Olympic Hotel where both groups were staying. Shriners and their interpretation of oriental splendor had also shared public attention with HIM at Princeton, where they had begun a downtown parade just as the emperor's motorcade was leaving.

On June12, the royal party had an afternoon departure for San Francisco on the Sothern Pacific Railroad's streamliner the *Klamath*. The emperor complained to Seattle reporters that he was so close to the Pacific Ocean but had not had an opportunity to see it. That travel goal was taken care of from the two special Pullman cars and an observation lounge on Southern Pacific's scenic route along the coasts of Washington, Oregon, and northern California.

On the night of June 13, the royal party arrived in Oakland at the Mole, the massive railways wharf and ferry pier that was still in use in the 1950s. The wharf was used to transport railroad freight cars across the bay to San Francisco. A crowd of 1,500 was at the station to greet the emperor, smiling and gracious, as he stepped down from his Pullman. Mayor Clifford Rishell of Oakland officially welcomed HIM and gave him yet another key to a city. The emperor made him a

Commander of the Order of the Star of Ethiopia.[22] The royals had arrived on Flag Day, and the *Oakland Tribune* had a welcoming editorial and a Lou Grant political cartoon showing Ethiopia under the jackboot of Italy and Haile Selassie telling an American, "Never take your flag for granted, my friend…."

The indefatigable little king then took his place in a nine-limousine motorcade with a motorcycle escort of six white-helmeted Oakland police for a ride across the Bay Bridge to San Francisco's Nob Hill. A throng of 500, who were waiting in the lobby of the Mark Hopkins Hotel, applauded when Haile Selassie strode in. The emperor was housed in the palatial Imperial Suite on the 17th floor that featured a glass-terraced bedroom commanding an inspiring view of downtown San Francisco, the Bay Bridge, and Oakland beyond. The suite was only two floors beneath the renowned Top o' the Mark, the hotel bar with famed view windows. A $60,000 refurbishment of the Imperial Suite had been completed only two days before, and the bathroom had 24-carat gold handles. HIM's first query was, "Where is the bathroom with gold knobs? I've been hearing about it." He was officially welcomed by City Attorney Dion Holm before setting out for the Veterans Administration hospital at Fort Miley. There he visited Ethiopian and U.S. soldiers who had been wounded in Korea and presented the hospital with a six-foot gold-plated cross for the chapel. The royals enjoyed a leisurely drive through Golden Gate Park and were received at the stately City Hall by Mayor Elmer Robinson just before noon. The mayor presented HIM with gifts—a gavel made of redwood and a Steuben Glass goblet. Haile Selassie gave the mayor two elephant tusks tipped with gold on a wooden base. He then bestowed Order of the Star of Ethiopia titles and medals on California Governor Goodwin Knight (Knight of the Grand Cross) and Mayor Robinson (Grand Commander). A reporter noted that Princess Seble "limped as if her feet were killing her."[23]

The royal party's motorcade drove down Market Street, which was lined with cheering spectators. Haile Selassie waved both hands in response and smiled. HIM addressed a luncheon meeting of the Commonwealth Club at the Palace Hotel, attended by 1,000 people. He told the members it was inspiring to see "the way of life of this great nation" and "the happiness and prosperity of its citizens." For three minutes the emperor praised California and its climate—so much like Ethiopia. He confessed to being fond of eating California fruits. In the late afternoon, the World Affairs Council of Northern California held a reception for HIM at the Gold Room of the Fairmont Hotel. The emperor expressed the hope that the strength of the United States would be a preventive of war. He asserted that big nations could best combat the spread of communism "by giving economic help to small nations." The very full day for HIM concluded with dinner at the Press and Union League Club. When asked about the U.S. Supreme Court decision *Brown v. Board of Education,* the emperor said, "The decision will not only strengthen the ties between Ethiopia and the United States but also will win friends everywhere in the world."[24]

The next morning, the royal party departed by car for Yosemite National Park. They had decided to drive from San Francisco to Los Angeles rather than fly, in order to see the redwoods and the spectacular scenery around Big Sur. The U.S. State Department had assigned John Utter as liaison officer to accompany Haile Selassie on the eight-hour drive. On the way, the emperor saw anchored in Suisun Bay a large number of ships that were not being used. Utter explained that these ships were in the U.S. "mothball fleet" and that they were largely old World War II ships that were being retained in this status as an emergency measure. They were not available for sale or transfer, and even if they were they would require considerable costly rehabilitation.[25] The emperor's vision apparently was better than his hearing, for he subsequently inquired about getting some of the vessels for Ethiopia's navy.

Utter also was involved in what John Spencer described as a rare moment of levity with HIM. At one point when conversation flagged, Haile Selassie asked, "How many children do you have, Mr. Utter?" "Sir, I am not married" was the reply. "But you have not answered by question, Mr. Utter" was Haile Selassie's wry retort.[26] The travelers had a brief rest stop at a hotel in Modesto, where the local press noted that they did not attract a large crowd. The royals arrived at noon at Yosemite, where they spent the night. In the park, they saw the Wawona big trees, the giant redwoods, Mirror Lake, and several waterfalls. On the following day, they visited Sequoia National Park en route to Los Angeles and saw Mount Whitney, the highest point in the contiguous 48 United States, and, at 14,505 feet, is slightly shorter than Ethiopia's tallest, Mount Ras Deshan.

After a 500 mile drive from Yosemite, the emperor arrived in Los Angeles the next evening escorted by state highway patrol cars and a dozen motorcycles officers. He registered at the Ambassador Hotel where near the lobby was a throne, a white velvet chair in the center of a dais that had been set up for the occasion. HIM, attired in a field marshal's uniform, sat on the throne with a rich canopy above with a backdrop of beige and aquamarine velvet. He looked tired but was unruffled by brilliant floodlights and flashing bulbs as he faced a battery of questions from reporters, movie news cameras, and television interviewers. His demeanor was serene and imperially august.[27]

The royal party went to Glendale Hospital and Sanitarium, a Seventh Day Adventist Church institution, where they enjoyed a reunion and vegetarian buffet supper with three married couples, missionaries and physicians, who had served in Ethiopia. The church maintained four hospitals that were established 28 years before in Ethiopia. One of the physicians, Dr. George C. Bergman, had not seen Haile Selassie in 10 years. At the reception, HIM met the 84-year-old mother of his supervisor of the palace, Della Hanson, also a missionary.[28]

The next morning the entourage drove through movie-land homes of Beverly Hills and Bel Air and toured the 20th Century Fox motion picture studio. In the studio they made their way through cowtowns, a New England fishing village, Egyptian temples, and Old South manses. The Royals witnessed the shooting of *Désirée,* a costume drama about Napoleon and Josephine, directed by Henry Koster. There Haile Selassie I met Napoleon the First, who was portrayed by Marlon Brando. Did HIM know he was seeing the model of antiestablishment behavior outfitted for the role of Napoleon in the film? The emperor told Brando that he had seen *Julius Caesar* on the *United States* coming over. Speaking in French he added, the picture was *tres jolie.* Brando gazed at the two medallions on his costume and at the 10 rows of decorations on the emperor's uniform (many of his own design) and remarked, "You've won more battles than I have." The emperor shook hands with actress Jean Simmons, resplendent in a 19th-century costume. She was one of a very few on the set who did not tower over HIM. The costumes were impressive, and *Désirée*'s costume design was nominated for an Academy Award the next year. The always technologically inquisitive emperor looked through the lens of a CinemaScope camera, a new wide-screen type of motion picture popular at the time. At the luncheon provided by 20th Century Fox, Marilyn Monroe did not appear as had been announced, but Rita Moreno attracted much interest in a low-cut dress. Before leaving the studio, the movie-loving monarch, who was like an overjoyed little boy at a candy store, also met and posed with film stars Merle Oberon (who was the Empress Josephine in *Désirée*), Dan Dailey, Bella Darvi, Edmund Purdom, Robert Wagner, Jeffrey Hunter, and Reginald Gardiner.[29]

At 12:00 noon, Mayor Norris Poulson held a private reception for the emperor at City Hall. Haile Selassie, wearing a jaunty sports cap, was cheered by thousands as he made his way to the city hall forecourt.

Though jaunty laid the head that wore that crown, there were, alas, no photographs of the L.A. sartorial headgear. The mayor stopped HIM at the threshold and pointed out the inscription quoting King Solomon carved in stone above the door: "Righteousness exalteth a people." In his private suite, the Mayor gave the king an illuminated leather-bound folio of his remarks, and Haile Selassie made Poulson a Grand Officer of the Order of the Star of Ethiopia. At the mayor's luncheon at the Ambassador Hotel, the 1,000 in attendance gave HIM a standing ovation. In brief remarks, the emperor compared California and Ethiopia:

> We have been impressed with the richness and importance of your state. The long trip through the Northwest has shown us the unending wealth of forests and streams and mineral resources, all of which remind us of Ethiopia. You are, at the same time, a rich agricultural state, and to cap it all, an industrial state, where the industry extends from oil to that of cinema. Surely you have reason to be proud of California.[30]

"Only in Ethiopia," he said, "can a climate equal to that of California be found." The emperor expressed the hope that the United States and Ethiopia could arrange for young Ethiopians to attend agricultural colleges in America. He said he was grateful for the great work of missionaries in his country and promised his continued interest and support.[31]

In the afternoon the royal party drove to Long Beach to tour oil wells and harbor installations, where the transient cargo sheds were the largest in world. They saw the new $40 million Richfield Refinery at Watson. Sinclair Oil, the parent organization of Richfield, had leases with the IEG to test for oil potentials in Ethiopia. The emperor anticipated the development of oil production in Ethiopia, so directional oil-well drilling as carried out in Long Beach captured his attention. The Long Beach Board of Harbor Commissioners made HIM an honorary pilot and presented him with a miniature ship's wheel of Philippine mahogany and a book of photographs of the harbor bound in redwood. While on a tour of the world's largest pier, Haile Selassie confessed to reporters that he had cultivated a taste for American milkshakes. Before driving to the foothills of the San Bernardino Mountains, where he would spend the night at Arrowhead Springs, the emperor received baskets of luscious fresh fruit and California-grown supreme dates picked in the nearby Coachella Valley.[32]

At this point in his travels in North America, the emperor made a singular stop in Stillwater, Oklahoma. The reason Haile Selassie went to this small town in the middle of the United States was to personally thank Oklahoma State University (then called Oklahoma A&M) for its work in assisting in modernizing agriculture and education in his nation under one of the first Point Four Programs. A dinner and reception for Haile Selassie and his 19-person entourage held at the college's new student union building on June 18 was the social event of the year (and possibly of the century) in Oklahoma and signaled the ascent of Oklahoma A&M to the top ranks of U.S. universities involved in technical assistance and international education. It was the first visit to Oklahoma by a reigning foreign head of state. At the time, the emperor was 61 years of age; the state of Oklahoma, only 46 years old.

The royal party had flown from the Ontario, California, International Airport to Stillwater aboard the *Star of Bombay*. The flight took about four hours, but the pilot, at the emperor's request, had circled over Grand Canyon and Hoover Dam for 20 minutes.

At 3:30 P.M., the *Star of Bombay* landed at Stillwater's Municipal Airport, where a crowd of 1,100—including national, state, and local dignitaries—was on hand to greet the emperor. It was a hot late spring day with a temperature near 100 degrees, and many women carried parasols. The Stars and Stripes and the tricolor banner of Ethiopia hung from two new flag poles erected for the occasion at the Searcy Field airport. The aircraft stairs were rolled out to the rear door of the plane, the official welcoming officials were poised in the heat at the foot of the stairs, and all was ready for a hearty greeting of the emperor. The A&M band played—and played—but no Conquering Lion of Judah appeared.

Inside the plane, HIM had his eyes fixed on his country's tricolor flapping in the breeze. The Okies had hung the flag upside down, reversing the three horizontal stripes of green, yellow, and red. The pilot of the *Star of Bombay* radioed the gaffe to the control tower. After a few minutes, the Ethiopian flag was lowered, reversed, and raised again.[33] HIM, assured that proper protocol had been followed, emerged from the plane dressed in a field marshal's suntan dress uniform and gave a smart salute to his audience. He was officially welcomed by A&M's president, Oliver Willham, Stillwater Mayor A. B. Alcott, and other officials. The emperor had requested an opportunity to see "an Indian," and Acee Blue Eagle, a well-known Native American artist from Okmulgee, in full Pawnee headdress and buckskin clothing, presented Haile Selassie with a war bonnet and gave him the name "Great

Buffalo High Chief."[34] Chief Blue Eagle evoked from the dead-panned emperor his most genuine smile of the Oklahoma trip.

An impromptu press conference ensued with Haile Selassie praising the area's cattle and grain production. He noted that modern coffee production in his country had been improved by the work of a number of scientists sent there under the Point Four Program. As a result of A&M's effort, Ethiopia had been able to "benefit other nations."

Some 17 A&M deans, professors, and administrative officials and their wives had been assigned as escorts for the visitors.[35] They shepherded the royal party into convertibles provided by a local automobile dealer for the occasion and traveled to the A&M campus in a parade of Buicks. The leather car seats were quite hot because the autos had been sitting for an hour in direct sunlight.[36] The guests took a quick tour of the library and classroom building, where they were shown original blueprints of the proposed Imperial Agricultural College, before going to their rooms at the "fashionable Student Union hotel."[37] A&M's new Student Union was described as "the Waldorf Astoria of Student Unions."

The emperor and his entourage stayed in the Presidential Suite, the entire third floor of the hotel. A snack bar was set up for the visitors on the fourth floor, and Prince Sahle had a jukebox in his room,[38] where he enjoyed listening to records of Frank Sinatra and other swooncrooners and occidental moaner-chanters. Prince Sahle also showed a fondness for the union's special-deluxe hot dogs and ice cream sundaes.[39] He and Acee Blue Eagle had both studied at Oxford, so the prince and the Pawnee chief enjoyed visiting about their student days.

At six in the evening, 300 guests were invited to a formal dinner in the Student Union that had been festooned with Ethiopian, U.S., and Oklahoma flags. The invitation list was a who's who of the Oklahoma power elite of the time. Among the guests were U.S. Senator Robert S. Kerr, Representative Carl Albert and other congressmen, Governor Johnston E. Murray, Lieutenant Governor James E. Berry, state legislators, mayors of six Oklahoma cities, the board of regents for Oklahoma A&M College and the Oklahoma state regents for higher education, 16 college and university presidents, A&M administrators, faculty, students, alumni, and business leaders and ministers from Stillwater.[40] Extra security guards were posted around the union building to protect the royal family and to help direct guests to their proper destinations.[41]

In his after dinner welcoming speech, Governor Murray mangled the pronunciation of Ethiopia, calling it "Oklamopia,"[42] but he praised Haile Selassie as "a symbol of the spark of freedom."[43] President Willham presented His Imperial Majesty with a scroll expressing respect and sincere admiration for Haile Selassie. The college gave the emperor a bronze plaque, given "in behalf of the citizens of Oklahoma," commemorating A&M's successful program of technical assistance and economic cooperation. The plaque read as follows:

> The Imperial Ethiopian College of Agriculture and Mechanical Arts was founded through the devoted interest and zeal of His Imperial Majesty Haile Selassie I, Emperor of Ethiopia, and his ministers with the advisement and cooperation of the Oklahoma A&M college in the interest of and welfare of the people of Ethiopia in the year 1952 A.D.[44]

Haile Selassie subsequently had the plaque mounted in the cornerstone of the administration building at the new Alemaya campus, where it is still on display today. The emperor gave citations and gold medals to three university officials and made them officers of the Order of the Star of Ethiopia.

Ambassador Simonson summarized the festive dinner by observing incorrectly that in the Amharic language something that was superlative was described as "*ishi.*" Said Simonson, "This, in Amharic, is a very *ishi* occasion."[45] *Ishi* means "okay," not a superlative. Those present might disagree with Simonsen's unintended understated evaluation.

After the dinner program, the emperor joined Governor Murray and President Willham and their wives in a receiving line to greet some 1,600 guests who were invited to a reception in the student union ballroom in honor of Haile Selassie.[46] After the first hour, those in attendance were asked to leave in order for the remainder of the guests to be able to get into the room.[47] Upon completing his handshaking ordeal, the emperor took a seat on a huge chair in the banquet room—A&M's best approximation of a throne. Newspaper reporters present described Haile Selassie as "stern and dignified," "a solemn but friendly man" "with the face of an aesthete."[48] The emperor, again in a brief talk, expressed his thanks to A&M:

> I have made an exception to my usual practice on this trip in leaving my itinerary entirely and making this 2,000 mile trip in order to express to you my deep appreciation. This trip has given me the opportunity to visit a truly great agricultural and mechanical college. What I have seen here this afternoon has confirmed my conviction in the enormous possibilities which lie as yet still to be uncovered in Ethiopia.[49]

When the reception came to an end at 10:00 P.M., Haile Selassie held a private audience with members of the family of the late Henry G. Bennett—a measure of the high regard in which the emperor held the former A&M president and Point Four director, who had tragically been killed in an airplane crash in Iran while on a tour of Point Four projects.[50] In a photograph taken at the audience, HIM holds one of Bennett's granddaughters in his lap—a very rare picture of a relaxed Haile Selassie holding a child. Even with his own family, the emperor was not publicly seen or much less photographed with a child on his lap.

During the night following the dinner, the emperor suffered an upset stomach and had to have medical attention. Stillwater physician George Gathers was called at about 3:30 A.M. He and the emperor conversed in French, and the doctor "administered opiates and sulfa drugs and advised the emperor to get more rest." For his services, Gathers was paid with a solid gold medallion commemorating the emperor's coronation.[51]

The dinner and reception were the biggest social events in A&M's history.[52] The attire for those attending was "strictly formal: "black ties and dark tuxedo coats for men (white jackets were acceptable for the dinner); formal dinner dresses either "ballerina or full length" for the ladies. Local merchants reported that tuxedo rentals exceeded all demands previously set by fraternity parties, and clothing stores in Oklahoma City and Tulsa reported a brisk business in formal attire. Tulsa newspaper columnist Roger Devlin reported that the "faint, tangy aroma which hung over the banquet hall was moth balls."[53]

¡VIVA MÉXICO! VIVA ETIOPIA!

On Saturday morning, the royal party left Stillwater at 7:45 A.M. for Mexico City and a five-day state visit. They were met at a new multi-million dollar airport by the President of Mexico, Ruiz Cortines, and his cabinet. The president walked up to the aircraft stairs and shook hands with the emperor. "My people have asked me to tell you that they are with Your Imperial Highness and the great Ethiopian people," said Corines. HIM was visibly touched by the warm welcome extended to him. It was the first time an emperor of Ethiopia had set foot in Latin America.[54] Thousands of people cried "Viva Etiopia!" and cheered the emperor on route to his hotel along streets lined with army troops, 10,000 of whom were on duty for the official welcome.[55] The royals' motorcade was accompanied by a mounted honor guard of cadets from the Colegio Militas. Throughout their visit, the Ethiopian ambassador to Mexico translated Spanish speeches into Amharic for the emperor and the royal party. Another granddaughter of HIM, Princess Sofia Desta, the younger sister of Princess Seble, joined the party in Mexico City from London, where she was studying.[56]

Haile Selassie took part in a solemn ceremony with the presidential guard at the towering Columna de la Independencia, or victory column. At the base of the column was a large statue of a Lion led by a child. Nearby, the Lion of Judah laid a wreath at the freedom statue. The royals visited the palatial Castle of Chapultepec with its monument to the boy heroes killed during the Mexican-American War in 1847. It was from the Battle of Chapultepec and the subsequent occupation of Mexico City by American forces that the line "From the Halls of Montezuma" in the U.S. Marine Hymn is derived.[57] With the mayor of Mexico City, the royal party saw the traffic circle Plaza Etiopia. The mayor explained that during the fascist occupation of Ethiopia, Mexico refused to recognize Italy's claim to Abyssinia and had named the plaza in honor of HIM's valiant country. The emperor was quite moved by this gesture and promised to repay this honor. The creation of Mexico Square in Addis Ababa was the result of this exchange.

Mexican culture was on display for the visitors at rancho de La Tapatia, where they saw a bullfight, a rodeo, an exhibition by national horsemen, and a dance performance. Afterwards, Haile Selassie was given a very wide-brimmed Mexican sombrero. At the National Palace, the emperor was honored with a champagne lunch, during which the two heads of state exchanged titles and medals. President Cortines presented HIM with the Order of the Aztec Eagle, the highest decoration awarded to foreigners in the country. In return, the emperor gave Cortines the Most Exalted Order of the Queen of Sheba. To conclude the program, Mexican youth sang the Ethiopian national anthem in Amharic.

At the striking, recently completed Ciudad Universitaria, the national autonomous university of Mexico, Haile Selassie gave the university a large photograph of himself. He told a gathering of the academic community that their campus was more beautiful than any university in the United States. The emperor presented the Greek Orthodox Church of Santa Sofia a special carpet woven in Ethiopia. The priest's homily delivered in Greek was translated into French for HIM. The Defender of the Faith also paid visits to the Mexico City Metropolitan Cathedral, the largest and oldest catholic cathedral in the Americas; the enormous Basilica de Nuestra Senorna de Guadalupe (Saint Mary's), where, according to tradition, the celebrated Catholic image of the Virgin Mary miraculously appeared on the cloak of a peasant in 1531 (the emperor made a gift to the shrine of a decorative Persian rug); and the 16-century Monastery Church of Saint Augustine with its elegant façade at Acolman where, according to myth, the first man was placed after being taken out of nearby Lake Texoco (would this be competition to early humanoid claims of the Omo River Valley in Ethiopia?). The royals also traveled 25 miles to the Aztec pyramids of San Juan Teotihuacán, "the place where gods were born," an appropriate destination for a monarch deified by Rastafarians.

In a ceremony at the Old Palace, "Palacio de Ayuntamiento," Mexico City's town hall, Haile Selassie gave the city gifts of elephant tusks, spears, and a shield. In Greater Mexico City, the royal party visited a modern steel factory and the public Hospital de la Raza, part of the ubiquitous Mexican health-care program IMSS, built at a cost of U.S. $4.5 million. The hospital uniquely featured spectacular frescos in its lobby by Mexican artists David Siqueiros and Diego Rivera. A diplomatic reception for the emperor was held at the Ministry of Foreign Affairs. The largest formal event of the trip to Mexico was the state banquet honoring HIM, hosted by President Cortines at the National Palace.

The royals went to Cuernavaca, "the city of eternal Spring," for a two-day respite. There, the movie-buff emperor enjoyed meeting Cantinflas, the comedian and film star, known as the Charlie Chaplin of Mexico. The roster of motion picture actor-acquaintances of Haile Selassie had grown considerably since Hollywood film star Tyrone Power had been a guest of the emperor in Addis Ababa in 1947 (just after he had completed filming the film noir "Nightmare Alley").[58] Film star Robert Wagner, who HIM had met on this trip, also later visited Haile Selassie in the palace.[59]

On June 25, 1954, Haile Selassie was seen off at the airport by President Cortines and a cheering multitude of Mexican well-wishers. The emperor gave a final sharp salute to the guard of honor before boarding the *Star of Bombay* and flying to New Orleans.

THE DEEP SOUTH

The red and white TWA plane arrived at New Orleans' Moisant International Airport with an enthusiastic crowd of 1,000 on hand to welcome the royal guests. When a 21-gun salute started and HIM, wearing a khaki field marshal uniform highlighted by red and gold lapels, gave a smart salute at the doorway of the plane, "into his eyes came an expression which made him look every inch the ruler"—wrote a reporter of the scene. After another prolonged military salute during the playing of the Ethiopian national anthem, the emperor boarded a yellow convertible and led a parade of open cars down historic Canal Street, with presidents or representatives of the seven principal business organizations and civic bodies that formed a citizens' reception committee. Spectators along the way cheered and waved.[60]

Centuries-old precedents and prejudices were shattered or ignored when the Deep South metropolis straddling the Mississippi River entertained and honored Haile Selassie. In a lively 26-hour program, the emperor saw more of New Orleans than many residents do in a lifetime. His visit initiated an unheard of display of racial tolerance, in which ancient segregation laws were forgotten. Although threatening telephone calls had been made to the Roosevelt Hotel, where the monarch occupied the International Suite, and to city hall and International House protesting the planned courtesies for the royal party, the elaborate schedule was carried out without an untoward incident. The hotel management reported more than 500 menacing calls. All were ignored, as were the others. Officials believed that all the calls stemmed from an organized source. Despite 90-degree heat, HIM moved with enthusiasm and interest in the "most unique" city in America.[61]

On the day of their arrival in "The City that Care Forgot," one of the few public sour notes about the emperor during his American tour was sent out on the wires of United Press (now United Press International). Congressman Usher L. Burdick (R-ND), who had vociferously opposed U.S. action in the Korean War, wrote a letter to his constituents, lashing out at Haile Selassie as a "perfectly ruthless dictator" who was trying to get U.S. aid under the guise of a democracy. In a racist, anti-foreign-aid diatribe, Burdick accused Haile Selassie of engaging in "a huge slave traffic." According to the congressman, during World War II, "Natives from the jungles were rounded up and driven like cattle to the slave markets operated by Selassie." Echoing Mussolini's fascists, Burdick asserted that the emperor's "antics indicated that he was an absolute and ruthless dictator, who had all the barbarous instincts of a complete savage." The sources of Burdick's information were not cited, but the letter was published in the *Los Angeles Times* and other UP-licensed print outlets.[62]

Haile Selassie was the guest of honor at an official meeting of the city council at city hall, during which all members of the royal party were made honorary citizens of New Orleans and were given golden keys to city (HIM's was solid gold). Mayor deLesseps S. Morrison greeted the emperor in French, and Haile Selassie presented the mayor with two battle spears and a war shield. HIM said he knew of the "worldwide reputation" of New Orleans and was proud to accept its citizenship. In the racially segregated Big Easy, the monarch held a precedent-shattering press conference in the mayor's private office during which he commented freely on the need for human equality in the world. He cited the Supreme Court's *Brown* decision as being "in accord with the Constitution and one which would give the U.S. greater prestige in the world." HIM again praised the virtues of collective security and emphasized that "if the smaller nations are heard by the General Assembly (of the UN), the peace will be surer."

The emperor was interviewed in French and quoted in the local newspapers in that language *On parle la Paix*. The monarch said he was *tres content* with New Orleans. The "gracious, easy-mannered" Prince Sahle told reporters that he had heard about New Orleans' fried chicken, shrimp, and hot jazz and wanted to investigate all of them.[63]

The royal party and city officials proceeded to Dillard University in open cars. There, the emperor received a citation in the presence of probably the largest mixed assemblage in New Orleans history up until that time. At a social reception at the home of university president A. W. Dent, "scores of the city's principal white business leaders mixed with prominent local Negroes in honoring Haile Selassie." The formal reception and state dinner that evening at New Orleans' International House was much more a racially segregated affair with 1,600 mainly white guests lining up to pay homage to HIM. The Chamber of Commerce, Board of Trade, Port Authority, City of New Orleans, Green Coffee Association, International House, International Trade Mart, and Greater New Orleans Inc., acted as hosts. White dinner jackets were de rigueur for the men present. The royal guests were toasted with champagne, and the emperor received a silver bowl from shipping magnate and chairman of the Citizens' Reception Committee, R. S. Hecht, who had visited Haile Selassie in Addis Ababa two years earlier. HIM added Mayor Morrison and Louisiana Governor Robert F. Kennon to the decorated initiates of the Order of the Star of Ethiopia. In the dining room, the emperor was presented with a handsome *café brûlot* set as a typical New Orleans gift, an apt present for the ruler of the country where, according to tradition, coffee originated.[64]

On Friday morning, the royal party, accompanied by Morrison and Kennon, had about a 30-mile tour of the city's chief residential sections and city park region, viewing some of the $60 million street and railroad improvement system of recent years. The tour ended at Eads Plaza (now the Spanish Plaza) at the end of Canal Street, where they boarded the yacht *Good Neighbor* for an inspection of the harbor and the famous Port of New Orleans as guests of the port commission. On board, they enjoyed a buffet luncheon with the city's principal business leaders, hosted by Governor Kennon, a vigorous critic of the *Brown* decision, who had left legislative matters in Baton Rouge to drive to New Orleans to meet Haile Selassie. The emperor told him about Ethiopia's regaining access to the sea only two years earlier. As the *Good Neighbor* passed the Algiers Naval Station, a 21-gun salute boomed forth, and the station's personnel, dressed in white, lined the decks of four ships at the wharf.

The royal party went to Loyola University, where they were welcomed by Archbishop Joseph F. Rummel to a gathering of representatives of New Orleans' institutions of higher education. HIM exchanged gifts with representatives of the five colleges and universities in the area. Doris Anderson, the wife of a U.S. serviceman at the time, attended the gathering and remembers Haile Selassie being surrounded by African Americans who were "thrilled to see HIM."[65] Prince Sahle and the royal princesses became real Crescent City tourists for an hour on this final day of their visit when they slipped off from the official farewells being said for a quick tour of the historic French Quarter.[66]

At 4:30 in the afternoon, the royal party flew to Fort Benning, Georgia, the home of the U.S. Army Infantry Training School, where they were the dinner guests of the infantry center commander, Major Gen. Joseph H. Harper. In a morning ceremony, HIM was officially welcomed with a 21-gun salute and a parade of an honor guard of crack troops and an 80-piece army band. The emperor was briefed on school operations, "witnessed an airborne demonstration which he mentioned as being especially impressive," and observed an infantry-tank team in an attack, a mighty display of military might. Prince Sahle and the royal princesses rode in an M-47 tank equipped with a 90-mm gun. The princesses visited a Girl Scout day camp and a Women's Army Corps (WAC) detachment and took a buddyseat parachute jump before having lunch with fort commanders' wives.

At an official luncheon hosted by the commanding officer, the emperor bestowed Order of the Star of Ethiopia on Harper and two other officials of Fort Benning and presented an ivory trophy to the infantry school "as a symbol of the contribution of Fort Benning toward strengthening the forces for the defense of world peace through collective security within the charter of the United Nations." Noting that there were then two Ethiopian officers enrolled in the infantry school, HIM expressed great confidence in his countrymen who trained there. In remarks at the luncheon, Haile Selassie said the following:

The new arms and techniques which you are developing here, and of which you have given today such a magnificent demonstration are, under an agreement concluded last year between Ethiopia and the United States, now being made available to my country. This association is a source of great pride and satisfaction to me and to my people. Moreover, our comradeship with you in arms under conditions of actual combat in Korea has already served for us, in far greater measure than for you, as another Fort Benning. Thanks to the Mutual Security Agreement, it will be possible for the Ethiopian soldier...to continue with you a comradeship in arms dedicated to the defense of collective security.[67]

Before taking off for New York in the *Star of Bombay* in midafternoon, the militarily attired ruler expressed "tremendous satisfaction" with his visit to Fort Benning. The royal party touched down at La Guardia on the night of June 26 and was driven to the Waldorf Astoria, where most of them would stay until July 14, when they would begin the journey back to Ethiopia. The party arrived at the hotel at 8:00 p.m. A State Department spokesman told reporters that the official phase of HIM's and the royal party's tour was over as of that hour and they were to be considered from then on as "private citizens."[68]

WORKING WHILE RESTING AND RELAXING
AT THE WALDORF ASTORIA

With the formal visit ended, the emperor could relax with his son and granddaughters and enjoy the cultural and entertainment treats that New York City offered. But first, he went to the Columbia-Presbyterian Medical Center for a routine checkup. He spent three days there for a general examination.[69] No news story about Haile Selassie during his stay in North America had wider coverage in the U.S. small-town press than the brief UP article about the emperor being declared to be in good health by the New York physicians upon his discharge from the hospital. The American public was concerned about the well-being of the little king whom they had come to admire.

Perhaps to demonstrate that he was feeling well on the day of his release from Columbia-Presbyterian, Haile Selassie paid a surprise late afternoon visit to the Bronx Zoo. During his hour's stay, the "usually stern-visaged little monarch who seldom is seen to laugh in public, did for once, and appeared to enjoy himself hugely."[70] The emperor laughed heartily when one of the attendants staged a wrestling act with Oka, the Lady Gorilla. He smiled as he petted a tiger cub and baby jaguars. HIM was, of course, no newcomer to being around big cats—even as cubs. His menagerie at Jubilee Palace always included African roaring cats. After making a complete tour of the zoo, the emperor said he especially enjoyed viewing fish in the aquarium, a 20-foot python in the reptile cage, baboons (who frequent many parts of Ethiopia), and penguins partaking of a late afternoon snack. He enjoyed everything but the weather, which he found too hot. When reporters inquired about the results of his medical checkup, the emperor said they were "very satisfactory."

While Haile Selassie was enjoying R & R in Manhattan, other members of his entourage were back in Washington, DC, attempting to make firm what each side thought had been agreed to during the meetings of the emperor with Eisenhower and other U.S. foreign policy makers. In a series of meetings at the State Department, Aklilou Habte Wold, Ethiopian Foreign Minister; Ambassador Yilma; and John Spencer presented the Ethiopian perspective to Secretary Dulles, Assistant Secretary for African Affairs Byroade, and Utter, representing the U.S. Government. On July 2, the foreign minister reiterated the requests the emperor had left with the president in his departing memorandum and the assurance the president had given HIM that they would be given sympathetic consideration. The Ethiopians were disappointed with the generally negative answers they had received to the requests for economic, military, and technical aid. According to the foreign minister, upon hearing the lack of positive U.S. responses, the emperor had been so deeply depressed he had been on the verge of leaving the country immediately, without awaiting the outcome of final talks scheduled for July 7.

Byroade remarked that he had been under the impression that the foreign minister understood that the talks they were engaged in should be in no way tied to the emperor's visit to the United States. The imperial trip, Byroade continued, "had been an outstanding success, and it would be too bad to have the Emperor's evident pleasure at the ovation he received throughout the country marred by disgruntlement at not receiving satisfaction in requests which he put forward to the U.S. Government." Byroade concluded that he would be opposed in the future to the visit of any chief of state from the areas he was responsible for "until it was clearly understood that the visit was only for goodwill and entailed no requests for help." The foreign minister assured the group that the emperor would not depart before hearing the outcome of the final discussion on July 7.[71] Despite that rather gloomy ending to the meeting, both sides continued to work behind the scenes in preparation for the concluding bilateral talk.

On the seventh, the emperor, the epitome of sangfroid, went to the Museum of Natural History with his youngest son and two grand-daughters. They inspected Akeley Hall of African Mammals, where they were pleased to see an Ethiopian Mountain Nyala, the last of the great African antelopes to become known to science. In Brontosaur Hall they saw skeletal forms of ancient reptiles, and in Whitney Hall of Pacific Birds, they marveled at "brilliant feathered creatures." The grand finale of the visit was a heavenly display staged for the special benefit of the emperor in the Hayden Planetarium.[72]

On the same afternoon Haile Selassie saw the heavens open, his stars were in better alignment in Washington. In a final meeting at the State Department between the principal diplomats of the two nations, Assistant Secretary Byroade expressed his appreciation to the Ethiopian foreign minister for taking additional time to work on the problems coming out of their previous conversations. He said he hoped the foreign minister better understood "the complicated nature of the U.S. Government."[73] Explained Byroade, "We had no doubts about the potentialities of a program of aid to the Ethiopian Government. Unfortunately, not even the President himself can act without legislative authority. What we have suggested is in the opinion of all interested American officials the best we can do." The State Department officials noted that the United States had many commitments throughout the world, and Congress was imposing increasingly stringent conditions and procedures on for-eign assistance. "When we refer to the possibility of help from lending agencies—governmental, private, international—it is simply because they are the only means for help available," said Byroade. "We have given the best response possible, and where there is any prospect of help we are continuing to study the case." It was not the definitive answer to his requests the emperor had wanted, but it was not a flat refusal and left the door ajar for further negotiations. Haile Selassie and his foreign minister could continue working in such a situation—especially with Kagnew Station an incentive to keep the Americans interested.

The next day, the emperor went to the police—or at least the New York City Police Headquarters. Police Commissioner Francis W. H. Adams greeted HIM and escorted the monarch into a darkened room to watch the morning questioning of prisoners who stood on a lighted platform. The emperor also toured the crime-detection laboratories, the identification bureau, and a museum in the police academy. In the communications bureau, Haile Selassie communicated with a patrol car by radio.[74] This was the last highly reported activity of the mon-arch's stay in the United States.

During his final week in New York, Haile Selassie traveled to Jones Beach Marine Theater, where he enjoyed a performance of the musical "Arabian Nights." Before the performance, he ate a hot dog with the show's star, heldentenor Lauritz Melchior, and producer–orchestra leader Guy Lombardo.[75] On their last evening in the country, the emperor, Prince Sahle, and the two princesses went to Ridgefield, Connecticut, to dine with Richard E. Southard, former minister to Ethiopia.[76]

On July 12, Haile Selassie left by air from Idlewild with planned stops in Yugoslavia, France, and Greece before returning to Ethiopia. The emperor said he found the United States even greater than he had expected. He thanked President Eisenhower and the people of America for a memorable visit and said he was leaving with regret and would return if he possibly could do so. The monarch showed "intense feeling" while speaking through an interpreter. Seeing HIM off were General C. L. Bolte, deputy chief of staff of the Army, representing Eisenhower, Simmons, Patterson, and Warren Lee Pierson, Chairman of the Board of TWA.[77] On the following day, the New York Times ran an eloquent farewell editorial, "Lion of Judah":

It is commonly believed that we Americans are deeply impressed by titles. Perhaps we are, but when it comes to choosing our friends we look behind the title to the man. In the case of the Emperor Haile Selassie . . . we would respect the man even without the title. It is correct to call Haile Selassie His Imperial Majesty, but if he were plain Mr., he would still be a man of courage, intelligence and great humanity. . . . Good wishes will follow the Emperor as he wings his way home after traveling over our country from coast to coast, and these good wishes will extend to his countrymen.[78]

The impact on Americans in meeting the emperor was eloquently described by Rabbi Harry J. Stern, who dined with HIM in Canada: "His presence in our midst evokes memories of historic pasts and breathes prayers within us all that peace prevail on earth and that nations great and small shall prosper and dwell in justice and brotherhood under the rule of the Supreme Father of all mankind." The Rabbi's brief interlude with Haile Selassie called to his mind the Song of David from the Psalms, "How good and how pleasant it is when brethren dwell together in unity." He concluded that "soon [in 1955] the Emperor will observe the 25th anniversary of his Coronation and all lovers of freedom will rejoice in the growth and advance of Ethiopia among the nations of the world."[79]

His countrymen gave their little king a regal ovation when his plane arrived in Addis Ababa. Scores of thousands of Ethiopians jammed the streets to cheer and ululate as the emperor passed by in his open Rolls Royce. The monarch had scored a resounding public-relations triumph at home and abroad. As far as the Ethiopian people knew, HIM's personal diplomacy had cemented an arms-for-base-rights agreement, with Ethiopia receiving weapons and a military training mission as well as economic aid and political support for union with Eritrea. Haile Selassie in his first public address after his return from the U.S. tour said that his reception in America "fully justified all my preconceptions of American friendship and hospitality."[80] For its part, the United States had solidified its claim to Kagnew Station and access to a strategic locale on the rim of the Middle East.

In the years following the emperor's first call on North America, state visits became "an almost annual compulsion" for Haile Selassie. He seemed to enjoy his status as a celebrity and cultivated a strong international image through state visits to many parts of the world. HIM thrived upon international travel and the social activities that accompanied it. Being treated as a head of state, with all the indulgences and condescension that it entailed was an exhilarating experience. His international fame and acceptance grew. In October 1954 he toured Western Europe. In Great Britain, the emperor received the royal treatment he craved. He wore a cocked hat topped by a lion's mane and rode in an open state landau with a household cavalry escort through London's flag-bedecked streets and the mall decorated with tall ceremonial poles bearing replicas of the crown of Ethiopia. He was the first head of state to visit West Germany after the end of World War II. The emperor's visit signaled the acceptance of West Germany back into the world, as a peaceful nation. He donated blankets manufactured in Ethiopia to the war-ravaged German people.[81] His subsequent state visits and official travel also would take HIM to South America and Asia.

ENTR'ACTE

The fruits of the emperor's personal diplomacy with Eisenhower were harvested soon after their meeting in Washington. In FY 1956, the United States committed to $5 million for the Ethiopian Army, a naval patrol craft, and economic assistance amounting to under $5 million for "soundly conceived projects mutually agreed upon." U.S. aid was tendered with a wary eye on possible security threats to Ethiopia: progressive young army officers along with young intellectuals and middle- and upper-class civil servants were dissatisfied with their place in society and were not optimistic about their future under the rule of HIM. But the IEG was in firm control of internal security. The Ethiopian government was dissatisfied, however, with the amount of U.S. aid and shifted toward a neutralist policy and the consideration of Soviet Bloc offers of economic aid. Indeed, in 1956, Soviet Bloc activity increased in the country.[82]

At the same time, the U.S. Point Four program proved to be a strong tool for the emperor in developing provincial areas and knitting the people more closely to the central government. Haile Selassie took a personal interest in the programs and insisted upon the location of the new agricultural college in Alemaya; an agricultural secondary school in Jimma; a hospital and health center at Mekele; a health training center at Gondar; a nursing and vocational school at Asmara; teacher training schools at Harar, Debra Berhan, and Addis Ababa; and water-well drilling in Eritrea and the southeast and southern border areas.

At a National Security Council (NSC) meeting in November 1956, Eisenhower told Herbert Hoover Jr., acting secretary of state, "You have your 'best drag' in [Ethiopia] when you do something for the Emperor." The president cited Haile Selassie's being sold a Lockheed Constellation so he could overfly neighboring countries. Unfortunately, the plane crashed and burned two weeks after its delivery. Secretary of Defense Charles E. Wilson expressed skepticism about the United States taking on further obligations in Africa because he feared a power vacuum when the colonial powers left. The consensus of the meeting was that Africa could suddenly become very important to the United States.[83]

In 1957, the emperor made a strong plea for substantially larger military assistance and requested aid to develop the IEG's air force— importunities given some effect by world politics. The Eisenhower Doctrine had been ratified that year, making it clear that the United States reserved the right to intervene in the oil-rich Middle East if it perceived its vital interests were threatened. Radical Arab nationalist opposition to the West, especially in Egypt, had sharpened in the aftermath of the Suez Crisis in 1956, and this resulted in accelerated delivery of U.S. equipment and training under a Military Assistance Program (MAP) to Ethiopia. After the British departure from Ethiopia in 1951, the IEG Army had seriously deteriorated. The MAP improved the army's potential and equipped units with U.S. weapons.

Vice President Nixon visited Haile Selassie in March 1957. The emperor complained that Middle Eastern friends were criticizing the IEG for supporting the United States in Korea and refusing to recognize the People's Republic of China. Further, the IEG had supported the U.S. position during the Suez crisis and had voted for the UN resolution about Hungary. He pointed out that U.S. privileges in Ethiopia were granted for an extremely long period, but American military assistance was maintained on a purely year-to-year basis. Nixon replied that this discrepancy resulted from the U.S. executive branch being dependent on annual appropriations from congress. The vice president assured HIM that a close collaboration with the United States "was entirely possible on the basis of a fresh and frank approach to the problems." In response, the emperor gave Nixon a shopping list of military and security items (a radio station "to offset radio Cairo and other insidious propaganda," helicopters, and police equipment), most of which the United States delivered to HIM within a few months.[84] The pièce de résistance came in June 1958, however, when U.S. funds for twelve F-86 jet fighters were approved. Eisenhower's decision to provide a modern weapon system that few other third world countries possessed reinforced Haile Selassie's belief that the key to enhancing Ethiopia's security as well as his own resided with the United States.[85]

Nevertheless, Haile Selassie contended that U.S. military assistance was delivered too slowly and was not of the quality deemed appropriate, and in July 1959 he visited Moscow (being the first African head of state to visit the motherland of actual, existing socialism) and Prague. Lost in the razzmatazz of diplomatic duplicity and protocols of the Kremlin elders was *Pravda's* harsh characterization of HIM not as the Lion of Judah but as the jackal of American imperialism. The unruffled IEG accepted Soviet Bloc aid of $100 million from the USSR (an amount far higher than what the United States had provided Ethiopia since the end of World War II) and $10 million from Czechoslovakia in long-term credits and embarked on a more neutralist foreign policy.[86] The CIA worried that these moves "might be the first major attempt by the Communist Bloc to penetrate into deeper parts of Africa." It was possible too that Haile Selassie "in his quiet way was attempting to blackmail the United States." There were even unconfirmed reports that the emperor had ordered the abrogation of the agreement that established Kagnew Station. "This, if true, could be extremely serious."[87]

In 1960, the emperor began what was already being called the Decade of Africa, confident that the United States would provide him with more and better military assistance or he would allow his new friends, the Soviets, to become more involved in key areas of his nation's life such as the armed forces, communications, education, and land resettlement—a move anathema to the Cold War–obsessed West. Although the United States had thwarted, for the most part, Soviet efforts to break into America's dominant role in the country, the USSR had recently opened and staffed a technical school in Bahar Dar. The former minister of foreign affairs, and now prime minister, Aklilou, requested U.S. financial assistance for a university (Ethiopia had only University College and the Imperial Agricultural College at that time) and arms and material for a fourth division of the Ethiopian Army. Eisenhower was enthusiastic about the university idea because he felt strongly that Africa should develop its own leaders at home. The president said he was less inclined to favor a buildup of armaments. Eisenhower thought the United States itself had too many, although he could not prove that thesis to his soldiers.[88]

Early in his presidency, Eisenhower had talked about his preference for aid over arms. He told his son, John S. D. Eisenhower, "Every gun that is made, every warship launched, every rocket fired signifies, in the final sense, a theft from those who hunger and are not fed, those who are cold and are not clothed.... We pay for a single fighter plane with a half-million bushels of wheat. We pay for a single destroyer with new homes that could have housed 8,000 people."[89] Is it little wonder that Eisenhower gave a farewell presidential address warning of "a military-industrial complex" thriving on war and threat of war?[90]

Eisenhower also made a memorable speech at the opening session of the 15th UN General Assembly on September 22, 1960, speaking to "the largest international galaxy of leaders ever assembled." The president appealed to all nations to "work for a true world community" and to join in settling the world's problems by negotiation and cooperation in the United Nations. He emphasized the need for new programs in Africa and expressed the hope that the Cold War might be kept out of that continent. Eisenhower envisioned a "consortium of African nations" to develop a sense of solidarity and prevent their domination by the big powers.[91] Unfortunately, the president's eloquent tribute to the UN did not receive the attention it deserved because the media focused on subsequent controversial speeches and actions by the grandstanding Khrushchev and Castro, among others. Nevertheless, Eisenhower had delivered a gracious and profound valedictory about Africa and the UN and had suggested that the UN be the principal instrument of U.S. policy in Africa.

While world attention was focused on the Congo, a new external threat haunted the emperor. Tensions along Ethiopia's eastern border were building with a growing fear of Somali nationalism. The former

Italian and British colonies became independent on July 1. Haile Selassie, who was 68-years-old then, had an obsession with security and
had not developed a fully satisfactory arrangement for dynastic succession. The monarch continued to hold the threat of Kagnew Station's
being in jeopardy if a substantial increase in U.S. grants for military
assistance were not forthcoming. In the United States a presidential
election in November would select a new chief executive. Would the
new man continue the friendly relations with the increasingly cantan-
kerous emperor? Was the era of good feeling between Ethiopia and the
United States coming to an end?

CHAPTER 8

The Rituals of U.S. and Ethiopian Diplomacy

President Dwight Eisenhower was presiding at the regular Thursday meeting of the NSC on February 26, 1959 in the Cabinet Room of the White House. On the agenda was discussion of U.S. policy toward the Horn of Africa, and Gordon Gray, special assistant to the president for national security affairs, had prepared a memorandum for the meeting that focused on the upcoming independence of French, British, and Italian colonies in Somaliland and Ethiopia's reactions to it. After Gray briefed the council on his memo, Secretary of State Christian Herter spoke first:

> I have only one comment to make about U.S. policy toward the Horn. We are in real trouble with the Lion of Judah. The British propose joining British Somaliland with Somalia when the former Italian colony becomes an independent state in December 1960. We have supported the U.K. proposal, and Haile Selassie dislikes both the British idea and our support of it. We're trying to cool him down and dispel the notion that we're ganging up against him with the former colonial powers.[1]

The president responded: "If the French still have the strength to hold on to French Somaliland with the important port of Djibouti, I don't think it would be wise on our part to ask them to give up their colony there. That area could be very advantageous to us from a geopolitical point of view as a means of blocking Soviet access. I would hate to see the Red Sea bottled up on both ends by people who might not necessarily be or remain our friends." Herter agreed with the president that the United States did indeed have a strong geopolitical interest in the Horn.

Secretary of the Treasury Robert B. Anderson said the council would have to face up to a major national security issue that was suggested in the memorandum:

> We are heading rapidly into a situation where a lot of little, newly independent countries are coming into being, and they will inevitably turn to the United States for support. All these little countries want to act like great big countries. This will mean increased demands on our resources for assistance. I'm afraid that sooner or later the bulk of financial support for Somaliland or similar newly developing countries will be expected to come from us. I doubt we can persist much longer in letting the entire world believe that we can and will support all these newly independent countries.[2]

The president said he had never been in the area of the Somalilands and wondered what it was like: "Did Somalia consist of wild jungle?" Allen Dulles, director of the CIA and brother of former Secretary of State John Foster Dulles, described Somaliland as mainly "dry and desert, and some of it is high in elevation." The president asked, "Are the Somalis primitive and aborigines?" Dulles replied, "A majority of them certainly fell into that category." Maurice Stans, director of the Bureau of the Budget, had traveled to Kenya and had "encountered Somali natives who were probably much the same as their brethren in the actual Somalia areas. They were certainly primitive. On the other hand, Somali women were said to be the most beautiful in Africa."

The president, who had served in Panama, the Philippines, and North Africa and had worked with what he called "primitive peoples" wondered how Somali natives thought they could run an independent nation and why they would try to do so. Dulles confirmed the president's doubts as to the capabilities of the Somalis to organize and administer a modern, civilized state.

Admiral Arleigh A. Burke, chief of naval operations, spoke in favor of a sustained effort "to bring to the United States young Somali natives who had displayed a potentiality for leadership in the area." He said, "Such young leaders should be trained very carefully and at some length in the United States. This is perhaps the most important single thing the United States can do to advance its interests in the Horn of Africa." Herter commented that Burke's suggestion could apply equally well to other sections of the African continent, an idea the president liked too.[3]

* * *

By 1959, the NSC system had evolved into the principal arm of the president in formulating and executing policy on military, international, and internal security affairs. The National Security Council had been created by Congress during the Truman administration in 1947, but the president only made regular use of it during the Korean War. Under Eisenhower, the NSC became a highly structured system of integrated policy review. Coming from a military career, Eisenhower appreciated careful staff work and believed that effective planning involved a creative process of discussion and debate among advisers who were compelled to work toward consensus recommendations. Eisenhower played a dominant role in foreign policy and national security issues, and the NSC system was a significant factor in his decisions.

The NSC session on the Horn of Africa was indicative of the broad sweep of such discussions. The members were concerned about U.S. policy towards Ethiopia, the end of colonialism and the creation of new nations of Africa, soviet expansionism in the Horn (with the threat of having the radical nationalism of Gamal Abdel Nasser of Egypt at one end of the Red Sea and the soviets on the other), the increasing pressure for America to provide aid to new developing nations, and the encouraging of bright young Africans to study in the United States. The NSC members did not evince much knowledge about the Horn or its peoples, although Stans' comment about the pulchritude of Somali women might be profound. By 21st-century standards, the vocabulary of the principals was not politically correct—perhaps indicative of how little was generally known about Africa at that time.

For Eisenhower and the Dulles brothers, U.S. foreign policy was the sum of external relations conducted by the United States in international relations. Deliberations of the NSC were strands of an elaborate tapestry of institutions and processes that made public policy. In the Cold War years, the question of how the United States related to the world beyond its borders—and how it should—became inescapable.

The Eisenhower administration inherited President Truman's containment theory to stop the international spread of communism and soviet expansionism. That strategy, started as the Truman Doctrine in 1947, shaped U.S. foreign policy in the 1950s and early 1960s. The

Korean conflict that had demonstrated that the USSR might use proxy forces for probes on the Eurasian periphery led to the geographical extension of containment from Europe to Asia and beyond and resulted in the modernization and expansion of U.S. military capabilities. In Africa and Asia, nationalist movements challenged colonial governments. U.S. officials suspected that communists dominated these movements and received support directly from the Soviet Union.

The United States poured military resources into Europe and the Far East and set about creating a global alliance system to complement the North Atlantic Treaty Organization that had been founded in 1949, the first peacetime alliance entered into by the United States. The Eisenhower administration sought to run the global containment strategy at a lower economic cost. This led to a renewed emphasis on U.S. nuclear deterrent and increased reliance on allies to provide conventional forces for local defense. In a January 1954 speech, Secretary Dulles advocated the threatened use of the "massive retaliatory power" of the United States to deter soviet expansionism. The first priority for U.S. military commitments was for Europe and the so-called rimland areas of the Eurasian land mass that were under threat of attack by the USSR or its surrogates.

In other parts of world, U.S. policy emphasized economic and technological development components of Point Four. General Andrew J. Goodpaster, staff secretary to the president, summarized Eisenhower's approach to development in third world nations. Freedom of choice and self-determination were central to the plan, which included explaining to aid recipients "what the West had to offer and what has been achieved by Western civilization."[4] At the same time they were to be provided "the assistance needed so they could begin to better the life of their farmers and improve their industry and trade." The president thought this would give them "a more reliable and more rewarding basis for development than the so-called shortcut of communism," to which Dennis FitzGerald, an overseas agricultural official during the Eisenhower administration, added, "But mostly technical assistance required the furnishing of American technicians to work in a foreign country, under foreign conditions, and with local people"; that is, "the ugly American" hero-protagonist of the 1958 novel of Burdick and Lederer.[5]

The fear of overextension in addition to the belief that there were primary areas where the Cold War would be fought relegated sub-Saharan Africa to the periphery of U.S. foreign policy concerns. During the reign of Haile Selassie, Ethiopia was not directly threatened by the

Strategic importance of the Kagnew Station put Ethiopia at the top of US interests in Africa!

USSR and was marginal to American global policy. The strategic significance of Kagnew Station, however, put Ethiopia at the top of U.S. interests in Africa. Also, the maintenance of an American presence in the Horn of Africa would provide stability for U.S. allies in the Middle East and security for oil exports from key Arab countries.

The main foreign policy concerns of Ethiopia were national security and the strengthening of the regime through U.S. military and economic assistance. The United States and Ethiopia shared common interests in sustaining stability in the Horn, preserving Ethiopian sovereignty and the sanctity of its borders, supporting the UN and collective security, providing Ethiopian hegemony over Eritrea and hence assuring a U.S.-friendly landlord for Kagnew Station, and blocking communist activities.

The making of Ethiopian foreign policy was from the top down by the emperor and his foreign ministry. An organization chart of the process would be simple: a giant arrow going down from the top box representing the monarch to the Ministry of Foreign Affairs and its agents in the field, the ambassadors in various countries. Could absolute rule in a feudal society be otherwise?

In American democracy, power to make foreign policy was widely shared. Under the separation of powers doctrine in the U.S. Constitution, the conduct of foreign relations is entrusted primarily to the president and Congress, although the judiciary may act as a check on the powers of the other two branches. An organization chart demonstrating the process would consist of a proliferation of boxes that would spread from all three branches of government in a policy-hill process. Although the buck stops at the top of the hill with the president, who is ultimately responsible for conducting foreign policy, participants are many and varied in the process. Commands issue from the State Department and the Pentagon. From these vast control centers, power is dispersed to representatives down the hill or on the ground—diplomats and warriors who work at home and in foreign lands to carry out the policy guidance that has laboriously been produced along the hillside. Key players include the White House staff, the secretary of state and the bureaucracy of the State Department, U.S. ambassadors to particular countries and their staffs, and military and intelligence officers in Washington and in the field. Foreign policy for a specific country takes place in a context of America's worldwide objectives as well as those for a continent or region.

Each of Haile Selassie's state visits to the United States was illustrative of U.S. foreign policy specifically toward Ethiopia but also toward

Africa in general. The Emperor's one-on-one meetings with the president and his interaction with Washington officials were parts of a complex web of diplomacy that existed between the two nations. Diplomacy is a system of communication in elaborate Byzantine rituals between states, an institution by which nation-states pursue their own particular interests or foreign policy. State visits are the highest form of diplomatic contact between two nations, and are marked by ceremonial pomp and diplomatic protocol.

Haile Selassie's state visits included all the traditional components: a welcoming ceremony with a review of military honor guards, parades, and the playing of the two nations' national anthems by a military band; a 21-gun salute; an exchange of gifts between the emperor and the president; a state dinner hosted by the president in honor of HIM; a formal address to Congress by the emperor; high-profile visits by Haile Selassie to national monuments such as the Tomb of the Unknown Soldier; and cultural events such as the display of Ethiopian books at the Library of Congress, celebrating links between the two nations. The emperor was accompanied by his foreign minister and a delegation of high-ranking officials who had an opportunity to develop economic, cultural, and social contacts with governmental and industry leaders, as well as Americans from a variety of walks of life. Throughout the emperor's visits, the state department's chief of protocol was on hand to ensure that the accepted rules of diplomacy were implemented. During the first visit, Ambassador John K. Simmons, in this role, carried out his duty to "plan and execute detailed programs for foreign leaders visiting the president and accompany them during their official travel in the United States." The costs of Haile Selassie's state visits were paid by the U.S. Treasury. After spending his first night in Washington at the White House, Haile Selassie subsequently stayed across the street at Blair House, the resident's guest house usually reserved for foreign visitors, during his visits to the capital.

Haile Selassie was confident that he would be in a better bargaining position in garnering rent for Kagnew if he could meet with President Eisenhower and personally discuss their mutual interests. Subsequent developments and the mechanics of carrying out decisions in a democracy would produce outcomes different from what the emperor thought had been agreed to. The exchange between Eisenhower and the emperor illustrated two significant factors in an autocracy's dealing with a parliamentary democracy. First, internal, economic, social, and political plans and policies can rival foreign and defense policies as claimants on limited resources. Eisenhower was limited in what he could do unilaterally about foreign aid by congressional control of spending, public opinion and its reflection in domestic politics, and his own predilections about striving for a balanced budget. Secondly, foreign policy decisions can be shaped by the contests for influence among groups and individuals. In the context of the vast array of U.S. global commitments, groups competing for limited resources to assist Ethiopia included various offices in the State Department, the Point Four Program, and the Department of Defense. Haile Selassie seemed flummoxed to encounter these restraints during his first visit to the United States.

In the 20th century, the foreign policies of both the United States and Ethiopia were influenced by two competing theories: realism and liberalism. Each nation played the realism or liberalism card whenever doing so advanced its power and security. Rare is the nation that would play one card exclusively.

Realism has been the dominant tradition in thinking about international politics. For Realists, order is created and maintained by states exercising power in interaction with other states. War and the use of force are the central problem of international politics. Strong states seek to dominate the weak and weak states resist the strong to preserve their interests and independence. There is no overarching institution or universal center of power in the world that is recognized by all states as legitimate. This anarchy in the world order requires states to defend themselves because they cannot rely on anyone else to do so (e.g., what was required of Ethiopia after its disappointing appeal to the League of Nations for collective security to protect it from fascist invasion). In defending themselves, states may come into conflict with one another. They try to manage this conflict through the reciprocal acquisition and use of military arms, or what is called the balance of power. During the Cold War, the United States and its allies were defending themselves from the Soviet Union and Eastern Bloc nations. Relations between Ethiopia and the United States reflected the ongoing process of balancing and adjusting of opposing power among the states on the two sides. So long as Ethiopia remained an ally of the United States and was felt to be useful to the super power, it received military aid and backing from the West. Should Ethiopia be deemed no longer useful to the strong nation, from a realist point of view, it would be in the interest of the United States to cease assisting it. Conversely, if Ethiopia felt that U.S. support was not what it should be, it could threaten to end its ties with America and become a friend of the Eastern Bloc, or it could curse both the houses and pursue an unaligned policy of neutrality.

In contrast to realism, liberal theories postulate a global society functioning alongside the states and setting part of the context for states. Liberal theories emphasize relationships and negotiations among non-state actors in international affairs. For example, trade crosses borders, people have contacts with each other, and international institutions such as the UN create a framework in which the realist view of pure anarchy is insufficient. Liberals advocate the growth of economic interdependence and the evolution of a transnational global society to establish rules to govern interactions among actors. Ethiopia and the United States were active in the founding and development of the UN and took part in its peace keeping activities. Both nations fostered reciprocal trade (e.g., coffee going to America and Coca-Cola to Ethiopia) and welcomed a flow of academics (e.g., Oklahoma A&M professors in Point Four; Fulbright students at U.S. universities) military (e.g., U.S. Military Assistance Advisory Group trainers; Ethiopian Army personnel at U.S. bases), and other personnel between them (e.g., TWA).

Hard and soft power also came into play in U.S. relations with Ethiopia. In its official external relations, the U.S. government attempts to influence other states by the direct or commanding method of exercising power. In getting other states to (1) do what they otherwise would not do or (2) not do what they would prefer to do (power relationships), traditional diplomacy can be based on inducements ("carrots") or threats ("sticks").[6] The president and Congress with their emphasis on treaties and geopolitical debates, exercise "hard" power. The military treaties and base agreements were classic examples of hard power in Ethiopia.

But there is another way to exercise power and to obtain desired outcomes through attraction rather than through coercion or payment. A country may achieve desired outcomes in its foreign relations because other countries admire what it stands for and want to follow its example or have agreed to a system that produces such effects. "In this sense, it is just as important to set the agenda and attract others in world politics as it is to force others to change in particular situations."[7] Getting others to want what you want might be called attractive or indirect power behavior, or what Joseph Nye calls "soft" power.[8] Soft power matters because countries that like you will want to be your allies. Soft power can rest on such resources as "the attraction of one's ideas or on the ability to set the political agenda in a way that shapes the preferences others express." Preferences can be influenced by such intangible power resources such as culture, ideology, and institutions.

One of America's greatest strengths during the Cold War was in leading the community of democracies and the nonaligned nations by example.[9] This was done through public diplomacy, interactions other than those between national governments. Effective public diplomacy involved dialogue; a two-way exchange of information and people-to-people contact were a significant aspect of that effort. U.S. public diplomacy emphasized the nation's core values and subtly built an image of a benevolent global leader.

In the 1950s, Chief Justice Earl Warren and other justices of the U.S. Supreme Court took up the challenge of exercising soft power through public diplomacy—especially that involving visiting foreign heads of state in the United States. From all accounts, the court's move into this previously unchartered area for the judiciary was a resounding success.[10] Any occasion honoring a visiting leader in such surroundings is bound to be a memorable event, even as only one aspect of a state visit. And the justices were among the most intelligent, knowledgeable Americans who, in their work, frequently interpreted the core values of the nation and who could well represent the nation in dialogue with foreign leaders. The visiting dignitaries had an opportunity to interact with the justices in an institution that was admired abroad for its independence from other branches of government and for its protection of human rights. The court's decisions ending racial segregation in public schools were especially lauded by the official visitors. Many were learned in the law and had an affinity for fellow professionals on the bench. The Supreme Court offered attractive ideas for emulation and thus was an ideal place to practice soft power. During a time of tense Cold War confrontations, the supreme court contributed to public diplomacy that successfully followed the sage advice of George Kennan in his "X" article, which appeared in the July 1947 issue of *Foreign Affairs*: "To avoid destruction, the United States need only measure up to its own best traditions and prove itself worthy of preservation as a great nation."[11]

As an individual, Haile Selassie was the practitioner of public diplomacy par excellence. He was canny and insightful in making public relations triumphs of his trips overseas or in his receiving foreign guests in Addis Ababa. "He radiated majesty from a light frame."[12] Unfailingly soigné, the Emperor's commanding presence combined with graciousness at public occasions made HIM an ideal ambassador of good will at home and abroad. He had the ability to understand and influence foreign populations—not only in their councils of state but in their cities and villages, as was seen in his reception when he had the opportunity to be with the common people. He magisterially presided over events throughout the country, for however crowded and official the scene, Haile Selassie was always in the picture, and more often than not in its center, all ribbons and propriety. He stood untouched and seldom spoke or smiled. He was emblematic of the era of monarchy that was drawing to a close. The emperor acquired in the eyes of many foreigners what the Romans called "gravitas"—patience, stability, the appearance of wisdom. Trouble only made him look a little graver. Such characteristics made Haile Selassie an appropriately venerated figure as an elder statesman of Africa. He also should be recognized for the significant role he played as one of the world's greatest practitioners of informal diplomacy.

Haile Selassie, accompanied by Vice President Richard Nixon and military brass, reviews an honor guard at Washington's National Airport to begin the emperor's first state visit on May 26, 1954. But where is President Eisenhower? (National Park Service/Dwight D. Eisenhower Presidential Library)

The Royal Party, Princess Seble Desta, Prince Sahle Selassie, and the Emperor, were greeted by President and Mrs. Eisenhower at the White House. (National Park Service/Dwight D. Eisenhower Presidential Library)

At the Library of Congress, the emperor saw a special exhibit of books, documents, and photographs highlighting Ethiopian culture and history, the first of its kind in the United States. (National Park Service/Dwight D. Eisenhower Presidential Library)

Artist Acee Blue Eagle presented the emperor with a feathered war bonnet and gave him the name Great Buffalo High Chief at Stillwater, Oklahoma, June 18, 1954. (#5403, OSU Photograph Collection, Special Collections & University Archives, Oklahoma State University Libraries)

Haile Selassie and JFK drove past admiring crowds on Pennsylvania Avenue in an open-topped blue limousine. (Cecil Stoughton, White House/John F. Kennedy Presidential Library and Museum, Boston)

At the White House, the emperor presented a leopard coat to Mrs. Kennedy and gifts to children Caroline and John Jr. (Cecil Stoughton, White House/John F. Kennedy Presidential Library and Museum, Boston)

Haile Selassie was the only African leader to make the gracious and expensive gesture of flying to Washington to participate in President Kennedy's funeral on November 25, 1963. At the burial service at Arlington National Cemetery with the emperor are General Charles de Gaulle; Ludwig Erhard; Queen Frederica; King Baudoin; and other mourners. (Cecil Stoughton, White House/John F. Kennedy Presidential Library and Museum, Boston)

The emperor with Kennedy-appointed U.S. Ambassador to Ethiopia Ed Korry, at a reception for the American community in Addis Ababa in December 1963. (© Hoyt Smith. Used by permission.)

Haile Selassie and President Johnson lead the procession "down the rather terrifying staircase" to the strains of "Hail to the Chief." (LBJ Library photo by Yoichi R. Okamoto)

The emperor had an eye for the ladies. Here he sits between Mrs. Robert McNamara and Lady Bird Johnson while the Strolling Strings serenade in the State Dining Room. (LBJ Library photo by Mike Geissinger)

Haile Selassie was the first African leader invited to visit the White House by President Nixon after his election in 1968. At the White House, the two leaders saluted while national anthems were played at the welcoming ceremony at the beginning of the fourth state visit on July 7, 1969. (Richard M. Nixon Presidential Library)

The last trumpet: the 80-year old emperor between President and Mrs. Nixon during his sixth and final state visit on May 15, 1973. That was a record number of state visits by any foreign head of state during the 20th century. (Richard M. Nixon Presidential Library)

CHAPTER 9

1960, The *Annus Horribilis* of Haile Selassie

At the end of the Eisenhower administration, the United States was caught off guard by the speed of decolonization in Africa. Most of the European colonies received little attention from the United States because they were in the sphere of influence of allies. Suddenly, U.S. policy makers had to pay increased attention to sub-Saharan Africa as 16 new independent nations came into being there between 1958 and 1960, and Africa replaced the Middle East as the primary Cold War arena. The State Department belatedly had created an African Bureau in 1959, finally taking Ethiopia out of a "Middle Eastern" category in the Bureau of Near Eastern Affairs. That year there were more foreign service personnel in West Germany than in all of Africa.

In the Horn of Africa, the termination of British and Italian colonial rule over lands neighboring Ethiopia would result in a redrawn political map. The area was inhabited by an almost homogeneous Muslim population, seething with ardor for a new united nation under the banner of Greater Somalia and harboring a long history of antagonism towards its predominantly Christian neighbor. As early as 1957, Emperor Haile Selassie had suffered from Somali angst. As the day of independence in 1960 neared for the possibly threatening Somali people living to the east, HIM's symptoms grew more pronounced, and building up the IEG military became his obsession.

The anachronistic feudal kingdom of Ethiopia continued in its traditional ways—with a veneer of progress. The emperor had proclaimed

a new constitution in 1955, emphasizing the religious origins of imperial power and providing for the continuing centralization of government power. The bicameral parliament featured an appointed Senate,
but the Chamber of Deputies was elected by popular vote in 1957. In
Addis Ababa, James P. Richards, special assistant to President Eisenhower, described this as a "façade of parliamentary government" but
with ultimate power resting with the emperor.[1] Richards noted that
Haile Selassie "did not exercise authority despotically but by working
out compromises among special interest groups: the Coptic Church,
nobles, land-owners, tribal elements, and now, a younger group of educated Ethiopians."

Ethiopia took stands on world issues against the Eastern Bloc motivated by friendship with the United States rather than by a fear of
communism—as seen by the IEG's cozier relations with the soviets and
their offer of financial aid. More worrisome to the Americans was the
"neutralist imperialism" led by Nasser's Egypt and abetted by Nehru's
India, which were trying to force Ethiopia to join the neutralist camp.
An unaligned, neutralist Ethiopia would have been to the soviets' lik-
ing too, rather than continuing the close U.S. ties to the country.

The emperor continued to be a leading supporter of United Nations
collective security, as demonstrated by his sending Ethiopian troops to
help quell the Congo Crisis in 1960. State Department historians called
the Congo Crisis "the single most important issue in U.S. policy in the
period." In July 1960, acting under a United Nations Security Council
Resolution, the UN dispatched a peacekeeping force to bring order to
the Congo (present-day Zaire). From 1960– to 1964, some 3,000 Imperial Bodyguard personnel—about 10 percent of the Ethiopian army's
entire strength at that time—and part of an air force squadron served
with the UN peacekeepers in the Congo.

Kagnew Station remained the driving force behind U.S. policy towards the IEG. Technological innovations made the listening post
ever more important to the Americans—especially after the 1957
soviet launch of Sputnik and the U.S. deployment of Polaris sub-
marines in the Indian Ocean.[2] The U.S. Army's worldwide communications system used Kagnew as a major link, and Washington's
diplomatic corps in Africa used it extensively to send and receive
messages. The National Security Agency—the government's cryp-
tologic experts—and the CIA used intelligence intercepted there.
Eisenhower noted "the importance of maintaining an atmosphere in
Ethiopia which would assure continued unimpaired use of the key
facilities at Kagnew."[3]

To maintain the proper atmosphere in Ethiopia, in August 1960, a secret executive agreement between the globalist-oriented Eisenhower administration and the IEG was approved. The agreement, still a quid pro quo, laid out an enhanced security framework for cooperation. In exchange for continued access to Ethiopian military facilities, the United States was to train and equip an imperial army of 40,000. U.S. military aid to Ethiopia was to be increased to $10 million annually over the next 15 years (more than double the average per year funding for the previous eight years). Washington reaffirmed its "continued interest in the security of Ethiopia and its opposition to any activities threatening the territorial integrity of Ethiopia."[4] The agreement ensured continued access to Kagnew without committing the U.S. MAP to a fixed timetable to complete its military mission in Ethiopia.

The operation of Kagnew Station had become indispensable to the United States, and by the end of August 1960, Haile Selassie had achieved the three political and military objectives he had sought since the early 1950s: the training and equipping of an Ethiopian Army of four divisions, support for a modern Imperial Air Force, and what he considered to be an explicit U.S. security guarantee. This strengthened Ethiopia at the very time that the independent nation of Somalia came into being, posing what Haile Selassie was sure would be a threat to his country of hostile Muslim encirclement and subversion.

GREATER SOMALIA

Throughout most of its history, present-day Somalia consisted of Arab and Indian trading ports along the coast while the interior was populated by scores of Somali clans. During the colonial era of the 19th century, Egypt became the dominant foreign power in the region, but in 1886 it was replaced by Britain in northern Somalia and in 1889 by Italy in the south. The French occupied the strategic port of Djibouti and surrounding lands. Ethiopia remained independent and partook in its own scramble for Africa by conquering and annexing neighboring territories. including those abutting lands.

Independently minded Somalis have never been welcoming to foreigners attempting to occupy their lands, and this animosity was demonstrated by the war of resistance against colonialists that raged from 1899 to 1920. The scourge of the colonial era to Ethiopian, British, and Italian forces alike was the "Mad Mullah," Mahammad Abdille Hasan, the religious and military leader of the Somalis who terrorized the region. Hasan lead the dervishes in one of the longest and bloodiest conflicts in the annals of sub-Saharan resistance to alien encroachment. The dervish uprising devastated the Somali Peninsula and resulted in the death of an estimated one-third of northern Somalia's population and the near destruction of its economy. The struggle was not quelled until 1920 with the death of Hasan, who became a hero of Somali nationalism.[5]

During World War II, the British military occupation of Ethiopia and neighboring areas from 1941 to 1952 contributed to the start of major problems in other areas of the Horn. In 1946, the British encouraged the idea of a "Greater Somalia" composed of British and Italian Somaliland and the Ogaden area of Ethiopia inhabited by Somali people—under a British trusteeship (the Somali areas of Northern Kenya were seldom included in such British plans).[6] Eisenhower complained that the British had made "a mess of it" in handling Ethiopia-Somalia situation.[7]

To the Americans and soviets, the idea of a Greater Somalia appeared as military expansion of the British Empire. There was no way that the British could convince the world at large, especially the Russians, of the purity of British motives in Somalia.[8] The possibility of oil in Italian Somaliland kept alive British interest in gaining a trusteeship of Greater Somalia, but international circumstances would not permit the establishment of a British regime.[9] Reluctantly, the British supported Italian trusteeship of its former colony—to solidify U.S., French, and Italian backing of British ambitions in Cyrenaica (a ploy muted by Libyan independence in 1948).

The Italian trusteeship was a relatively peaceful 10-year period leading to independence for Italian Somaliland in 1960, when it was united with British Somaliland to form the new nation of Somalia. In 1948, the British Military Administration was evacuated from Ethiopian territories in the Ogaden, and the Anglo-Ethiopian Agreement of 1954 formally confirmed the return of the Ogaden to Ethiopia. The process of decolonizing Ethiopia, which was considered complete only with the restoration of its internationally recognized pre-1935 frontiers, had taken one and a half decades.

Although the outlook for a new Somali nation was not promising because of the people's lack of experience in governing and inadequacies of the economy, the United States supported the unification of British Somaliland and Italian Somalia after they achieved independence in 1960. This perturbed Haile Selassie, who was extremely sensitive to any derogation of Ethiopian sovereignty. The emperor became paranoid in his fear that the United Kingdom and United States were pushing for a Greater Somalia while neglecting the concerns of their long-time ally.

The new Somali Republic fostered a Greater Somalia nationalism based upon reuniting all Somali people. The irredentist policy of the new nation was characterized by the national flag, a white five-pointed star on a blue field that symbolized the five supposed branches of the Somali nation—the peoples of British and Italian Somalilands and the Somalis still living in French Somaliland (Djibouti), Ethiopia, and Kenya. Hopes were high for Somali's national cohesion. The people shared a common language, a sense of cultural identity, and a dominant religion—Islam. But competing clan and subclan allegiances were always potentially divisive to the society. Traditionally, clans were governed by experienced wise men who would need wisdom to keep national loyalties paramount over blood ties.

Somalia's independence exacerbated tensions with Ethiopia over the status of 350,000 Somali tribesmen living in the Ogaden and nearby areas, and several hundreds of thousands others who regularly sought water and forage in Ethiopia in the course of their seasonal migrations. The constitution of the Somali Republic proclaimed that all ethnic Somalis, no matter where they resided, were citizens of the republic. The new government demanded that Somalis living in adjacent territories be granted the right to self-determination. Pan-Somali nationalism was encouraged by virulent Egyptian propaganda directed at subverting the Somali people who were subjects of Ethiopia and inciting Somalia against colonial powers and Ethiopia. Recurrent border incidents kept Ethiopian police alert, but there were no major outbreaks of violence in Somali areas of the IEG immediately after the birth of the Somali Republic.

THE COUP THAT FAILED

While the threat of a Greater Somalia remained Haile Selassie's idée fixe for the rest of his reign, he felt confident enough about his kingdom's security to go on another series of state visits in the winter to West Africa and South America. During his absence, there was an attempted coup d'état led by the emperor's body guard on December 14. Many of the educated elite of the country, returned from study in the United States and Europe, were critical of the lack of progressive reform in Ethiopia and influenced the body guard to attempt a coup.[10]

Leading the insurrection were two brothers, Brigadier General Mengistu Neway, commander of the Imperial Guard, and Girmame Neway, a provincial governor and intellectual educated at Columbia University. The effort to depose the emperor was supported by students and the educated classes and seemed to be succeeding early on. The conspirators proclaimed Haile Selassie's eldest son, Crown Prince Asfa Wossen, as Emperor. The plotters attempted to win the collaboration of the army, air force, and police, but the outcome was still uncertain at the end of the first day. The coup attempt lacked broad popular support, however, and was denounced by the Ethiopian Orthodox Church.

In Brazil, Haile Selassie had been made aware of the coup by his son, Prince Sahle Selassie's use of his ham radio. Sahle was loyal to his brother the crown prince and was cognizant of the gap between the haves and the have-nots in Ethiopia, but nevertheless, he was persuaded to send the message by his mother, Empress Menen. His broadcast was picked up in several places around the world and made public in the press.[11]

The recently arrived U.S. ambassador, Arthur L. Richards, feigned American neutrality but actually authorized the transmission of a message to Haile Selassie from forces loyal to the emperor. The embassy had concluded that the loyalists would prevail.[12] On the morning of the second day, U.S. military advisors moved to meet their agreement obligations and provide advice to loyalist government forces.[13] With most of the IEG military rallying to support the emperor, the rebels were crushed on the third day—but not before they slaughtered a host of leaders of the IEG in the Green Salon of the Royal Palace. Ambassador Richards jumped out a palace window just before the carnage ensued.

The United States facilitated Haile Selassie's return to Addis Ababa on the evening of December 17. At the Addis Ababa airport, the emperor, with some emotion, expressed his sincere gratitude to Ambassador Richards for the assistance given those who put down the revolt. He asked that his gratitude be conveyed to President Eisenhower. With exceptional security measures in place, HIM's motorcade then proceeded through streets lined with cheering crowds to Jubilee Palace.[14] Eisenhower sent HIM a letter of congratulations upon his safe return. The wily emperor, with some help from the U.S. military, had survived to resume his absolute rule, but there had been a shaking of the foundations. The monarchy had been stripped of its claim to universal acceptance as the coup attempt "for the first time questioned the power of the king to rule without the people's consent,"[15] The tensions between traditional and modern forces within the country had been exposed, and they would continue to plague the little king.

The CIA reported on "Ethiopian Prospects after the Abortive Coup" and concluded that Haile Selassie remained "the dominant force in a far from united Empire," where "the potentialities for sustained conflict and fragmentation" are flagrant "when the Emperor leaves the scene."[16] The CIA, like most Ethiopians, worried about succession and speculated upon the disastrous outcome of open conflict between the ruling and educated groups if a power struggle ensued in a post–king-of-kings empire.

Thus ended 1960, the *annus horribilis* for Haile Selassie. In carrying out the U.S. foreign policy objectives of keeping the emperor on the throne and his nation secure, the United States had preserved Haile Selassie's reign—but for how long? Would the Lion of Judah live up to the findings of American President Theodore Roosevelt, who knew quite a bit about lions? Wrote Roosevelt: "The darker the night, the bolder the lion."[17]

CHAPTER 10

The Lion of Judah at Camelot: The Second State Visit, 1963

Why wag your head with turban bound, yellow, red and green? Are the things so strange and marvelous you see or have seen?
—Walt Whitman, "Ethiopia Saluting the Colors," 1871

On the first day of October 1963, a Pennsylvania Railroad train pulled out of Philadelphia at 9:35 A.M. sharp bound for Washington, DC's Union Station. Included in the train set was the private railway carriage of Emperor Haile Selassie of Ethiopia on his second state visit to the United States. He was the guest of President John F. Kennedy, who had responded positively to the emperor's lobbying to come to Washington to meet face to face and engage in personal diplomacy. In the emperor's rail car sat the 10 members of the official party, ministers and family members,[1] who listened to Ambassador Angier Biddle Duke, the U.S. State Department's chief of protocol, speaking in French and pointing out scenic landmarks along the way.

After leaving the suburbs, the train picked up speed and traveled southward at 75 miles per hour. The 72-year-old emperor wore a field marshal's uniform of tan and red and carried a long swagger stick. His Imperial Majesty sat ramrod straight in his seat, a bit on edge. Official visitors to Washington usually flew from Andrews Air Force Base to the White House lawn by helicopter, but Haile Selassie thought such an entry undignified for a man of his stature and demanded that he arrive by train. The State Department made arrangements for that to happen, and the entire visit was choreographed with grace and precision.

At 11:59 A.M. the train backed into Union Station and docked at the exact location where the emperor could alight on the 140-foot-long red carpet laid out for the occasion. As Haile Selassie stepped out of the car, the herald trumpets of the military band sounded a welcoming fanfare, and President Kennedy shook the emperor's hand. Mrs. Kennedy, dressed in a black Oleg Cassini suit and wearing a signature pillbox hat, greeted the emperor in flawless French. Haile Selassie bowed to her and then proceeded down a receiving line of Washington's top brass official welcomers and a host of diplomats, many from African nations, as cannons fired a 21 gun salute at precisely three-second intervals from the bottom of Capitol Hill. Rousing shouts of "Long live the Lion of Judah" in Amharic roared through the vault of Union Station.[2]

In ceremonies at the station, President Kennedy said that since Haile Selassie's earlier visit in 1954 the world had seen "one of the most extraordinary revolutions in history," the appearance of 29 independent countries.[3] "Africa and Asia have been transformed into continents whose people are almost entirely removed from the subjugated status which was the lot of so many of them but a few years ago." The President paid tribute to the emperor as a man "whose place in history is already assured." But "perhaps the most celebrated of all, is his leadership in Africa," said Kennedy, referring to Haile Selassie's role in the Summit Conference in Addis Ababa a few months earlier that had launched the Organization of African Unity (OAU).

The diminutive emperor replied in Amharic that he came to "explore ways and means of strengthening our cooperation; a task especially important when the face of the globe has so vastly changed, and the struggle for liberty for everyone, irrespective of race, continues and must be of concern to all of us." The president, who suffered from severe back pain, gamely and graciously stood attentively while Haile Selassie made a lengthy response in a language he did not understand.

With the preliminary formalities completed, the Kennedys escorted the emperor through an honor cordon comprised of personnel from all the branches of the military to a waiting limousine. The two heads of state rode in an open-topped blue limousine behind marching bands and troops in a motorcade on sun-dappled Pennsylvania Avenue. Thousands of Washingtonians lined the curbs between the station and the White House and cheered and clapped. The emperor waved and saluted the enthusiastic crowds as Mr. Kennedy sat smiling beside him. Mrs. Kennedy followed in the next car, a bubble-top limousine, accompanied by the 33-year-old Princess Ruth Desta, Haile Selassie's granddaughter, and the Ethiopian ambassador to the United States, Berhanou Dinke.

After the parade, the Emperor began a three-day marathon of speaking engagements and banquets. Chief Justice Earl Warren, joined by Attorney General Robert Kennedy and others, entertained Haile Selassie and some members of his royal entourage aboard the secretary of the navy's white yacht *Sequoia,* the "Rolls Royce of yachts," for luncheon on the Potomac. The Warrens had been the personal guests of the emperor at Jubilee Palace in Addis Ababa earlier in June and probably knew him better than any other Washington officials. Warren had received head-of-state treatment while in Ethiopia, and some American diplomats thought this a non-too-subtle hint as to how the emperor expected to be royally treated during his state visit to the United States. At 4:30, the emperor attended a tea party, a spur of the moment affair, in the private presidential apartments of the White House just before his conference with President Kennedy. Mrs. Kennedy and daughter Caroline, almost six years old, greeted Haile Selassie and enjoyed iced tea with him. The emperor presented gifts: a large golden filigree jewelry case and a full length leopard coat for Mrs. Kennedy; a carved ivory Ethiopian girl figurine and Ethiopian dress and *shama* made especially for Caroline by the Empress Mennen Handicraft School; and a carved ivory Ethiopian warrior bearing a spear for John Jr., who was almost three. Mrs. Kennedy donned the coat and thanked Haile Selassie in French for the wonderful coat and added, "I am overcome." She escorted the Emperor down to the Rose Garden where the president greeted them. Said the president, "I wondered why you were wearing a fur coat in the garden," and then added his thanks.[4]

Kennedy and Haile Selassie formally met at the White House for one hour and 25 minutes. The emperor took the opportunity to affirm his favored bond with the United States, discussed African issues including Ethiopia's border strife with Somalia, Salazar's Portugal and Angola, apartheid South Africa, the civil war in Yemen with increased arms traffic in the Red Sea area, and the shifting balance of the Cold War. According to the official record, the emperor also requested U.S. economic aid to promote stability in his kingdom and military aid including the training of Ethiopian military personnel in Ethiopia. Kennedy thanked Haile Selassie for the continued use of Kagnew Station. The emperor pointed out that African nations criticized him for allowing the Americans to operate the communications center. Dr. Minase Haile, who was interpreting for the emperor during the meeting, recalls the president raising the question of constitutional reform for Ethiopia with the need for community development and civic action in the feudal regime. Kennedy also delicately brought up the matter of succession, which was far from clear at the time. HIM was obviously not happy with the introduction of these issues and dismissed them outright. This exchange clouded the atmosphere of the visit up to a point, although it was not recorded in any minutes of the meeting. The two heads of state did agree, however, to maintain a private channel to keep in touch.[5]

That evening, the president honored HIM with a white-tie dinner at the White House, the highest social occasion in Washington. While the guests were gathering, Jacqueline Kennedy was flying to New York on the first leg of a two-week, strictly private visit to Greece. In her absence, Rose Kennedy, the president's mother, who was a year older than the emperor, acted as hostess for the evening. In the high theater of the state dinner, Haile Selassie wore his court uniform: an olive jacket, dark blue trousers, and myriad ribbons, medals, and gold braid. Princess Ruth wore the Order of the Queen of Sheba. Altogether 129 guests, the important people of Washington and other VIPs, dined in formal splendor on green-bordered Truman china with gold tableware at 10 candle-lit round tables and were entertained in the East Room by the Robert Joffrey Ballet. The performance resembled a vaudeville or nightclub act, and the president later expressed his displeasure.[6] In an after-dinner toast, Kennedy hailed Haile Selassie as a giant in world affairs for the last three decades. "There is really no comparable figure in the world today who held high responsibilities in the 1930s, who occupied and held the attention and the imagination of really almost all free countries in the mid-1930s, and still could, in the summer of 1963 in his own capital dominate the affairs of his continent.... This is an unprecedented experience in the twentieth century, and I know of only a few experiences in recent history which are in any way similar."[7] The emperor replied to the toast with deep feeling, thanking Kennedy for the aid and friendship given by the United States over the years to Ethiopia.

Like other heads of state who visited the Kennedy White House, Haile Selassie had fallen under the spell of the wit and charm of the president and first lady and the uniquely hospitable treatment lavished by both Kennedys. In meetings with HIM, the president spoke simply and directly, as one world leader talking in confidence to another. He set forth American policy without apology, even when he knew it might disturb or displease the emperor—as was the case in discussing Somalia. Kennedy was candid in not promising HIM things he could not deliver.[8] In turn, the Emperor seemed to admire the sensibility of the young president and his respect for the dignity of his guest.

Of course, Jackie Kennedy, *"la belle Américaine,"* with her flawless French and dazzling grace captivated the emperor from the moment he stepped off the train. In short, the monarch was privy to the culture, beauty, and sophistication of a short-lived era that upgraded American pageantry and public discourse—Camelot, before it became known as such. Events would soon create the mythology of Kennedy's Camelot, a gallant place of courageous deeds, glamorous spectacle, and enduring mystique, but the Lion of Judah had drunk deeply from the stream of life-enhancing zest that flowed through that Washington kingdom in the autumn of 1963.

Haile Selassie had made a special request to lay a silver wreath at the Lincoln Memorial, and on the next morning, he did that in a stirring and somber ceremony. The emperor ascended the memorial steps between two cordons of American soldiers. He carried a glittering wreath made from 580 Ethiopian coins and weighing almost 50 pounds. The emperor placed the wreath at the foot of the imposing statue of Abraham Lincoln, a man Haile Selassie said had been "a symbol to all men who cherish freedom and equality as the most precious of God's gifts."[9] Secretary of the Interior Stewart Udall then led the emperor to the side of the memorial where Lincoln's Gettysburg Address (delivered in November 1863) is chiseled in five-inch letters, and where an interpreter read it in Amharic.

Next, it was off to Capitol Hill, where the emperor met congressional leaders and addressed the U.S. Senate, expressing the hope of his nation that independence will come soon to those African people "who are still under the bonds of colonialism."[10]

Haile Selassie then gave a state luncheon in honor of President Kennedy at a country club in Rockville, Maryland. The president and his party traveled to and from the event in two helicopters from the South lawn of the White House. At the luncheon, gifts were exchanged. The emperor gave the president a handmade, filigreed silver centerpiece in the shape of a fluted bowl, a silver statue of a striding lion wearing a gold crown, an autographed portrait photograph, and two Bibles—one a priceless, 200-year old relic in Ge'ez, and the other, a beautifully bound and inscribed New Testament. Kennedy gave Haile Selassie a replica of the Washington-Bailey Sword, which General George Washington carried in battle during the Revolution; a Tiffany silver desk set; a 16-milimeter motion picture projector with gold plaque; and an inscribed photograph in a silver frame.

At 3:15 P.M. the emperor was at Georgetown University, where an honorary degree of doctorate of humane letters was conferred upon HIM. At four o'clock, Haile Selassie arrived at the White House, where he had a final 45-minute meeting with the president. The two leaders again discussed current problems of the African continent. Kennedy repeatedly emphasized the warmth of American friendship for Ethiopia and also affirmed U.S. support for Ethiopia in her border dispute with Somalia. Washington's position was that the United States also needed to supply arms to Somalia to prevent that nation from turning to communist powers for military aid. The Somalia issue was the only matter, officials said, that presented any problem during the conversation that was described as extremely friendly and smooth. The president promised to give careful consideration to Ethiopia's request for loans and other economic assistance to help finance its five year plan, especially with the developments of the nation's rivers. In response to an invitation to come to Ethiopia extended by Haile Selassie, the president "expressed his desire to arrange such a visit as soon as his schedule permitted."[11] The meeting ended with the heads of state issuing a joint communiqué declaring that the still dependent territories of Africa had the right to freedom and independence.

The emperor then went to the Shoreham Hotel, where he held a reception for the chiefs of diplomatic missions and friends of Ethiopia in Washington. He and his party stood in a receiving line and shook the hands of 1,126 guests. This was followed immediately by a reception in honor of HIM given officially by the Ethiopian ambassador. The guests were served scrumptious food and drink worthy of royalty.

The next morning, readers of the *Washington Post* were treated to an editorial entitled "Lion of Judah" that praised Haile Selassie but added that "sentiment cannot blind the Emperor's well-wishers to signs of inefficiency and ruthlessness in the country's [Ethiopia's] government. But nevertheless the balance is highly favorable, and few African nations have brighter prospects."[12] The editorial concluded that HIM's "gallant resistance (to the Italian Fascists) has earned him his prestige and the right to a respectful audience." The emperor's star still was bright, but some of the luster of a previous time had faded.

The emperor's breakneck schedule continued on the third day in Washington. At 10 o'clock in the morning, Acting Secretary of State George Ball met Haile Selassie at his guest house, and by 11:00, HIM was at the State Department's West Auditorium for a press conference. The hall was largely filled with U.S. government employees, to swell the crowd to a size befitting royalty. The emperor talked about the goals of Ethiopia's five-year economic plan and his meetings at the White House. He characterized his discussions with the president as very cordial but expressed regret that he was not successful in his efforts to get President Kennedy's full support in Ethiopia's dispute with Somalia. Even as Haile Selassie was speaking heavy fighting was reported in the Ogaden. HIM was not satisfied with Kennedy's explanation of why the United States was giving military aid to Somalia. With Assistant Secretary of State G. Mennen Williams at his side, the emperor said, the "validity" of the explanation "did not impress us very much."[13] Haile Selassie asserted that if Ethiopia did not receive military aid matching what Somalia had obtained, she too would be forced to turn to the East. Kennedy agreed only to take HIM's request under consideration. The undisclosed U.S. strategy was to partially satisfy the emperor's request as inexpensively as possible while assuring a stable, cohesive, and friendly government in Ethiopia.

The audience applauded when the emperor took leave of the podium for the elevator to the John Quincy Adams Room, where Secretary of State Dean Rusk was the host of a state luncheon for 130 guests. The U.S. Army Band string ensemble serenaded the diners seated at a horseshoe table for another sumptuous meal provided by French caterers. After lunch, Rusk accompanied HIM to the Naval Observatory, where the emperor again received military honors and passed through a final receiving line of ambassadors and officials before boarding a helicopter. The herald trumpets blew a farewell fanfare as Haile Selassie ascended into the clouds on his way to Andrews Air Force Base and an awaiting plane to fly him to New York City, where his state visit continued.

PRELUDE TO THE WASHINGTON VISIT

While the Byzantine ritual and splendor enthralled the American public and stroked the egos of the Ethiopian visitors, events before and after the emperor's state visit were to have an impact on American foreign policy. Much had happened since Haile Selassie had brought his brand of personal diplomacy to Washington in 1954. Although Ethiopian government spokesmen frequently complained that the United States was not providing adequate support, there had been a sharp increase in military and economic cooperation during the Eisenhower administration. Eisenhower had approved basically an arms-for-base-rights agreement, and Ethiopia received most of the arms the emperor had requested and a military training mission. In addition, Ethiopia sought aid in the development of its economy, and political support for the incorporation of Eritrea, control over the Ogaden, and backing against any threats to its sovereignty. For its part, the United States had solidified its claim to Kagnew Station and access to a strategic locale on the rim of the Middle East. Other major goals of American foreign policy included keeping soviet and Egyptian influence out of the Horn of Africa and a pro-Western government empowered in Ethiopia. There had been a remarkable gain in goodwill toward Ethiopia by Americans as a result of HIM's first state visit, and Haile Selassie had become a bona fide international celebrity.[14]

At the time of Haile Selassie's second state visit, what were U.S. attitudes toward Ethiopia, and who were the major actors bringing reality to policies? Ethiopia was still recovering from the unsuccessful coup of December 1960. Assistant Secretary Williams had visited Ethiopia early in 1961 and reported that the country had been deeply affected by the rebellion and would never be the same again. The events of 1960 had brought to the fore as never before challenges to the status quo from Ethiopians and lingering questions about the future of imperial rule. Haile Selassie seemed either unwilling or incapable of taking necessary steps to accelerate programs and make desired changes.[15] The attempted coup was followed by a period of deep personal sorrow—for the disconsolate Haile Selassie. His wife, Empress Menen, died in August 1961, and a little more than a year later, his son, Prince Sahle Selassie, also died. Arthur Richards, the U.S. ambassador to Ethiopia at the time, speculated that these deaths had made Haile Selassie "tired and depressed" and a lonely figure of a man.[16]

As more African countries gained independence, the nonaligned movement gathered strength and there was growing anti-Americanism among nonaligned nations. Haile Selassie attended the 1961 nonaligned conference in Belgrade hosted by his friend Marshall Tito. There he took part in proceedings condemning nuclear testing and U.S. policy in Southeast Asia. Although he maintained close ties with America, the Emperor occasionally would publicly criticize the United States to demonstrate to the world his nonaligned bona fides.

Haile Selassie remained perturbed by Somalia's hostile activities on Ethiopia's eastern borders. The emperor feared that Somalia, armed by the soviets and backed by the United Arab Republic, would follow the Italian example and invade his nation.

The election of John F. Kennedy in 1960 brought to the office a president with a unique record on Africa. Kennedy had served on the Senate Foreign Relations Committee and became chair of the African Subcommittee. Early in his presidency, Kennedy recommended "a strong Africa" as a goal of American policy. He lent rhetorical support to African nations, doubled their foreign aid, and sent Peace Corps Volunteers to serve in many of the sub-Saharan countries. According to Kennedy aide Arthur Schlesinger Jr., the president "became, in effect, Secretary of the State for the Third World. Assistant Secretaries of State in charge of developing areas dealt as much with him as with the Secretary of State."[17] Further, Kennedy "conducted his Third World campaign to an unprecedented degree through talks and correspondence with heads of state"—especially those of African nations (he liked one-on-one meetings). An important milestone in this campaign was the passage early in the Kennedy administration of the Foreign Assistance Act of 1961 that reconfigured the government's development assistance activities and created the U.S. Agency for International Development (USAID) as the primary vehicle for foreign aid.

Kennedy preferred using the term *international security* instead of international development.[18] Strengthening the security of the Free World was a phrase he liked. Said Kennedy, "We hope we can tie this whole concept of aid to the safety of the United States. This is the reason we give aid. The test is whether it will serve the United States. Aid is not a good word. Perhaps we can describe it better as 'Mutual Assistance.'"[19]

When the newly appointed ambassador of Ethiopia, Berhanu Dinke, presented his credentials to the president in August 1962, Kennedy talked about Ethiopian development and affirmed "our desire to be associated intimately with the peoples of Africa in your quest for those things which you desire for yourselves: peace, your continued development as free and independent nations, the opportunity to develop your institutions in your own way."[20] To assist Ethiopia in attaining such goals, the first group of 244 Peace Corps Volunteers, the largest contingent sent to any country at that time, arrived in Addis Ababa in September 1962. They were greeted by the emperor, who thanked the volunteers for coming to "help drive out ignorance" from his country.[21]

Meanwhile in the Horn of Africa, Eritrea that since the 1950s had been "an autonomous state federated with Ethiopia" was absorbed into Ethiopia as a province in 1962. This action, seen by some as a violation of a UN mandate, provoked strong international opposition—but not from the United States, which viewed Haile Selassie as a preferable landlord of Kagnew Station to other possibilities.[22] While the emperor gained Eritrean ports on the Red Sea, he encountered heavy seas in the U.S. Congress. Members of the House Appropriations subcommittee criticized foreign aid officials for giving Haile Selassie what some of them called a "royal yacht," complete with air conditioning and gold-colored wallpaper in his stateroom. The ship, actually a converted U.S. seaplane tender, was to serve as the flagship of the Ethiopian Navy. The storm about the "floating palace" that had been given to Ethiopia as a "political consideration" soon blew over.[23]

Two months later, the United States was at sea with weightier matters on its agenda: its naval blockade of Cuba during the missile crisis. At its conclusion, the emperor cabled Kennedy: "We commend the statesmanship and judgment which have averted the catastrophe in Cuba where only a few short days ago the future of humanity appeared to hang in the balance. We urge that the settlement of the Cuba problem be used as a point of departure for the resolution of other pressing problems which threaten the preservation of peace."[24]

In the early 1960s, Haile Selassie played a role in bringing about what many observers thought might brighten prospects for peace in Africa. The emperor enhanced his reputation as an elder statesman of the continent by his astute leadership in the creation of the OAU. He also had continued his role as a Cold War ally of the United States and as a supporter of United Nations collective security by maintaining a force of Ethiopian troops in the still unstable Congo.

In October 1961, in Addis Ababa, HIM made a splendid gift of one of his palaces, the Guenete Leul, and its grounds to the people of Ethiopia for a newly founded Haile Selassie I University, the nation's first university. USAID was to play a prominent role in the early success of the university. Another significant U.S. initiative was agreed to in January 1963: a $10 million, four-year project for the aerial photographing and mapping of the entire country.

On the eve of Haile Selassie's state visit in 1963, the U.S. country team in Addis Ababa analyzed the situation in Ethiopia and recommended possible U.S. actions to speed reforms. The Americans noted that "even without Kagnew, U.S. influence would be of great importance because of heavy public commitment U.S. has already made here."[25] The size, population, and location give Ethiopia strategic importance. "For better or worse" the United States was "inescapably identified with Haile Selassie and the present regime." The country team worried about the "repressive nature of present police state alienating increasing numbers of Ethiopians from all classes." The analysis concluded: "We believe that regime is too aware of the tangible benefits which flow to Ethiopia as a result of Kagnew to attempt to secure its removal. They realize it accounts in large measure for generous military assistance programs and other evidences of U.S. favor, both past and anticipated."

The State Department viewed the emperor's visit as an opportunity for the United States to do honor to HIM as an important world figure. Indeed, at that time Haile Selassie was a more significant world leader than he had been during the previous decade. In meetings at the White House, Kennedy and the emperor could discuss major issues confronting the world and those of specific pertinence to relations between the two countries. Finally, State hoped that the personal relationship between leaders established during the visit would contribute to the success of whatever negotiations might subsequently ensue.[26]

In the spring of 1963, Kennedy's newly appointed ambassador to Ethiopia, Edward M. Korry, a former journalist and editor for *Look* magazine, arrived in Addis Ababa and was to be a significant presence in U.S. policy towards Ethiopia and Africa during the next four years. In a letter to the president, Korry described the positive impact Kennedy's speeches on civil rights and the Cold War had on the emperor, who described them as "masterpieces." Wrote Korry, "All these recent events made him that much more eager to meet you again (HIM says he met you in your Senatorial capacity in 1954)."[27]

Korry was a proactive ambassador, and shortly after his arrival he began to entertain Ethiopians at the embassy in a manner never before seen. As he described it, he "threw 'an enormous bash' which produced the highest percentage turnout and the greatest number in absolute terms of invited Ethiopians in the history of our [U.S.] presence here—some 300 of the best minds in the country."

But the new ambassador soon encountered problems in U.S.-Ethiopian relations from the perspective of frustrated officials of the Imperial Ethiopian Government. They informed Korry that the emperor was only going through with the state visit to the United States "because it was too late to back out."[28] The IEG was convinced that "nothing would come out of it." For Korry, the Ministry of Foreign Affairs rehearsed the accomplishments of the IEG that had provided the U.S. government with vital military facilities, refrained from recognizing the Peoples Republic of China (PRC), steered clear of any close ties with the soviets, provided troops for the UN's Korea and Congo operations, been a moderating influence in African affairs, and been responsible for the best possible OAU charter at the summit, "for whose success it also was largely responsible." By comparison, pointed out the IEG spokesman, Somalia had done none of those sterling deeds, but the United States was granting help to the new nation. By hearing the foreign ministry's lament, Korry was introduced to the IEG's now you-see it, now you don't, one step forward, two steps back rhythm of policies for getting the maximum amount of dollars from the United States as rent for Kagnew Station. Always implied in these rhetorical exchanges was the subtle threat that if a substantial increase in grants of military assistance was not forthcoming, the Asmara facility would be in jeopardy. Such ploys frequently were used by the IEG to demand U.S. attention to its perceived needs just before an important importunate moment. Public criticism of the United States of this sort played well with some segments of Ethiopian society and also burnished Ethiopia's nonaligned credentials.

There were two essentially unquestioned central goals of Kennedy's foreign policy: containing communism and preventing world war.[29] Kagnew, as one of four world-wide U.S. bases for future satellite communications in addition to regular military uses, played a role in both of these goals. Ethiopia made full use of this fact in negotiations for economic and military aid—even though the IEG remained solidly in the pro-Western camp. As part of a secret executive agreement in 1960, the U.S. Department of Defense and the IEG carried on negotiations to expand Kagnew by more than 800 acres, build enormous installations including larger antennae, and double the U.S. personnel on the base in anticipation of future space probes. In exchange, the United States was to give the IEG $2 million in military assistance over a five-year period. A new Kagnew Station lease finally was signed on July 29, 1963.

Three weeks later in a meeting at the Dire Dawa Palace, the emperor subjected Korry to what the ambassador called the "lengthiest and bitterest criticism of U.S. policies in the Horn."[30] In a 30-minute "excoriating of Korry," Haile Selassie, "loaded for bear" but in a tone courteous and dignified, lambasted the United States for every perceived slight, shortcoming, or error committed against Ethiopia. Bewailed the emperor, "What had the Ethiopian people done to deserve such treatment at the hands of the U.S. Government? It fills our hearts with sorrow." HIM said he intended to make a similar presentation to President Kennedy during his upcoming state visit. This exchange was followed by attempts by well-placed Ethiopians to cancel the emperor's trip to the United States.

Cooler heads prevailed, however, and the state visit occurred as scheduled. Haile Selassie was persuaded that U.S. aid was the key to Ethiopia's development efforts to affect substantial tangible improvement in his people's well-being and thus bolster his prestige and undercut his critics.

On September 29, HIM and his party were flown by presidential jet from Addis Ababa to Geneva. The next day they flew nonstop to

Philadelphia, where amid pomp and ceremony, Haile Selassie paid a late afternoon visit to Independence Hall. James H. J. Tate explained to HIM how the Liberty Bell got its crack. At City Hall, the mayor conferred honorary citizenship of the city upon the emperor. After an overnight stay at the Bellevue Stratford Hotel in the City of Brotherly Love, the royal party left by train for the U.S. capital. They were escorted on their eight-day trip to the United States by Ambassador Korry.

A TRIUMPHANT RETURN TO NEW YORK CITY

Having concluded his business with the U.S. government, HIM continued his state visit with the international community and the American public. Accompanied by Secretary of State Rusk, the royal party arrived at New York's LaGuardia Airport at 4:45 P.M. on October 3. There the emperor was greeted by Mayor Robert Wagner, Adlai Stevenson, the chief U.S. delegate to the UN, and 50 members of foreign delegations to the UN. That evening, Mayor Wagner was the host at a reception in honor of HIM at the Grand Ballroom of the Waldorf-Astoria Hotel.[31]

At noon on the next day, Haile Selassie joined a very select group of people—those who have been honored two or more times with New York City's traditional welcome—a ticker-tape parade up Broadway. An enthusiastic crowd of onlookers, about 10 deep, cheered the short, black-clad figure who got out of his limousine to walk the last five blocks of the hero's mile from the Battery Park to City Hall. He was greeted in Amharic by some Ethiopians shouting, "May he live long for our glory." They were rewarded with a wide smile by HIM. The emperor "worked the crowd" and veered to the curb to shake hands and to exchange personal greeting with admiring spectators. He was even accosted by a woman seeking his autograph. U.S. protocol officers and New York police officials described the city's welcome as the warmest since President Kennedy's first visit after his inauguration.[32]

At the conclusion of the eventful, confetti-strewn procession, Haile Selassie was greeted by Mayor and Mrs. Wagner at City Hall. The emperor, dressed in a dark double-breasted business suit, and the image of royal dignity, recalled his 1954 visit and parade and his receiving the city's Medal of Honor. He added, "We hope our second visit helps to strengthen the already good relations between Ethiopia and the United States."[33]

Haile Selassie then was driven to the United Nations, where he was guest of honor at a formal luncheon for 60, hosted by Secretary General U Thant. The emperor deposited with the secretary general the charter of the OAU signed by the heads of 32 African states at the Addis Ababa conference earlier in May.

At 3:00, HIM addressed a jam-packed attentive general assembly session. A hushed silence hung on his measured phrases. He recalled a day 27 years earlier when he made a vain appeal to the League of Nations to help his country against aggression. In his remarks, the emperor referred to the League as the UN's "discredited predecessor."[34] Haile Selassie said, "History testifies to the accuracy of the warning that I gave in 1936." He had words of praise for the organization that succeeded the League. The UN's action in Asia, in the Congo, and in Suez "has thus far proved an effective safeguard against unchecked aggression and unrestricted violation of human rights." The monarch stated proudly: "The UN is perhaps the last hope for world survival." Speaking at a time when the Civil Rights Movement was struggling to end de jure segregation in the United States, the emperor said, "There is no one who is not sad about the current racial conflict in the United States." But he found consolation in the efforts of the Kennedy administration to find a just solution. The emperor concluded, "It is the sacred duty of the UN to win real equality for all men everywhere." When he finished his 35-minute speech, the audience rose as one and gave HIM a standing ovation. It was the general assembly as theater, and gripping, even if the outcome, like much of theater, was understood all along. It was in its way historic compensation for Haile Selassie, now so widely hailed and so deferentially received. At that moment, his appeal to the League of Nations that had seemed so fruitless was in vain no longer.

The emperor's address to the UN was the highlight of his New York stay. He also enjoyed meeting General Omar Bradley and having power luncheons and dinners with Mayor Wagner and the Sulzbergers of the *New York Times* and a mining executive aboard his 190-foot long yacht in New York Harbor. HIM received 100 Ethiopian students in his suite at the Plaza Hotel and later in the day went to the RCA Building to make a videotape for a Sunday broadcast of NBC's *Meet the Press* radio-television show. He wore a military uniform and spoke in Amharic with a member of his cabinet, Dr. Menassie Haile, translating for him. The emperor forcefully said "the UN should seek to solve the problem of colonialism. If all other methods fail, the African states will have to consider the use of force against the remnants of colonialism on the continent."[35] He still believed in the efficacy of collective security.

The royal party had planned to fly to Florida and tour the National Aeronautics and Space Agency, but a hurricane caused the tour to be cancelled and Haile Selassie to prolong his stay in New York City.[36]

During that interval, HIM spent four hours in a routine checkup at the Harkness Pavilion of Columbia-Presbyterian Medical Center. The emperor's state visit to the United States ended on October 7 with Haile Selassie saying some extremely complimentary things about America at Idlewild Airport. He said his talks with President Kennedy had strengthened the existing cordial relations between Ethiopia and the United States. Then he flew on a Canadian Department of Transport plane to Ottawa, where he began a three day state visit.

CANADA REDUX

The royal party was met at the Ottawa airport by Prime Minister Lester Pearson, Governor General Vanier, and two 13-year old Ethiopian "Michaels"—Prince Michael Makonnen, the emperor's grandson and Lij Michael Mengesha, HIM's great grandson. In a private talk with the prime minister at Government House, the emperor discussed the possibility of Canada providing assistance to Ethiopia in farm and technological matters, especially in livestock production and maintenance. Escorted by the commissioner of the Royal Canadian Mounted Police (RCMP), HIM was given a special performance of one of Canada's most celebrated pageants, the RCMP Musical Ride. Afterwards, in brilliant autumn sunshine, he took a tour of the stables of the RCMP Rockcliffe Barracks and talked about one of his favorite subjects, horses, with the ride's commander. In a field marshal's uniform, Haile Selassie inspected troops of the Second Battalion of the Canadian Guard, who were dressed in full-dress red uniforms, complete with tall bearskin hats, at the War Memorial, the granite cenotaph in Confederation Square. He laid a wreath in honor of Canada's war dead at the foot of the memorial. The emperor also visited Ashbury College, where his young relatives were students.[37] On the morning of October 9, Haile Selassie left on a Royal Canadian Air Force plane for Bermuda, where he later continued his world tour that would take him to West Africa.

RESULTS OF THE SECOND STATE VISIT
TO THE UNITED STATES

The emperor's second state visit to the United States was again a resounding public relations triumph. The monarch's Q rating—how well people are known—was astronomical. Still a commanding figure, slight of stature, whose beard was flecked with gray, Haile Selassie won over the American public with just the right combination of exotic royal spectacle and dignity. He was an iconic personality—that is, anybody who is celebrated. And celebrated he was! At a time when there was no Internet, no satellite communications, no CNN, no network television news, much less Twitter or iPods—no way of knowing quickly or reliably what was going on 7,000 miles away, the emperor seemed to stand tall for ideas then deemed virtuous in the United States. His Christian genteelism, reliability as a Cold War ally, service as a moderating voice in the councils of African nations and among the nonaligned countries, and staunch support of the United Nations and the concept of collective security played well in the provinces and on the sidewalks bedecked in fluttering flags and royal crests in America's political and cultural capitals. Whenever he appeared in public there was still a critical mass of spectators, whose graying heads testified to memories of 1935, to lead successive waves of applause. The emperor basked in the admiration, and having learned from his first state visit, played up every opportunity to enhance his celebrity—especially with the photogenic Kennedys.

Upon his return to Ethiopia in October, HIM played a mediating role in settling a dispute between Algeria and Morocco—an action appreciated by the United States that sought order in the Maghreb. More troubling to Americans was the withdrawal of Ethiopian troops from the UN force in the Congo on November 20. Haile Selassie ordered two battalions home because the troops were urgently needed in view of Somalia's decision to accept a soviet offer of $30 million in military assistance.[38] The United States immediately terminated its half-million dollar military aid program to Somalia but stayed in that country with limited economic assistance and a Peace Corps program. Three months later, when Somali forces attacked Ethiopia and Kenya to create Greater Somalia, HIM might have said "I told you so" while repulsing the invaders.

Although Ambassador Korry had admonished the president that "trying to out-Byzantine" the emperor "would be futile and counterproductive" and that Kennedy therefore should "spell out details of the U.S. program and justification from the start,"[39] Washington tried to outsmart HIM by providing a few of the IEG's requested items but holding back on others by insisting that first a survey team should be sent to Ethiopia to determine what was really needed. The United States shied away from the emperor's new military requests, believing that economic and governmental reform and a better-trained military were more pressing needs.

After reviewing the survey team's findings, the United States offered to give the Ethiopian Army additional training but no more equipment. The emperor had requested $20 million in military assistance, but the United States only agreed to give $2 million over a five-year period. More significant in terms of military hardware was the agreement for the Americans to send a squadron of twelve F-5 jet fighters for delivery in 1966. By that action, Ethiopia became the first country in sub-Saharan Africa and one of the few third-world countries to receive supersonic jet fighters. For its part, the United States expanded Kagnew with the Stonehouse project, which added in 1964 huge parabolic antennas (12 to 15 stories high) to intercept soviet space transmissions and to aid in development of U.S. ballistic missiles.[40]

Did the personal diplomacy between the heads of state of Ethiopia and the United States pay off? If friendship on the international political scene is a pay off, then the answer is yes. The emperor returned to Addis Ababa a closer friend of the president and of the United States than before he arrived. Throughout the rest of his reign, he remained a staunch ally of America, a rarity in sub-Saharan Africa during the Cold War. From another perspective, the end result of the short-lived Haile Selassie–Kennedy diplomacy was that both sides got what they wanted: the Ethiopians the military hardware they desired—although not as costly or as modern as they had sought—and the United States expanded facilities at Kagnew Station and the maintenance of a strong presence in Ethiopia in the face of spreading soviet and Chinese activities in the region.

The emperor later confided in Dr. Minassie Haile, chief of the political section of HIM's private cabinet, who translated for Haile Selassie during the 1963 state visit, that he liked Kennedy the best of the American presidents.[41] JFK treated HIM as a respected elder and courteously introduced him to the White House secretaries and other ladies on the staff. The president also made informal promises to the emperor that he was sure would be kept.

As the end of 1963 approached, Ambassador Korry prepared a trenchant policy paper for the State Department reviewing the accomplishments of U.S. programs in Ethiopia. The ambassador found that the United States had an "overwhelmingly predominant presence in military, transportation, communications, public health, and educational fields," and the new elite of the country owed "their status to education in U.S. institutions."[42] Where else in Africa, asked Korry, has the United States such an invitation to extend its influence and such a base on which to build its hopes? "Where else do we have opportunity for influence in all key sectors?" Where else in the underdeveloped world do we find responsiveness to the demand of U.S. foreign policy in the form of actions in Korea and the Congo, in the formulation of all-African institutions and attitudes, and in the commitment to a U.S. military installation? Korry concluded by saying it was essential for the United States to commit additional resources at specific places and times to help induce change and help assure Haile Selassie's plan for a peaceful transition to a constitutional monarchy. There was New Frontier optimism in the U.S. Embassy in Ethiopia at the end of the Kennedy administration, although the State Department never gave answers to Korry's cogent queries.

Who knows what further political outcomes might have resulted from the Haile Selassie-Kennedy friendship and the possible visit of the President to Ethiopia? Would the private communication and candor preferred by Kennedy have paid off to the mutual benefit of both nations in additional ways?

The questions remain academic. The personal ties between the leaders were ended by the assassination of the President in Dallas only a few weeks after Haile Selassie's visit and three days after the Emperor withdrew his troops from the Congo.

CHAPTER 11

He Shall Have a Noble Memory: The Kennedy Funeral

The two splendidly uniformed heads of state walked out of the White House where they had been conversing in French and took their places in the orderly rows of foreign leaders. The tall, slender President of France, Charles de Gaulle, dwarfed the diminutive but impressive figure of Emperor Haile Selassie of Ethiopia. They were among a mighty gathering of chiefs of state, heads of government, and other representatives of foreign governments, 220 in all, who had come to Washington, DC, to pay their last respects to the slain American president, John F. Kennedy. They had been invited to join Mrs. Jacqueline Kennedy and the new U.S. president, Lyndon B. Johnson in the procession of the state funeral on November 25, 1963.

At 11:40 A.M., the visiting dignitaries, the choice and master spirits of that age, joined the cortege behind the Kennedy family and the president and began the eight-block walk to Saint Matthew's Cathedral, where the Archbishop of Boston, Richard Cardinal Cushing, would celebrate the pontifical requiem low mass that had been requested by Mrs. Kennedy. There was virtually no conversation among the world's leaders as they walked in a loose crowd up Connecticut Avenue to the cathedral. The State Department's protocol office had arranged no special lineup for this walk, leaving it informal, and soon the orderly rows of rulers broke apart into a formless mass. Haile Selassie, dressed in the most colorful, most decorated garb, was easy to spot in his black uniform set off by brilliant green and gold trim, by colorful medals and by a black and red hat and sword belt. He walked between the militarily attired King Baudouin of Belgium and President Diosdado Macapagal of the Philippines. As they moved forward, nine pipers from the Black Watch of the Royal Highlanders Regiment played "The Brown Haired Maiden," "The Barren Rocks of Aden," and other slow march elegiac tunes.

Approximately one million people lined the route of the funeral procession, which had begun that morning at the Capitol before going to the White House, then to Saint Matthew's Cathedral, and finally, after the mass, to Arlington National Cemetery. Millions more across America watched the funeral on television. International celebrities such as Haile Selassie and de Gaulle who had drawn huge crowds in their state visits to the United States were now being seen by far more Americans than ever before. For one brief day, they had been a part of the grandest assembly of world statesmen ever gathered in Washington, DC. Their presence added color and splendor to the funeral, but it also created the greatest security and protocol problems ever encountered in the capital. Because the 19 heads of state and government and members of royal families from 92 countries, five international agencies, and the papacy were not official guests, they were responsible for their own lodging and arrangements. Most stayed at their own embassies.

Mourners watched as the procession passed: the coffin of the late president, draped with the Stars and Stripes on a gun carriage drawn by six grey horses; a caparisoned horse; the Kennedy family led by Kennedy's widow and his two brothers, Attorney General Robert F. Kennedy and Senator Edward M. Kennedy; President and Mrs. Johnson; a black limousine carrying the Kennedy children, Caroline, and John Jr.; and finally, the foreign delegations.

Former presidents Truman and Eisenhower already were in the church when the cortege arrived. Seated near the emperor at the requiem mass were Canadian Prime Minister Lester B. Pearson, the Duke of Edinburgh representing Queen Elizabeth II, British Prime Minister Sir Alec Douglas-Home, Irish President Éamon de Valera, and Japanese Premier Hayato Ikeda. At the funeral, Rose Kennedy, the president's mother, turned to Haile Selassie and said: "It's wrong for parents to bury their children. It should be the other way around."[1]

After the mass, the casket of the late president was borne again by caisson on the final leg of the procession to Arlington National Cemetery in Virginia. Virtually everyone else followed the caisson in a long line of 107 black limousines, passing by the Lincoln Memorial and crossing the Potomac River. Protocol officials had established some

formal precedence for the trip, and the visiting dignitaries were assigned places in an alphabetical listing of their nations. Accordingly,
the first was Belgium's King Baudouin, immediately behind President
Johnson. Then followed the cars of Haile Selassie, de Gaulle, President
Heinrich Lübke of West Germany, and others in alphabetical order.[2]

At Arlington, the emperor stood next to de Gaulle at the head of the
grave during the ceremony. The two uniformed leaders saluted while
a 21-gun salute boomed, followed by the Third Infantry firing party
delivering three volleys, and the bugler sounding taps. After the ceremony at Arlington, the foreign visitors went to the White House to
pay their respects to Mrs. Kennedy and, later, to the State Department,
where President Johnson greeted them individually at a reception.[3]

* * *

Upon hearing news of Kennedy's assassination, Haile Selassie had
addressed his nation on the radio, saying, "Let each Ethiopian today
pause for a moment in his daily tasks and lament the passing of this
man, a good friend to Ethiopia, who understood our problems, who
sympathized with us in our struggle and who shared our dearest de-
sires and hopes for the future."[4] All government and private offices
were closed, and flags flew at half mast. Memorial services were held
in a number of churches in the capital and in the provinces. The largest memorial mass was at Trinity Cathedral and was attended by
Crown Prince Asfa Wossen, members of the royal family, ministers of
the crown, the diplomatic community, and distinguished Ethiopians.
Hundreds of people went to the United States Information Service's
Library to get news reports. Portraits of Kennedy were ubiquitous
throughout the country—including many in very humble homes.
Long queues waited at the American Embassy to sign a special reg-
ister. Several men present, including Acting Foreign Minister Ketema
Yifru, shed tears, saying in Amharic, "He was a good man." Similar
scenes were played out throughout the continent. Thirty-two independent African states paid last respects to the young president.[5]

The U.S. government had not encouraged mass visitation from
abroad for the funeral. Foreign governments had been notified that
the presence of their regular envoys stationed in Washington would be
sufficient. So many world leaders wanted to attend, however, that the
State Department relented and sent out formal invitations. Before that
decision had been made, Haile Selassie already was flying in a special
Ethiopian Airlines plane directly to Washington. The emperor said he

felt honor-bound to attend the funeral of Kennedy because he had had a very pleasant visit with him only weeks before. He was accompanied by Ras Andargatchew Massai, the emperor's son-in-law; HIM's grandson Commander Iskander Desta; Teferra-Work Kidane-Wold, scholar and private secretary to the emperor; Lij Kassa Wolde-Mariam, president of Haile Selassie I University; Brigadier General Assefa Demissie, and U.S. Ambassador Korry. Their plane was met at Dulles International Airport by Secretary of State Dean Rusk. Security was tight at Dulles, with newsmen being kept 15 feet away from arriving dignitaries by rope barriers. The memory of Jack Ruby's killing of Lee Harvey Oswald was still vivid in the minds of U.S. officials. Ruby had been standing in a crowd of newspaper reporters just before he fired.[6]

A small contingent of Ethiopians welcomed the emperor at the airport. One of them, Attorney General Teshome Gabre-Mariam Bokan, remembers the emperor ruefully saying, "Only two months ago We were together in this city. Now he is no more. We put all our hopes on him as the guardian of international peace. Now he is fallen. We [the royal "We," i.e., HIM] had to attend his funeral."

When the emperor went to the White House on the next day, Monday, to await his participation in the funeral procession, he had a reunion with Kennedy's brother-in-law, Sargent Shriver, who had been in charge of making arrangements for JFK's funeral. As director of the Peace Corps, Shriver had visited Haile Selassie at Jubilee Palace in Addis Ababa. Surrounded by many other heads of state, the emperor "remarked to all those within hearing that Ethiopia had no need to build a physical monument to the memory of Kennedy; the American president would always be remembered through the work of the Peace Corps in East Africa. This set off a torrent of praise for the Peace Corps, as each leader of a country hosting Peace Corps Volunteers strove to outdo the last in his effusiveness for the program."[7]

At the requiem mass at the cathedral, Haile Selassie had seen Chief Justice Earl Warren who had been his guest in Addis Ababa earlier in the year. The emperor sponsored a major address, "Equal Justice Under the Law," by the Chief Justice that Ambassador Korry said was "considered the major intellectual event of the year if not of the decade" in Ethiopia.[8] On the day Haile Selassie had arrived for the funeral, Warren had given a memorable eulogy in the Capitol Rotunda, expressing the feelings of many mourners present: "John Fitzgerald Kennedy, a great and good President, the friend of all people of good will, a believer in the dignity and equality of all human beings, a fighter for justice, an apostle of peace, has been snatched from our midst by the bullet of an assassin. Our Nation is bereaved. The whole world is poorer because of his loss."[9]

During a break in the funeral events, Haile Selassie had met for half an hour with Anastas Mikoyan, soviet ambassador to the United States, about his country's supplying Somalia with military arms. Mikoyan replied with "honeyed words," saying that press reports of soviet arms programs were exaggerated. The soviets tried to convince the emperor that the IEG should not take precipitous action vis-à-vis the USSR, such as canceling a planned soviet oil refinery in Ethiopia.[10]

***

Mrs. Kennedy received the foreign dignitaries at White House after the funeral. The somber spirit of the day still held them in silence. Haile Selassie, de Gaulle, and de Valera, Ireland's president, were the only heads of state who met privately with Mrs. Kennedy in the family quarters in the Yellow Oval Room before she mingled with other foreign guests.[11]

That evening at the State Department, President Johnson held a reception for the visiting rulers, an unusual event viewed as an expression of gratitude by the U.S. government for the spontaneous outpouring of sympathy over Mr. Kennedy's death from all parts of the world.[12] The foreign dignitaries had spent a quiet, ceremonious day, but when they arrived at Foggy Bottom, they were again their usual voluble selves. They were once more representatives of a world suddenly looking forward and making a final salute to Kennedy and getting a close look at the new president in his new role.[13]

President Johnson stood before a fireplace in the ornate, candlelit reception room of the State Department overlooking the Capitol, the Potomac, and Arlington Cemetery. The president began to practice his own brand of personal diplomacy by standing for more than an hour in the eighth-floor reception hall to greet the visiting personages. He shook the hands of more than 200 members of royal families, presidents, chancellors, premiers, foreign ministers, legislators, and representatives of the UN and other international organizations. In demonstrating the warmth of his personality, Johnson used a firm handclasp held until condolences and wishes had been expressed. For special friends he used the "super sincere handshake—a normal clasp with the right hand, reinforced with a semi-embrace of the subject's elbow or upper arm with the left hand."[14] Johnson had met Haile Selassie briefly during HIM's earlier visits to Washington, and when the emperor came through the receiving line he received not only the prolonged handshake but also the covering clasp of the left hand, held through longer remarks and usually broader smiles. The *Voice of Ethiopia* reported that LBJ pumped the emperor's hand 20 times.[15]

The president mingled with his guests after leaving the receiving line and then retired to a side room for brief conversations with the delegations of several countries. By that time, some of the foreign visitors had broken into small groups for the first time to assess the American scene and their new problems. A roaming photographer took a shot of LBJ, de Gaulle, and Haile Selassie sitting with their heads huddled together. What a collection of political acumen was crowded into that photograph. The new president was besieged with requests for formal audiences by visiting heads of state. Only a few were chosen to meet with LBJ in a tightly scheduled day of audiences on the following day, Tuesday.

The next morning at nine, Haile Selassie was the first foreign dignitary to confer with the president at the White House. For half an hour the two discussed relations between their nations.[16] Johnson told the emperor that he wanted to look to HIM, as Kennedy had done, for advice and counsel because of the monarch's many years of experience. Haile Selassie had suggested to Kennedy that they address one another not as an emperor to a president but rather as two friends holding frank and open discussion. According to the emperor, Kennedy had acceded to this request and had always spoken frankly with HIM. Indeed, Haile Selassie signed his later letters to Kennedy as, "Your good friend." Johnson responded, "We'll speak to him as frankly as he has to us."[17] The emperor then asked the president if U.S. policy toward Ethiopia would remain the same. Johnson's affirmative answer was interpreted by Haile Selassie (unfortunately, according to the State Department) to mean the United States will respond positively at least in part to the IEG's requests. A short time later, Johnson sent the emperor an autographed photograph of the two of them together with the inscription, "I hope for the benefit of your counsel and for the continued cooperation of our two countries."[18]

Haile Selassie was the only African leader to make the gracious and expensive gesture of flying to Washington for Kennedy's funeral. By playing an impressive role in the greatest assembly of mourners since the funeral of King Edward VII in London in 1913, the emperor showed the IEG's appreciation of U.S. policies, programs, and purposes in Ethiopia. The little king who took pride in his friendship with American presidents did his part in assuring that John F. Kennedy would have a noble memory. But would Ethiopia retain its status as "the most favored among African states" under the LBJ administration?

CHAPTER 12

The Winter of Discontent: The Third State Visit, 1967

And each man shares The strength derived from head held high…As holds his head, the King of Kings…Our symbol of a dream That will not die.

> —Emperor Haile Selassie on Liberation Day, May 5, 1966, reading from *The Collected Poems of Langston Hughes*[1]

A little before eight o'clock, the motorcade of black limousines pulled up to the North Portico entrance of the White House after making the ridiculously short journey from Blair House, the official state guest house of the president, just across Pennsylvania Avenue. On a blustery, cold February evening, the automobiles went through the White House gates, where 12 herald trumpets greeted them with a rousing fanfare. Two Marine musicians played a drum roll as Emperor Haile Selassie, attired in a black, double-breasted tuxedo, stepped out of the lead limousine accompanied by his granddaughter, Princess Ruth Desta. They were warmly greeted by President Lyndon Johnson and Mrs. Johnson, who walked down the front steps through the glaring lights of the photographers and into the icy weather to usher them into the warmth of the mansion. Johnson, standing six-feet, three-inches tall, towered over the little king, although Mrs. Johnson was only two inches taller than HIM. The other limousines carrying the emperor's official entourage of distinguished Ethiopians followed close behind; among them, Commander Iskender Desta, HIM's grandson; Ethiopian Minister of Foreign Affairs Ketema Yifru (one of a very few IEG officials known to talk back to HIM and get away with it); and the Ethiopian ambassador to the United States Tashoma Haile Mariam (described by the State Department as "intelligent, discreet, confident, well-trained"), and their State Department handlers (including Korry and Symington) and security officers.

President Johnson was hosting a black-tie dinner in honor of the emperor on his third state visit to the United States. The president and first lady escorted the royal guests upstairs to the Yellow Oval Room for an intimate gathering and presentation of gifts (the part of the evening Mrs. Johnson "liked best").[2] A small number of guests, among them Vice President Hubert Humphrey and Acting Secretary of State Nicholas Katzenbach, were already there enjoying cocktails when the heads of state arrived. Chief Justice Earl Warren, who knew the emperor better than any of the other officials present, was the first to greet HIM.

The president and the emperor sat on a couch and engaged in lively conversation before making a formal exchange of gifts. To commemorate his visit, Johnson gave Haile Selassie a portable pocket dictating machine, IBM's latest (to the delight of HIM, who adored electronics and took great interest in things practical); a set of surgical implements, including a bronchoscope, which allowed direct examination of areas of the lungs that are not accessible with stethoscopes or seen on X-rays, in a chest with a gold plaque to be given to Princess Tsehai Hospital in Ethiopia, named after the emperor's daughter, who died in 1942; a sterling silver tray with edging in vermeil bearing the presidential seal and an engraved inscription from President and Mrs. Johnson (her only gift to HIM); leather-bound books, *The Living White House* and *Washington: Magnificent Capital*; a book box in vermeil with the seals of the emperor and the president engraved on top; and an autographed photograph in a vermeil frame. Mrs. Johnson confessed that she was sometimes "vaguely unhappy that our gifts seem less imaginative and less meaningful than the gifts that foreign monarchs make to us."[3] This was one of those times, for Haile Selassie presented LBJ with a silver box, a set of cufflinks, and tie pin and gave Lady Bird Johnson and her daughters jewelry boxes, traditional Ethiopian dresses, and sets of gold jewelry.

By the time of the emperor's visit, Lady Bird was accustomed to entertaining royalty in the Executive Mansion and had personally endured alleged faux peerage jibes by the nobility-conscious in Europe who inquired about "Lady who?"[4] She, along with Ethiopian poet laureate Tsegaye Gabre-Medhin, who, to the English ear, was "Sir Guy Gabre-Medhin," were peerless in confusing the class-conscious British wags of their day. Mrs. Johnson had met Haile Selassie at the White House state dinner in 1963, and she would renew the acquaintance-ship by sitting next to the emperor at dinner.

Following the presentation of gifts came what Lady Bird Johnson described as "the always thrilling removal of the colors, the forming of the line, and the marching downstairs," "down the rather terrifying staircase," to the sound of four ruffles and flourishes followed by *Hail to the Chief*[5] echoing throughout the White House. This stately salute accompanied the president and the emperor as they led the proces-sion of dignitaries down the Grand Staircase. The party stopped for photographs at the bottom of the stairs before standing in line in the East Room, where approximately 150 guests, a cascade of Washing-ton society converging on the White House, filed by to shake hands. The president introduced the guests—Supreme Court justices, cabinet members, congressional couples, and big donors to Johnson's Demo-cratic Party—to Haile Selassie. The emperor with mournful eyes and tremendous dignity grasped the bejeweled and manicured hands of a variety of Americans bearing greetings to emperor and king.

The heads of state then walked down the Cross Hall to the State Din-ing Room, where a Marine string ensemble, wearing red jackets with light blue trousers, awaited them. While the guests were being seated, the 22-piece string ensemble played and the music reverberating in the White House created an irresistible holiday mood. During the ban-quet of European splendor, the dress-blue-uniformed U.S. Air Force Strolling Strings came with the salad course and played on either side of the head table. In front of a huge fireplace and beneath a portrait of Abraham Lincoln, President Johnson leaned on his right elbow to talk to Vice President Humphrey over Princess Ruth, who was seated between them.

The president called over his shoulder to Charles "Steve" Gillispie, a Peace Corps executive on loan as a translator for the evening, who was standing immediately behind him throughout the dinner. Said LBJ, "I want you to translate every word of my speech for the emperor. *Every word*."[6] Fortunately for Gillispie, Ambassador Korry heard the president's command and alerted Dr. Minassie Haile, the emperor's primary translator for important events, who quietly provided HIM with a running translation during LBJ's remarks.

Johnson toasted the emperor, saying, "With God's help, we have al-ways stood proud and free upon our native mountains."[7] LBJ said how pleased he was to "exchange views on international affairs with one whom I consider to be one of the world's greatest elder statesmen."

The president drew subtle parallels between the fascist aggression that Ethiopia had survived and that faced in the 1960s by South Vietnam. He recited Haile Selassie's words to the League of Nations and added, "We all know, to our shame, the reply your majesty received." Johnson concluded, "It is my genuine and most earnest hope that succeeding generations of our peoples will continue to reinforce the solid edifice of American-Ethiopian amity and understanding." In reply, Haile Selassie said, "We take this opportune moment, Mr. President, to express our deep gratitude for the numerous forms of assistance which Ethiopia has benefited from your Government, be it in the form of technical knowledge or in human resources in all walks of our country's endeavor for national development."[8]

After coffee and liqueurs, the party went to the East Room, where Lady Bird always introduced the after-dinner program with grace and a touch of humor.[9] Performing for the first time at the White House that night were Metropolitan Opera stars, tenor Richard Tucker and soprano Nedda Casei. They sang songs very appropriate for Ethiopia: "Celeste Aida," a special salute to one of Haile Selassie's granddaughters, Princess Aida; "You'll Never Walk Alone;" and the duet, "Make Believe."[10] At the conclusion of the program, the president and first lady accompanied their guest of honor to the front porch to say good-bye. Johnson had considered having Haile Selassie at his ranch in Texas (which might have produced some interesting photo opportunities), but his schedule was such that he chose to play host to the emperor in Washington, where the president again performed with meticulous correctness the duties of a head of state within the confines of protocol.

Dr. Minassie, who was with the emperor on several of his state visits to the United States, recalls Haile Selassie's not being beguiled with LBJ.[11] Unlike other presidents, Johnson did not signal his recognition of HIM as a world leader—at least in the manner that the monarch thought appropriate. The emperor found LBJ to be absent minded (perhaps he was distracted at the time by the Vietnam War), and he resented the president's interrupting him when he was speaking. In official correspondence, one would never sense a cacophony in their relationship. Whatever the personal chemistry of the two, Johnson ultimately satisfied Haile Selassie's rapacity for military aid.

* * *

President Johnson brought some experience in Africa to bear on his foreign policy toward that continent. As vice president, he had gone twice to Senegal and thought he had some perspective into "what life in an African village was like and what its problems were."[12] As a senator, he had met leaders of African states and knew of their displeasure at being considered pawns in the Cold War games. He knew there was a need for "a coherent American policy to deal with the African continent, at least that portion south of the Sahara." Foreign aid had been more plentiful during the Kennedy administration when there were fewer countries, and Johnson faced tighter budgets due to increased U.S. involvement in Vietnam. Thus, the president looked for new ways to be responsive to the challenges of development in Africa and to review aid programs with the aim of improving them.[13] A major problem was what to do with traditional bilateral programs. With 36 independent African states in existence and the number growing, and most of them requesting U.S. aid, how could the Johnson administration best meet its obligations during a time of tight budget restrictions?

Advising Johnson in the State Department was Assistant Secretary of State for African Affairs, G. Mennen Williams, a carryover from the Kennedy administration who opposed apartheid in South Africa and the still extant European colonial rule and who supported African unity. Mennen encouraged the president to correspond with African heads of state and to invite them to Washington to share ideas and plans for cooperation. During the LBJ administration, there were some 20 visits by African chiefs of state and heads of government, and the president's skills at personal diplomacy with them was described as "damned good" by an assistant secretary of state.[14]

Johnson set up an active program of taking Ambassadors on the presidential yacht down the Potomac, and the Africans were the first to go. The ambassadors also were invited to informal luncheons in the White House Fish Room hosted by the president's staff, usually Walt Rostow or Ernie Goldstein, and occasionally Vice President Humphrey. Johnson would drop in during desert and spend 15 to 30 minutes with them. According to a state department observer, the president related quickly and well to the African diplomats. "He did everything he possibly could to give them a feeling that he was concerned."[15] Ethiopian ambassadors Tashoma Haile-Mariam and his predecessor Berhanou Dinke were recipients of such special treatment.[16] Berhanou, who represented Ethiopia in Washington from 1961 until mid-1965 made headlines when he resigned to protest the oppression of HIM's absolute monarchy and sought asylum in the United States. A *Washington Post* editorial on the resignation referred to Ethiopia as one of Africa's most backward countries and criticized the IEG's massive military expenditures.[17]

The president had laid out the principles and plans of his foreign policy in a major address at the Associated Press luncheon in New York City on April 20, 1964. At a time when U.S. involvement in Vietnam was escalating, Johnson cited military might as the bedrock of the administration's policy. In a prophetic statement about what would be his attitude about Southeast Asia, he proclaimed, "Surrender anywhere would mean defeat everywhere."[18] Resistance to communist expansion and the strengthening of allies, and encouragement of developing countries, while still pursing lasting peace would continue to be basic. The president mentioned certain areas of concern: (1) to build military strength of unmatched might; (2) to resist efforts by communists to extend their dominion and expand their power; (3) to revive the strength of allies, to oppose communist encroachment, and to protect the American future; (4) to aid the independence and progress of developing nations and to help them resist outside domination; (5) to pursue peace through agreements that would decrease danger without decreasing security. The language and thrust of Johnson's principles were remarkably similar to those proclaimed by the State Department during the Kennedy administration. Citing a "Great Society" parallel, the president asserted that America could wage war against poverty in the new nations of Asia and Africa—as well as at home. In conclusion, Johnson said the United States could never again retreat from world responsibility and would have to get used to working for liberty abroad as well as at home.

U.S. domestic politics during the height of the civil rights movement also were of concern to African leaders. In March 1965, Johnson addressed a joint session of Congress, announcing his signing of the Voting Rights Act of 1965 that outlawed discriminatory voting practices that had disenfranchised African Americans in several states. Johnson said passage of the act spoke "for the dignity of man and the destiny of democracy."[19] A few weeks later, the president sent a letter to African heads of state, 39 in all, enclosing what he called "The American Promise," a copy of the Act that was the "definitive statement of the policy of my Administration." Johnson wrote that the Act also reflected "the determination of the American people to utilize all the resources at their command to achieve rapidly the goal of full and equal rights for all citizens." This indeed was "The American Promise," proclaimed the president. It is not just African Americans, "but it is all of us, who must overcome the crippling legacy of bigotry and injustice. And we shall overcome."[20] The speech was made on March 15, 1965, a week after deadly racial violence had occurred in Selma, Alabama, as African Americans were preparing to march to Montgomery to protest voting rights discrimination.

Likewise, LBJ's inspiring June 4, 1965, commencement address at Howard University on race relations, "To Fulfill These Rights,"[21] had an impact in Africa because a defamatory book called *The Invisible Government* had been published a few months earlier and was being used in Africa against the United States. The book that was read by Ethiopian university students sensationalized "America's intelligence and espionage apparatus with the CIA at its center that conducts the clandestine activities of the Government."[22] *Atlanta Journal* editor Ralph McGill reported to the president that "among the questions most frequently asked" about the book by Africans, "are those about American civil rights, the CIA and the young people, American national politics, Vietnam, and foreign aid."[23] Johnson's eloquent statements in the Howard address; for example, "We seek…equality as a fact and equality as a result," took some of the steam out of the affect of the supposed exposé.

On May 26, 1966, President Johnson gave the first major speech by an American president on Africa since Eisenhower's address to the UN in 1960. At a White House reception marking the third anniversary of the Organization of African Unity, the president spoke about "U.S. Africa Policy" to the ambassadors of 36 African member states and an audience of 300. The speech was given to demonstrate that the administration was capable of new foreign policy initiatives. Johnson took a firm stand in support of truly representative government and the termination of white racial rule in Africa, believing that such a stance would have a positive impact on African attitudes toward the United States. The president expressed sympathy for African efforts toward economic development and made several specific proposals for channeling aid into more useful fields: first, to strengthen the regional economic activities; second, to increase the number of trained Africans; and third, to develop effective communications systems for Africa.[24] Although Johnson did not offer an increase in aid, he indicated that the United States would increasingly channel assistance into regional and subregional economic groupings. The president expressed aspirational thoughts for the OAU: "Our dreams and our vision are of a time when men of all races will collaborate as members of the same community, working with one another because their security is inseparable, and also because it is right and because it is just…It is this deepening appreciation and respect for the diversity of the world—each man and nation in it—that increases the possibilities for peace and order."[25] With the Civil Rights Act of 1964 and the Voting Rights Act of 1965 only recently enacted, the president probably had an African American audience in mind during his speech too. Johnson's civil rights policies and diplomacy in Africa doubtlessly played a role in his reelection by a large margin in November 1966.

Johnson also announced that a team of specialists headed by Ambassador Korry would prepare a major comprehensive report on U.S. development policy and programs in Africa. His study would examine needs for economic growth expressed by Africans, prospects of multilateral cooperation, application of regionalism and subregionalism to African development, and ways for the most efficient use of U.S. resources.

Korry's report was completed on August 8, 1966, but Johnson ordered it kept secret.[26] At the heart of the Korry report was the question of regionalism versus bilateral aid. The report contained 42 recommendations spread over 16 categories and included initial proposals in regional activities, communications, education, transport, power, and agriculture, and proposed ways in which policy and programs could be made more effective. Korry recommended that the United States concentrate aid on a few "development-emphasis countries" and lend support to the World Bank for external aid. In 1967–1968, USAID adopted a new policy that reduced its regular bilateral programs from 30 to 10 by phasing out existing programs and not undertaking new ones.[27] The 10 nations to retain bilateral programs were those where development prospects were best or where there was a special U.S. interest or relationship. Ethiopia was one of the 10 "development-emphasis countries" and one of five in the "special relationship" category. As soon as possible, USAID projects in other countries would be limited to support for regional institutions, regional projects, and multidonor projects. Also as soon as possible, the United States should consider transfer of funds to multilateral institutions, such as the World Bank, for their use in providing capital and technical assistance. The Korry report advocated a renewed and expanded emphasis on self-help by African nations. In a short time, Korry had reviewed an extremely complicated subject and had explained it in his usual trenchant and understandable English. Later, Johnson would praise the report as "the most comprehensive study of Africa and our role there ever compiled for a President."[28]

To implement the report, Johnson named a committee of experts in the State Department and USAID to work with White House representatives. A steering committee was formed with members from the United States, the UK, Italy, Belgium, and Canada to consider the plans. Interdepartmental and interagency rivalries and bureaucratic turf battles kept the plan from ever reaching its full potential, but during the Johnson administration, the Korry report was a center of controversy and kept Africa foreign assistance as a focus of attention at a time when Vietnam was of central concern. As Johnson explained, "Economic and social development is a slow business, especially among nations in a very early stage of modernization."[29]

During his term as U.S. ambassador to Ethiopia, Korry, a political appointee and outsider to career foreign service officers, received glowing official reviews of his work. National Security Council staff member Edward Hamilton, in a memo to Walt Rostow, said Korry had "thrown great intelligence, energy, and imagination into a job which has probably never before been filled by a man of his ability. He has managed a good relationship with the Emperor without becoming in any sense a captive. In short, he has done quite a job."[30] Harry C. McPherson Jr., the president's counsel and top speech writer, informed Johnson about an Inspector General's report on Ethiopia, in which Korry and his embassy came out very well. Korry was described as "providing the Embassy with dynamic, imaginative, and purposeful leadership."[31] The ambassador was well-informed and made his presence felt throughout the staff. He had "affected a substantial revaluation of the importance of Ethiopia to the U.S. and this, in turn, under his initiative, has led to a significant shift in U.S. policy toward the country. He has taken advantage of every opportunity to press his view." The inspectors complained mildly of the embassy's excessive use of cables. Korry put many ideas on the African desk in the State Department, and State had "its hands full trying to process them."

With the appearance of Korry in Addis Ababa, cable traffic flowing to Washington enjoyed a new birth of literacy and pungency. He was an intrepid watcher and an unsurpassed commentator. His writing was knowledgeable and gracefully expressed, thoroughly researched and full of uncontrolled zest for the subject. This was a welcome relief from lack-luster Foggy Bottom speak that permeated the telegrams from the embassy that preceded and followed Korry's prodigious tenure in Ethiopia.

While still in his first year in Addis Ababa, Korry put Ethiopia in perspective in the State Department in a memo to the secretary of state: "In past 7 years (since 1956) Ethiopia became first nation in modern times which succeeded changing its geography, moving from isolated Middle Eastern country of no particular consequence to committed African nation with considerable role in continental affairs. Ethiopia rapidly attaining aspiration of becoming fulcrum of Africa."[32]

By 1964, a series of events had made Ethiopia, if not the fulcrum of Africa, at least more significant to American foreign policy. Ethiopia was increasingly openly nonaligned, and Haile Selassie again was waging a charm offensive on the communists by visiting the USSR and by extending a warm welcome to Premier Chou En-lai of the PRC in Addis Ababa. The soviets offered Haile Selassie anything he wanted if he would break off ties with the United States. While the possibility of defection by the feudal state was not likely, the threat of losing the investment in Kagnew gave the United States impetus to pay the rent in a timely way and more in keeping with the expectations of the land-lord. It also inspired the U.S. Department of Defense to give thought to alternatives to the Kagnew technologies. In 1966, the Defense Satellite Communications System was launched and successfully used satellites to transmit reconnaissance photos and other data that held the promise of making land-based communications posts obsolete. Also in 1966, the United States signed a secret agreement with the UK to use the Indian Ocean coral atoll of Diego Garcia, 1,000 miles south of India, for joint defensive needs that might include those of a listening station. Kagnew was still prime real estate, but it was obvious that its valuation might be going down.

Continuing disagreements between the United States and Ethiopia over the types of military arms being given and the speed of their delivery exacerbated frustrations on both sides. Squabbling until the heavens fall was the trademark of the Ethiopian-U.S. relationship about military assistance from its origins, and it would continue to plague diplomatic ties between the two nations. Korry was perturbed by an anti-American tone in the government-controlled Ethiopian press. The State Department began to ponder just how long-term American military assistance could be continued. And always in the background was concern about royal succession, should, God forbid, the emperor die.

By this time, the Johnson administration's policy was reminiscent of the Eisenhower-Dulles years. The United States was playing a stricter zero-sum game in assessing political trends and alignments. Washington was choosing sides forcefully in combating communist expansionism and insurgencies in the third world. The Kennedy strategy of preparing for United States disengagement from potential political hot spots came to be viewed as an unacceptable option under

LBJ. Threats to U.S. interests should be faced down, and Johnson believed that "U.S. political, economic, and military interests could be safeguarded by a better effort and greater investment of resources."[33] There was no shortage of threats to American interests in the mid-1960s in Africa.

Mounting concerns about Africa resulted from the outbreak of the Biafran War in eastern Nigeria, the unilateral declaration of independence by Rhodesia, the growing threat of Eritrean dissidents, and the soviets' providing sophisticated arms to Somalia, which were used against Ethiopian forces in combat. The two Horn nations fought over the Ogaden region in southeastern Ethiopia, dominated by ethnic Somalis and claimed by Somalia. Since independence in 1960, Somalia had rejected the border demarcation by colonial powers that gave the Ogaden to Ethiopia. In the ensuing struggle, the United States served as the proxy for Ethiopia, and the Soviet Union for Somalia.[34] The Ethiopian military blamed its lack of success against the Somalis on inadequate military aid from the United States, and the soviets, in becoming arms merchants in Somalia, had made their profound entrance into the Horn. In May 1966, the IEG got delivery of four of the much-anticipated F-5 jet fighters, but the number was smaller than foreseen and the schedule of future deliveries was vague.[35] The emperor had won a qualitative battle: Somalia's Soviet MiG-17 combat fighters were thought to be of lesser quality.

Early in 1967, the IEG Defense Ministry submitted a large request to the embassy for arms and training for the next five years. Included was a list of major equipment requirements totaling well over $150 million, including tanks, armored personnel carriers, antitank and anti-aircraft guns, C-130 Hercules aircraft, more F-5 jet fighters, and helicopters. The IEG justified the request on the basis of soviet military aid to Somalia and the Sudan and support from various sources to armed dissidents operating within Ethiopia in Eritrea, the Ogaden, Bale, and Sidamo. Korry tried to dissuade the Ethiopians from making such an impractical proposal while the United States was heavily involved in Vietnam and budgets were tight. The emperor, however, thought it a propitious time for HIM to practice his personal diplomacy in America and to again seek to raise the rent for Kagnew.[36]

It was the threat of a saber-rattling Somalia that most influenced Haile Selassie to seek a meeting with President Johnson to request additional military arms. At the time of Haile Selassie's February 1967 state visit, Johnson was preoccupied with the escalating war in Vietnam, and his administration was more susceptible to the argument that the communist bloc was actively advancing its interests worldwide and campaigning to dislodge the United States from the Horn of Africa.

***

The emperor had been a fair-weather friend of America during his first three visits to the New World, having been there during spring and summer and mild autumns, but he gamely faced Washington's harsh chill when he arrived for his third state visit. Haile Selassie was in the United States as part of a 21 day tour that included the USSR, Turkey, and the Sudan in the itinerary. He arrived on February 13, 1967, at 4:30 in the afternoon at Andrews Air Force Base, where he was met by Vice President Humphrey and Ambassador Symington. They departed by helicopter for the President's Park on the Ellipse and continued to the North Portico of the White House where President Johnson welcomed HIM. Full military honors were rendered the visiting head of state by an honor guard from all the armed services. The weather was bitter and windy, and the 74-year-old emperor looked cold even in his heavy double-breasted military overcoat. Welcoming ceremonies quickly were moved inside to the East Room for an exchange of brief remarks by the leaders. Johnson said Haile Selassie "believes men are closer than ever to achieving a better, more peaceful world."[37] The emperor in response stressed friendship among nations as a worthy goal in Africa and all through the world. He added, "I believe that leaders must from time-to-time come together, face each other, and discuss problems they share in common. It is not enough that we deal through diplomatic channels." The royal party then went to Blair House for the evening.

A *Washington Post* editorial the next morning welcomed the emperor, because at the age of 74 he had "seen more history and held power longer than any other living Chief of State. Because relations between the United States and Ethiopia throughout his long rule have been both cordial and constructive, and remain so, the Emperor might be said to be this country's oldest friend."[38] The *Post* continued, "For all that may seem antiquated about his ancient monarchy, his rule in recent years has been increasingly progressive. His standing among younger, more volatile African leaders is astonishingly high." The emperor still was esteemed in Washington as a wise friend on a troubled continent.

More cautionary was an editorial published in the *Christian Science Monitor* two days later. In Ethiopia, there is a risk, warned the *Monitor,* that the United States should not overlook.

> So long as Emperor Haile Selassie is on the throne, his peculiar and remarkable qualities will probably guarantee security and stability within his Empire. But it is an empire whose unity might be severely put to the test once Haile Selassie were no longer at the helm. And it would be unfortunate indeed if the United States, through too close a commitment, became involved in civil war in the Horn of Africa.[39]

The *Monitor* concluded, "Such strife is something which Emperor Haile Selassie prays will never come. And so do we."

At 10:30, the hardy emperor walked through the chill with Ambassador Symington and party from Blair House to the White House without a top coat. He met with President Johnson to discuss shared concerns about the United Arab Republic and soviet advances in the Red Sea basin, and the soviet-sponsored Somali threat to Ethiopian security. Haile Selassie's primary objective was to convince the president of the need for the United States to provide Ethiopia with more arms.[40] They talked for more than 90 minutes on world problems but not about more aid for Ethiopia. The leaders discussed economic development in Ethiopia and the country's problems in education, health, and agriculture. They touched on Vietnam only in passing, Johnson mentioning it as a problem he faced.[41] The emperor described his talks with LBJ as "completely satisfactory."[42] Haile Selassie was concerned with the build-up of soviet arms in Somalia and sought accelerated U.S. assistance in modernizing the Ethiopian armed forces. "We achieved a great measure of understanding," he said.

In preparation for the meeting, the State Department had sent the president a packet of information including a secret memorandum for the president from the undersecretary of state summarizing the foreign policy implications of the visit (e.g., the United States could not satisfy the emperor's demands for more military assistance, but "on the other hand, friendly relations with Ethiopia" were important to American interests in Africa) and suggesting talking points on questions for discussion with the emperor (e.g., "Topics the Emperor will raise: threats to the Red Sea Area and Ethiopia. I recommend that you say.... Topics you might raise: The danger of a continued arms race in the Horn of Africa..."); the emperor's itinerary; "confidential" biographies of the 12-member official party in order of precedence, with personal descriptions in pithy language (e.g., "on occasion he becomes arrogant and 'uppity'"; "his tastes run to American clothes and whiskey"), their titles and manner of address, and a guide to pronouncing their names; a copy of a confidential country fact sheet including information about governmental structure, natural resources, human resources, economic activity, defense forces, and Americans in Ethiopia; confidential "suggestions on approaching the Ethiopians and topics of conversation" (e.g., "Ethiopian court etiquette makes the Hapsburgs look breezy…Ethiopians are generally aware of what is going on in the United States and also follow with some interest developments in Vietnam, China, the Middle East and Europe;" "Subjects to be avoided, if possible…Somalia, controversial African issues, such as Rhodesia, South Africa").

After leaving the president, the emperor and the royal entourage drove to the Supreme Court, where the emperor would be the honoree at a rare luncheon for a visiting head of state in that stately temple of justice. His Imperial Majesty was met by Chief Justice Warren and escorted to the East Conference Room, where a reception was held. In hastening the royal party and getting as many as possible into the elevators, uniformed U.S. security guards apparently shoved people so tightly that the emperor's black-and-red military hat was knocked askew—a misfortune doubtlessly galling to the ever-meticulous ruler. Although the incident was quickly passed over, some of the Ethiopians interpreted the zealous security arrangements and the actions of the guards as showing a lack of respect for the emperor and the royal party.[43]

After the 45 guests had arrived, the party moved to the West Conference Room where lunch was served. Many of those invited were attorneys working in a variety of federal government positions and included "at least some of the important persons who [were] not going to the White House dinner" later that evening.[44] Among the eclectic roster of guests were Secretary of the Interior Stewart Udall; Senator Frank Lausche (D-OH); Congressman Ross Adair (R-IN), who later would serve as Ambassador to Ethiopia in the 1970s; former ambassador to Ethiopia Arthur L. Richards; an admiral and a general; a half dozen State Department officers; representatives of the Peace Corps, USAID, and USIA; and the *Washington Post* columnist Joseph Kraft. At the head table, Haile Selassie was flanked by the chief justice and Senator Frank Carlson (R-KS), who, on the next morning, hosted a prayer breakfast at the Capitol that the emperor attended. Warren was a charming host who, in his remarks, made several comparisons of California to Ethiopia. He and the emperor competed with bragging rights about their homelands and urged the guests to visit them to see for themselves their natural beauty. In his toast, the chief justice said:

When mention is made of the Emperor of Ethiopia, Americans today recall with pride and affection your many courageous and far-sighted actions which have contributed to the freedom of mankind. Yet, on this occasion as we are breaking bread at the Supreme Court of the U.S. where all Americans who come here pursue our national ideal of equal justice under law, I think it is more appropriate to salute Your Majesty for your contribution to Ethiopia's legal system."[45]

Warren concluded with "a toast to Your Majesty—a great statesman, a valued friend, a wise law-giver."

After the luncheon the emperor attended a reception at Howard University during which he again was awarded an honorary degree by the university.

The emperor returned to the White House office for a 4:30 meeting with Katzenbach and Secretary of Defense Robert S. McNamara. They talked for one-and-a-half hours about continuing military assistance. Haile Selassie again expressed his concern about soviet arms in Somalia and repeated his oft-repeated mantra that peace can be assured only by collective security measures. He spoke strongly in favor of a nuclear nonproliferation treaty and of the importance of multilateral and regional approaches to development problems. HIM asked the secretaries for a doubling of the Military Assistance Program and a new program of support for the IEG budget. Katzenbach reminded HIM that the United States already was supporting his nation's budget through revenues from PL 480 shipments of cotton. He asked the emperor to put his requests in writing for reply by Ambassador Korry in Addis Ababa. Taking leave of the cabinet officers, Haile Selassie briefly met astronauts Charles Conrad Jr. and L. Gordon Cooper before receiving the Chiefs of the Diplomatic Missions of African countries in the White House. That evening the Johnsons held the state dinner in honor of HIM.

The next morning, after attending a prayer breakfast at the Capitol hosted by Senators Carlson and Mark Hatfield (R-OR), the emperor left by helicopter from the South Lawn of the White House for Andrews Air Force Base, where he departed for New York City.

The Ethiopians' plane landed at JFK International Airport just before noon, and at 12:30 the emperor was at UN Headquarters to meet

Secretary General U Thant for a discussion centered on current attempts to bring peace to Vietnam. Haile Selassie was the guest of honor at a state luncheon at the UN, where he exchanged remarks with soviet ambassador Nikolai T. Federenko. Lunch concluded with a toast to HIM and the Ethiopian people by Secretary Thant and a toast by Haile Selassie expressing his hopes for the continued success of the UN and continued good health of Thant. At a press conference that followed, the emperor expressed his willingness to take the initiative in seeking peace in Vietnam if any of the countries concerned requested that he do so.[46] His remarks in Amharic were translated by Ethiopia's permanent representative to the UN Endalkachew Makonnen, who had performed the same service for HIM during his first state visit to the United States in 1954.

In the afternoon, Mayor John V. Lindsay gave a tea for the emperor at his residence at Gracie Mansion.[47] On the porch of Gracie Mansion, Mayor Lindsay's youngest child, John, was introduced to HIM by Mrs. Lindsay. John bowed from the waist and shook the emperor's hand, drawing a broad smile from the usually stoical king. At the tea, the mayor presented Haile Selassie with a silver cigarette box adorned with a lion on its cover. The tea was attended by a dozen city officials and their wives and by 10 members of the royal party. After the tea, the emperor met members of the Council on Foreign Relations at their headquarters at Pratt House on East 68th Street. That evening Haile Selassie hosted a reception for the permanent representatives to the UN at the Carlyle Hotel, where he was staying.

On the following morning, Haile Selassie gave an interview to *New York Times* reporter, Sam Pope, in his suite on the 34th floor of the Carlyle. The emperor sat on a large satin sofa, while his pet Chihuahua, Lulu (a male), who would be HIM's traveling companion throughout the day (except at lunch), romped over HIM, "pawed at his hands and lay down against his thigh and went to sleep."[48] The emperor spoke to Pope about his personal diplomacy and said it was wise to talk not only with the executive branch but also with senators and representatives "to ask them to help President Johnson to strengthen relations with Ethiopia." At 11:00 A.M. the emperor was interviewed by a distinguished group of reporters, including Christian Daniels of the *New York Times* and Pauline Fredrick of NBC News, for "Today," the NBC television program. Dr. Minase Haile served as interpreter for the program that was tape-recorded for later broadcast.

In the afternoon, HIM privately received King Hassan II of Morocco at the Carlyle, and at four o'clock he held a reception for the Ethiopian community at the Bronxville residence of Endalkachew. That evening, the emperor attended a performance of Wagner's *Die Meistersinger* at the Metropolitan Opera at Lincoln Center.

On Saturday morning, New York Governor Nelson A. Rockefeller called on HIM at the Carlyle for a half-hour conversation. The governor petted the frisky Lulu without untoward results. Haile Selassie addressed a luncheon meeting of the African American Chamber of Commerce, an organization with about 75 large corporations as members, at the Plaza Hotel. The emperor made an appeal to American businessmen to put more private capital into Ethiopia to speed its general development. He said his countrymen already were doing all they could for themselves and getting aid from foreign governments and international organizations but that still more was needed from the private sector. He told his audience of 250 that Ethiopia had enacted liberal legislation to encourage private capital and that his country had "vast untapped natural resources" to be developed by such capital.[49] In the afternoon the emperor called on Jacqueline Kennedy for a brief visit at her home on Fifth Avenue.

Before departing from the United States on a private airliner for the USSR in the late afternoon, Haile Selassie thanked President Johnson and the people of the United States "for the spontaneous and warm welcome accorded us during our short stay in your country."[50] Two weeks later, when HIM was on the Turkey leg of his tour, the U.S. ambassador there reported that the emperor made unsolicited comments about his stay in Washington. Wrote Rostow to LBJ, "Obviously there is a certain amount of diplomatic blarney involved, but he seems to have gone out of his way to let you know he enjoyed himself."[51]

* * *

After his 21-day trip to the United States and other ports of call, Haile Selassie was back in Addis Ababa and ready for what Korry called "unwrapping the package" of U.S. aid. The contents had good news/bad news aspects. There would be no increase in funding, and the United States could not make a five-year commitment for military assistance. The United States, however, would provide Ethiopia with seventeen M-41 tanks, four helicopters, and, eventually, eight more F-5 fighters. In addition, augmented MAAG training would continue for another year.[52] A high level of economic assistance would be maintained. The emperor's personal diplomacy—playing on U.S. vulnerabilities in its costly commitment to the defense of South Vietnam, its acceptance of the domino theory of communist expansion and fear of the Soviet's displacing the United States from its dominant place in the Horn—paid off. America's great stall on providing modern weaponry to Ethiopia had come to an end. Johnson's largesse was influenced by Kagnew's continuing significance in U.S. research in satellite communications and in the development of ballistic missiles. U.S. policy also sought to assure a stable, cohesive, and friendly government in Ethiopia. The emperor was facing stiffer resistance to his regime at home, and he no longer was the international celebrity he once had been. The White House meetings of the emperor and the president underscored the complexities of Ethiopia's problems at the time and also the nature of U.S. governmental operations.

The State Department reported to the White House that "our limited response to the emperor's requests for significantly more military equipment during his February visit was a disappointment to him (despite his satisfaction with the personal aspects of the visit). We have been attempting in a number of ways since then to sweeten the pill."[53]

One of the sweetened pills that Haile Selassie seemed to enjoy was being sent high-level officials for visits to the palace. Among the American VIPs received by HIM were Governor Soapy Williams, to discuss the problem of achieving an honorable and peaceful settlement in Vietnam; LBJ's "trusted colleague," Governor Averill Harriman, "to obtain your wise counsel and advice;" and Senator Robert Kennedy with wife Ethel, who petted HIM's cheetah and laid the cornerstone of the John F. Kennedy Memorial Library at Haile Selassie University.[54] Under Secretary of State Nicholas Katzenbach spent two days in Addis Ababa and met with HIM as part of a 17-day, 12-nation tour of Africa in May 1967 to demonstrate that the United States remained interested in its problems and opposed to white rule in South Africa.[55] Former Vice President Richard Nixon came to Ethiopia on a fact-finding tour of Africa, and Vice President Hubert Humphrey and wife Muriel, leading a 10-member party touring nine African nations in January 1968, called on HIM.

Humphrey's trip was remarkable for what he saw and learned in his travels. In a report to the president, Humphrey said, "Among African leaders, I found a fierce self-pride and healthy nationalism, combined with a sense of pragmatic realism."[56] Traveling in his party were Supreme Court Justice Thurgood Marshall; Leonard Marks, director of USIA; and Dr. Samuel Proctor, a former Peace Corps executive and future pastor of the Abyssinian Baptist Church in Harlem. The vice president demonstrated the continued concern of the United States and the American people with the African continent. He spoke to the OAU at its headquarters in Addis Ababa on January 6, 1968.

The vice president "found emperor Haile Selassie vigorous, alert and clearly feeling in charge of his country's affairs." The emperor "warmly reminisced with enthusiasm about his visit" with the president in 1967. "If Ethiopia continues to play its role as balance wheel in the changes of the Red Sea Basin and Horn of Africa, and as moderator in the broader spectrum of Africa's problems, it then rests with us to respond affirmatively, as best we can, to meet the legitimate needs of this country," wrote Hubert Humphrey. Haile Selassie specifically asked that the United States "maintain the tempo" of its delivery of military equipment and provide special training in counterinsurgency. "I think we should respond affirmatively to both requests," Humphrey concluded.[57]

The vice president also was favorably impressed with the situation in Somalia, where there was a thaw in relations with Ethiopia. Somalia had been the first country in Africa to peacefully replace a government in power through the vote. Praising President Abdirashid Ali Shermarke and Prime Minister Mohamed Ibrahim Egal, Humphrey asserted that Somalia may well deserve the label of "the most democratic country in Africa." As one of the fathers of the idea of the Peace Corps, Humphrey spoke most favorably of that organization's work throughout the continent and especially in Ethiopia and Somalia.[58]

Haile Selassie also enjoyed playing royal host to a stream of admiring American celebrities. Most noteworthy was the visit of the African American poet Langston Hughes, who visited Addis Ababa in 1966 as part of a State Department–sponsored tour of Africa. Hughes participated in the First World Festival of Negro Arts in Dakar and, after spending a month in Senegal, continued on to Nigeria, Tanzania, and Ethiopia. While in the Ethiopian capital, he wrote a stirring poem, "Emperor Haile Selassie on Liberation Day, May 5, 1966," that he personally presented to the emperor at Jubilee Palace.[59]

***

Haile Selassie maintained his own busy schedule of international travel and state visits during the 1960s. One visit to the New World was especially noteworthy. On April 21, 1966, HIM made a historical call on Jamaica and was greeted upon his arrival at the then Palisadoes Airport in Kingston by an estimated 100,000 Rastafarians from across the country. A haze of holy smoke generated by the faithful engulfed the landing site. The crush of the boisterous crowd prevented Haile Selassie from coming down the mobile steps of the airplane. He returned into the plane, disappearing for several minutes, but eventually order was restored to the island universe, and the Rastas met the man they considered to be God. The visit became part of their mythology and is commemorated by Rastafarians as Grounation Day, the second holiest holiday after November 2 , the emperor's coronation day.

A few weeks after the emperor's return from his three-week tour of the United States, the USSR, Turkey, and the Sudan, he took off again for North America on what he described as a private trip. On April 23, 1967, after a brief layover in Bermuda, Haile Selassie and a party of 24 flew on LBJ's Air Force One, the president's private jet, directly to Los Angeles. Upon his arrival at Los Angeles International Airport, he was given the key to the city by Mayor Sam Yorty. During a three-day visit in California, Haile Selassie sailed around Los Angeles and Long Beach harbors on the luxury corporate yacht *Argo*, inspected offshore drilling operations in Long Beach, and enjoyed the Magic Kingdom of Disneyland, where he shook hands with Mickey Mouse. He was Charter Day speaker at UCLA's Pauley Pavilion, where Chancellor Franklin D. Murphy conferred an honorary doctor of laws degree upon HIM. The motion picture-loving emperor was pleased that one of the other five honorary degree recipients was film director George Cukor, who had won an Academy Award in 1964 for his work on *My Fair Lady*. The emperor's praise of the California system of higher education brought his audience of 4,000 to its feet for four standing ovations. UCLA was an appropriate place to honor Haile Selassie. Almost 1,000 Peace Corps Volunteers had trained there for service in Ethiopia and other countries, and its law school had a cooperative program with Haile Selassie I University.[60] Haile Selassie presented the UCLA library with antique illuminated manuscripts written in Ge'ez on parchment during the visit.[61] The university's professor of Semitic languages, Dr. Wolf Leslau, would have been one of the few people in the country who could have read the manuscripts.

On his last day in the Golden State, the emperor flew by military jet to Palm Springs to visit briefly with President Eisenhower at the airport. He then departed by plane to Vancouver, British Columbia, on April 26, 1967, to start a state visit to Canada, the first such visit arising from Canada's celebration of its centennial year.[62]

The royal party made its way across Canada from west to east in three Canadian Northern Railroad business cars, passing through British Columbia's scenic Canadian Rockies and the prairie provinces of Alberta, Saskatchewan, and Manitoba on the way to Ontario and Quebec. The emperor entered Canada in Vancouver and flew on to

Victoria, British Columbia. His arrival was upstaged by his pet dog Lulu, who turned out to be the media star of the royal Ethiopian entourage during its stay in Canada. Lulu charged off the plane ahead of Haile Selassie when they landed in Victoria and played "ring-around-the-legs" of U.S. Secret Service agents and Canadian police. By law, any dog from Africa arriving in Canada is required to be quarantined for three months. Canadian officials apparently gave Lulu diplomatic immunity, or at least looked the other way while HIM's canine slipped through customs and frolicked across the country.

Lulu, a brown dog identified in the press as a Chihuahua, although the emperor said he wasn't, was HIM's constant companion. He was to receive a bad rap from Polish journalist Ryszard Kapuscinski who, in his fantasy biography *The Emperor,* made the undocumented claim that Lulu was trained to irrigate the shoes of Jubilee Palace visitors that HIM did not like.[63] Lulu did travel to Iran's 2,500-year celebration of the Persian Empire at Persepolis in 1971, however, where he again would be the center of attention because of a diamond-studded collar he sported in the midst of the rich and famous.

Haile Selassie was the first of some 60 heads of state to visit Canada's centennial celebration. His eight-day sojourn was marked by controversy. En route to Ontario, he issued an announcement that all questions for his press conferences had to be in writing and submitted in advance. This edict apparently was made in response to what the emperor thought had been rude treatment on the west coast by Canadian reporters who peppered HIM with embarrassing questions about what was happening in Ethiopia. His pronouncement was anathema to the proud Canadian press. At the same time, 14 Ethiopian students were demonstrating in front of the Ethiopian mission to the UN in New York City, protesting the IEG's treatment of fellow students at Haile Selassie I University. The protestors were carrying signs saying "Down with Haile Selassie and his Clique." Although there had been antiemperor Somali protestors at the UN earlier in the year, this was the first time Americans saw Ethiopians demonstrating against HIM. Times were changing in Ethiopia.

In Ottawa, Prime Minister Lester B. Pearson greeted the emperor and accompanied HIM to a guard of honor ceremony at Canada's 100th birthday flame in front of the gothic parliament buildings. Haile Selassie received assurances from Pearson that Ethiopia would receive more foreign aid from Canada. The emperor announced that he soon would appoint an Ethiopian ambassador to Canada. In Addis Ababa, there was already a Canadian ambassador at work.[64] That evening at a state dinner, Lulu stood quietly by his master in the receiving line.

As the receiving line followed guests down long corridor to the dining room, Lulu let out a series of high-pitched barks preceding the party down the hall.[65] If the press was skimping on coverage of HIM, it was making up for it with canine scoops.

The emperor took a train to Quebec City's Central Station, where he arrived during a light spring shower. HIM was welcomed by Daniel Johnson, premier of Quebec, and informed that he was the guest of Quebec and no longer of Canada. Haile Selassie, on a state visit, should have been greeted by the representative of Britain's Queen Elizabeth, but that gentleman was ill and recuperating in Florida and was unable to perform his duty. The protocol-conscious emperor made his way to City Hall, where Quebec, rather than Canada, gave HIM a most regal reception.

The royal party flew from Quebec to Montreal on an RCAF Cosmopolitan, the Canadian standard VIP aircraft. Upon arrival, Lulu sprinted out of the aircraft and down the red carpet toward the official greeting party. The dog responded to the call of nature at a huge white concrete flower pot and proudly sprinted back to the airplane and his imperial owner.[66] The royals proceeded to the Queen Elizabeth Hotel, where, according to Paulos Milkias, waiters at the hotel competed to clean up any carpets that Lulu spoiled, "as they got $200 tips for their services."[67]

During his two-day visit in Montreal, the emperor was among the first dignitaries to attend Expo 67, the 1967 International and Universal Exposition, ultimately considered to be the most successful World's Fair of the 20th century.[68] HIM presided over his country's national day and passed by a heraldic lion in front of the red and gold Ethiopian pavilion, where he saw replicas of the imperial throne and St. George's church in Lalibela, as well as works of artists and artisans. Accompanied by an honor guard of RCMP, he was the recipient of the first state dinner at the Pavillon d'Honneur on Île Sainte-Hélène. Lulu wandered around the restaurant, and a disgruntled reporter, who could not get close to the royals, groused, "The dog, in fact, had a good deal more freedom granted members of the press."[69] HIM also attended the first performance in the new Théâtre Port-Royal, featuring the Haile Selassie I Ethiopian Theatre Folkloric Ensemble, composed of 10 musicians and 24 dancers from Addis Ababa.[70]

In Quebec City, the African monarch ended his state visit with a 10-minute meeting with Pearson and a brief public address praising cultural diversity as enriching nations. At City Hall, the little king thanked Canadians for "a warm welcome."[71] When Haile Selassie stepped out of the elevator at Chaâteau Frontenac for the trip to the

airport, a crowd of about 200 at the main entrance broke into ap-
plauses. Lulu, seizing the moment, sprinted out down the red carpet,
an imperial charge beating HIM to his black limousine. The emperor
left Canada from Montreal on an Ethiopian Airlines Boeing 721 jet-
liner for Geneva, concluding another public relations triumph. The
emperor's burnish, however, was not what it once had been in North
America.[72] Only a few days later in May, Haile Selassie, spending
little time in his homeland, continued his international travels by
going to Cambodia for a four-day state visit. Was the king of kings
aware of what was happening in his ancient kingdom?

* * *

Haile Selassie's third state visit to the United States, the winter visit,
was highlighted by discontent. President Johnson was focused on deepening crises in Vietnam, and although he still was willing to pay the
rent for Kagnew, he also had begun investigating alternatives to the listening post on the roof of Africa. The war in Southeast Asia, with all its
costs, had torn apart traditional American cohesiveness, and a dispirit-
ing malaise hung over the land. All the hard knocks were taking their
toll on the president. The emperor remained depressed about Somalia
getting more and better military assistance from the soviets than he,
the long-time friend and supporter of the United States, was receiving
from his Eritrean real estate lessee. Payment was never enough, nor
was it delivered fast enough. The monarch's travels in North America
were receiving far less notice in the media, and the aging king was
showing a crotchety side in some of his dealings with the press. Open
demonstrations against his government were being held at home and,
what was even more disgruntling, in the foreign countries where he
traveled. The Lion in winter was enmeshed in malcontent.

In April 1968, the U.S. government postulated optimistically about
"the Outlook for Internal Security in Ethiopia." The emperor's foreign
neighbors had backed down from aggressive behaviors. Ethiopia's military countermeasures had been successful. Somalia under Egal sought
détente with the IEG and was reducing aid and encouragement to ethnic Somalis in the Ogaden. Even Eritrea was quieter than it had been
a year before. Nevertheless, Haile Selassie was much more concerned
with building his country's military strength to meet possible external aggression than with nation building through economic and social
reform. When the United States did not meet urgent requests for increased military aid, Ethiopia bought Canberra bombers from the UK

and other war materials from France and Italy. The emperor's army of nearly 40,000 and well-equipped air force gave Ethiopia by far the strongest military capability in the region. Both had been trained by U.S. MAAG units for more than a decade. HIM continued to harbor a nightmare scenario of his isolated Christian empire being under siege from hostile Muslim neighbors backed by the soviets. The IEG spent about a quarter of the national budget on military expenditures.

The nation's fundamental problem was the remarkably low level of government revenues from domestic sources. The people were poor and lacked education; the few gentry and the Ethiopian Church were unwilling to pay taxes on their substantial land holdings, and the IEG had little interest in national development. Dissatisfaction with the emperor's arbitrary rule and the slow progress of modernization was muted but growing. The feudal regime still basically ruled by court intrigue that undermined the efficiency of the civilian and military ministries and cooperation among their leaders. The emperor was receiving his Kagnew rent, but despite spiffy U.S. military aid, HIM was chronically dissatisfied with the level of deliveries. To complicate matters, the United States was considering reducing yearly deliveries as part of a general cutback in foreign aid. Because of his perceived internal and external threats, Haile Selassie would almost certainly continue to seek increased deliveries.[73]

What the U.S. Embassy and the IEG were missing was that the Ethiopian student movement, bolstered by Western education, had become very antiemperor and anti-United States, and the influence of the young radicals was being widely dispersed. Young intellectuals were beguiled by the soviets' glib and appealing quick fix for Ethiopia's chronic problems of poverty, ignorance, and disease through Marxist-Leninism. The Americans' slow but steady development strategy of demonstrating the virtues of freedom of choice and self-determination and explaining the accomplishments of democracy and capitalism lacked immediacy. Besides, the United States was propping up the repressive IEG and wallowing in the slough of despondency with the hapless old guard. In metropolitan areas the soviet-financed Crocodile Societies were winning the hearts and minds of the students who lacked the maturity to appreciate the meaning of Jefferson, Madison, Mill, and Lincoln. Many Ethiopians in the universities distrusted U.S. motives in Vietnam, foreign aid, student exchanges, and military assistance. They also feared that continuing racial strife in America revealed a state of mind which precluded meaningful understanding of the African commitment to independence and self-sufficiency.[74] U.S. government informants, secret police, and CIA agents did not realize the significance of the battles in and around the classrooms then underway.

But in the greater scheme of foreign policy, the United States paid little attention to Africa and its affairs during the last years of the Johnson administration. Leading African leftist leaders, such as Ghana's Kwame Nkrumah, Algeria's Ben Bella, and Mali's Modibo Keita, had fallen, and anticolonialist guerrilla movements in Angola, Mozambique, and Rhodesia seemed on the wane. In 1968, LBJ, having boldly attempted to build a Great Society at home, was hoist with his Southeast Asia petard abroad. There simply wasn't enough in the U.S. larder to pay for a domestic war on poverty and a war on communism overseas. Despite the deployment of more than 500,000 U.S. troops in Vietnam, U.S. forces achieved only a costly stalemate. Under attack at home by opponents of the war, Johnson saw his plans for reelection in the 1968 presidential election collapse in the face of turmoil within his Democratic Party. On March 31, the president announced that he would not run. There would be change in the chief executive's office.

Change was afoot too in the embassies in Washington and Addis Ababa. Menassie Haile, the emperor's trusted translator during his most recent U.S. state visits, was appointed Ambassador to the United States. In Addis Ababa, Ed Korry had been appointed Ambassador to Chile by LBJ, and he departed leaving behind a nonpareil legacy of accomplishment. "More than any other American chief of mission in Addis Ababa either before or since, he had the greatest impact on U.S. policy towards Ethiopia," wrote an ambassadorial successor David Shinn.[75] "He was not only a highly capable ambassador but served there during the highwater mark in relations and at a time when there was frequent tension in the relationship." Korry was replaced by a Career Foreign Service Officer William O. Hall, who had been assistant administrator of administration for USAID and who relaxed by jogging in the rarified heights of Addis Ababa. Would Hall run into difficulties as the Horn entered into a season of volatility? Would his more traditional leadership make a difference in U.S. programs and actions in Ethiopia?

A larger question was whether change would come to feudal Ethiopia at a fast enough pace to ease the pressure mounting for a drastic reordering of the entire system. Robert Kaplan observed that "pushing [Haile Selassie] for reform would have been like tinkering with the divine order."[76] The enigmatic emperor seemed confident that governing would continue as it had for almost 40 years under his enlightened rule. He would adhere to the lesson of the old Ethiopian folk saying: "Slowly, very slowly, the egg walks upon its own two feet." Would a glorious summer follow the winter of discontent for HIM?

CHAPTER 13

Götterdämmerung: The Nixon State Visits, 1969, 1970, and 1973

The hope and expectation of thy time Is ruined, and the soul of every man Prophetically do forethink thy fall...For thou hast lost thy princely privilege With vile participation. Not an eye But is a-weary of thy common sight.

—Henry IV, Part 1

The group of young people was neatly dressed for a muggy July afternoon in Washington. Thirty-five youthful Ethiopians had assembled around their country's chancery on Kalorama Road, NW, two miles from the White House, to demonstrate against the expected arrival of the Emperor of Ethiopia Haile Selassie, who was coming on a state visit at the invitation of President Richard Nixon. As they marched peacefully in front of the two-story brick building, they shouted, "Down with Haile Selassie!" "Down with the Tyrant!" Two police guards had been assigned to keep an eye on the chancery in light of increasing violence against embassies and their staffs in the nation's capital. Already in the first six months of 1969 there had been 261 such incidents, up from only 34 in 1965, according to the State Department. Embassy-bashing had become a blue-chip protest during the years of the Johnson and Nixon administrations. Earlier in the year, a small group of Ethiopian students had occupied the IEG's embassy in Washington for a short time in protest of the emperor's closing down some Ethiopian high schools and curtailing operations at Haile Selassie I University, but in that era of lock-ins on U.S. college campuses, the episode received little notice.[1]

One of the guards glanced at his watch. The demonstrators had been at it for about five minutes. Maybe they would grow tired of their unobserved marching and disperse. Suddenly, one of the taller men in the group yelled "Jan Hoy!" a name of the emperor in Amharic, and the students ran by the startled guards to the chancery door. It was locked, but the tall leader of the group soon kicked it in. The youngsters knew the layout well and scrambled to their wreaking places. Some of the men carried rocks under their shirts and used them to smash windows on both floors. Kitchen crockery went flying, photographs of the emperor were yanked off the walls, and furniture was overturned. The guards charged in and flayed away at the demonstrators. Some were injured. Some had cut themselves on broken glass from the smashed windows. Fourteen were arrested inside the building.[2] The others made their way out and disappeared. Bloodstains were still on the sidewalks when reporters showed up half an hour later. The arrested, who claimed to be students, were disappointed to learn that the emperor's arrival had been delayed by bad weather and that Ethiopian Ambassador Minasse Haile was not in the building when they had made their grand entrance.[3] But they had made their point. There was opposition to the rule of the 76-year-old emperor and his policies, even in the United States—and the story of the Washington protest would be widely disseminated by the media. The United States vowed to pay for the heavy damage at the ransacked chancery, as was customary under international law.[4]

At the same time, 3:30 in the afternoon, 50 Ethiopians demonstrated peacefully on Pennsylvania Avenue across the street from the White House. Under a rule invoked by metropolitan and U.S. park police, they could not march within 500 feet of Blair House, where the emperor again was staying. They were permitted, however, to march in a circle on the north side of Pennsylvania Avenue, where they carried signs and handed out pamphlets. The protestors were members of the Ethiopian Student Association from several American universities, who claimed to represent 300 Ethiopians studying in the United States. They accused Haile Selassie of repression, extravagance, and exploitation. Their pamphlets reflected student unrest in Ethiopia and accused the regime "of imprisoning students in labor camps, torturing political prisoners, massacring peasants, breaking strikes, and arbitrarily raising taxes."[5] The demonstrators claimed that the United States was "fulfilling its bargain to suppress all opposition to Haile Selassie's reactionary regime in return for maintaining its most important military base in Africa on Ethiopian soil." They shouted "Down with the

Tyrant!" and "Haile Selassie must go!" among other epithets. Their signs in Amharic and English proclaimed, "Feudalism no; People's democracy, yes!" and "The Lion to the Zoo!" After the emperor arrived at Blair House at 6:10, they left peacefully but vowed to return.

The presence of Ethiopian protesters was not the only change that had occurred since Haile Selassie's visit in 1967. American small-town newspapers had begun to write editorials questioning the emperor's being "in a good light or bad light." Some opined that he had "outlived his friends and his enemies."[6] Syndicated columnist Andrew Tully, in his feature "Capital Fare," which appeared in 150 papers throughout the country, wrote derogatorily: "In Selassie's country, there is approximately the same amount of human liberty as there is in the calaboose in Hattiesburg. Mississippi."[7] National newspapers reporting on Haile Selassie's state visits during the Nixon administration decreased their coverage of the events. They simply were not as newsworthy as they had been in the past. The *Christian Science Monitor* set the new tone by burying a brief three sentence article on page 8 in "Inside the News—Briefly" with a subheadline "Haile Selassie Visits Washington Again."[8] Familiarity was breeding diminished column inches of coverage.

* * *

The careers of Haile Selassie and Richard Nixon had continued on uneven trajectories following their inauspicious initial meeting in 1954, when President Eisenhower had not welcomed the emperor at the airport upon his arrival in Washington for his first state visit to the United States. The emperor had returned to Ethiopia after his public relations triumphs in North America and proceeded to garner vast sums of military and economic aid for his country. Having tasted the elixir of international celebrity, HIM began a recurrent ritual of international travel justified as exercises in personal diplomacy. He encountered rough spots in surviving an attempted coup, provincial rebellions, and armed conflict with Somalia. More positively, he garnered accolades for his leadership in the founding of the OAU, in championing African independence, and mediating African disputes. He endeavored to maintain a moderate voice in African affairs but found it increasingly tricky to navigate around the shoals of neutralism and U.S. clientelism. Perceptions of his being in the American camp resulted in Arab hostility and, as the Cold War escalated, gave the soviets a bridgehead in Somalia.

Nixon, during his tenure as vice president, became the most significant holder of that position in American history up until that time. He had little formal power, but he caught the attention of the media and the Republican Party. Like the emperor, he frequently traveled abroad on missions of diplomacy and goodwill, although he suffered much more indignity at the hands of angry crowds abroad, especially in Venezuela.[9]

When Eisenhower sent him to Moscow for the opening of the American National Exhibition, Nixon staged his famous "Kitchen Debate" with Soviet Premier Nikita Khrushchev and emerged as a respected champion of capitalism and democracy. The vice president conducted National Security Council meetings in the president's absence and gained broad experience in international affairs. In 1957 he went on an extended tour of Africa, visiting eight nations accompanied by a press corps of 30, more than half of whom were African Americans. In Ethiopia, he renewed his acquaintance with Haile Selassie, who received him in the throne room and held a state dinner in his honor at Guenete Leul Palace. The vice president asked HIM for more acreage at Kagnew and for the emperor's support of the Eisenhower doctrine of direct American intervention in the Middle East to safeguard Western interests. Nixon's visit formerly activated the U.S. MAAG mission.[10]

The vice president, after observing the especially large U.S. presence in Ethiopia, returned from Africa convinced that there were too many American overseas.[11] In his report on the trip, Nixon predicted that Africa "could well prove to be the decisive" factor in the determination of the struggle between the West and communism. The vice president's rhetoric had little effect, however, because Eisenhower did not have much interest in Africa.[12]

For Nixon, as well as for Haile Selassie, 1960 was a year of disaster. He lost a close presidential election to John Kennedy and returned to his home state, California, where he practiced law and wrote a bestselling book, *Six Crises*, that kept his name in the national limelight. In 1962, Nixon ran for the governorship of California but lost by a substantial margin to the Democratic incumbent Pat Brown. The loss was thought to be the end of Nixon's political career. He moved to New York City and joined a leading law firm that he used as a base to maintain ties with mainstream republicans and to advise them on politics and international affairs. In the 1966 midterm elections, he campaigned for republican candidates and traveled to South America, parts of the Middle East, and Africa in 1967. He visited the pope, part of every presidential aspirant's ethnic stations of the cross.[13] In Addis Ababa, as part of a private fact-finding tour, Nixon had a four-hour audience with the emperor and also called on Telli Diallo of Guinea, Secretary

General of the OAU.[14] The African trip left Nixon discouraged about the continent's future. He wrote Eisenhower that it would be "at least two generations before...anything [Americans] would recognize as freedom" would take hold in Africa.[15]

At the end of 1967, Nixon was ambivalent about running for president the following year. After some soul searching and encouragement from Republican Party leaders, he formally announced his candidacy for president of the United States on February 1, 1968. From what politicos called "the wilderness years," the Nixon phoenix emerged ready for political battle. Two months after his candidacy announcement, President Johnson withdrew from the race. In late April, Vice President Humphrey announced his candidacy and eventually was nominated by the Democratic Party at its troubled Chicago convention. In a twist of fate, Nixon again was in an extremely close presidential election, but this time he won—with less than one percent of the popular vote. As president, he reveled in foreign policy. As he told his aides, "I didn't come here to build outhouses in Peoria."[16]

NIXON VISIT I, 1969

Continuing his personal diplomacy with U.S. presidents that had produced increased military and economic aid for Ethiopia from 1954 to 1968, Emperor Haile Selassie sought and received an invitation for a state visit, his fourth, to the United States from the newly elected Richard Nixon in July 1969. The emperor was the first African leader invited to visit the White House by Nixon after his election in 1968, and the President wanted to show HIM that the new administration would continue to hold Ethiopia as its closest friend in Africa. By that time, the monarch was well acquainted with the protocol of White House arrival ceremonies and even with weather-inspired changes in plans.

His endless paranoid importunities were familiar. He contrived an epochal whine. The emperor was the hero victim leading an Ethiopia surrounded by hostile Muslim and communist foes intent on intruding on the sovereignty of the land of the Elect of God. Aggressive minatory neighbors in Somalia and the Sudan, armed with superior weapons provided by the soviets, threatened war and aided rebels in Eritrea and the Ogaden. The only salvation would come from increased U.S. military aid with state-of-the-art armaments and equipment. And if the United States did not deliver the necessary hardware with celerity, Ethiopia would be forced to turn to the Eastern Bloc and become even more neutralist and unaligned. Worse yet, the landlord might evict the tenant in Kagnew Station. The emperor, with his kingly granite profile, was inscribing the palimpsest of his personal diplomacy—a parchment that has been used two or three times, the earlier writing having been erased. How many more times would he write the same mendicant homily? And how many more times would his U.S. auditors be willing to patiently listen?

Thunderstorms with winds up to 35-miles-per-hour were forecast for July 7, 1969 at the 4:30 P.M. landing time of the emperor's plane at Andrews Air Force Base. Thirty minutes later, Haile Selassie and his 11-member official party were at the White House, where Mr. and Mrs. Nixon greeted them. The herald trumpets sounded Sir Arthur Bliss's "Fanfare" followed by "Hail to the Chief." The Marine Band played the two nations' national anthems while a 21-gun salute was fired simultaneously with the music. The president and the emperor reviewed the troops at a quick march, and then moved into the mansion's North Portico.[17] The emperor's official party again included his grandson, then commodore Iskinder Desta, and Ketema Yifru, minister of foreign affairs. Ambassador Minassie Haile repeated in his role as HIM's principle translator.

In the East Room with an audience of 150, the president welcomed Haile Selassie, saying, "No visit to this house has greater historical significance." Indeed, the gray-bearded emperor epitomized a sense of history. When he came to power in 1916, there was still a czar ruling Russia and the United States was opposed to any war on foreign soil. During the half century he had held power, he had seen 10 U.S. presidents pass in and out of power, scores of European dictators rise and fall, and most colonial rule give way to independent nationhood. Criticized by some of his subjects as "an autocrat whose reign is as anachronistic as the two chained lions that stalk outside his office in his capital, Addis Ababa, as symbols of his power," his admirers credited HIM with trying to bring his country "from the Middle Ages to the 20th Century in 30 years."[18] Nixon apologized to HIM for having to move the ceremonies inside and saw the royals off to their residence at Blair House.

Early the next afternoon, the stately ruler and the president spent an hour and 45 minutes in "a general exchange of views" at the White House. They agreed that a stable, secure, and prosperous Ethiopia was an objective shared by both countries. The leaders focused on continuing crises in Nigeria and the Middle East and expressed mutual concerns about soviet influence in Somalia, Sudan, and parts of the Arabian Peninsula. Enjoying détente with Egal of Somalia, the emperor felt the soviets were the greatest danger to his country. Working through the UAR as a client state, their vessels had penetrated the Red Sea and were attempting to make it into a soviet-UAR lake. The president sought HIM's advice on Biafra and the Middle East, and on how to work with Nasser of the UAR and Israel's Abba Eban. The emperor noted that many young Ethiopians were opposed to the policy of friendship with America and were worried that Kagnew endangered the nation's security. Therefore, Haile Selassie concluded, his country needed U.S. military assistance to demonstrate to the people that Ethiopia's pro-U.S. policy did meet the nation's security needs. He added that U.S. military assistance, once judged to be adequate, no longer met the country's needs because of the deteriorating security situation. The emperor, operating from what NSC director Henry Kissinger, called a siege mentality, was displaying his appetite for U.S. arms that the administration could neither satisfy under congressionally mandated military arms limitations or justify in terms of U.S. estimates of his position. He hoped to interest Nixon in making Ethiopia a bulwark against a Communist-Muslim thrust into the Horn.[19] More realistically, Haile Selassie sought economic aid for his country's third five-year plan. The president noted that Ethiopia received 60 percent of U.S. military funds available for Africa, a level that would be difficult to sustain. The United States, however, recognized Ethiopia's problems and what it stood for and would continue to assist its development as a strong and independent nation.[20]

In the evening, Haile Selassie was honored at a White House state dinner given by the president, who basked in his role as host. Protestors continued their vigil in Lafayette Park across the street as the 102 guests arrived. At a predinner exchange of gifts, the emperor gave Nixon a magnificent gold and silver bowl and Mrs. Nixon and the daughters beautiful gold jewelry. Haile Selassie received from the president a vermeil and leather engagement book engraved with the president's seal and the emperor's crest with an inscription for presentation. Nixon was more formal at state dinners than had been Johnson. Richard Nixon came down the stairs alone, in contrast to LBJ, who was followed by his entourage. The receiving line was in the Blue Room. Nixon disliked this part of state dinners, because he hated small talk.

Protocol for the order of being served food was changed in the Nixon White House, with the president being served first. If Pat Nixon were present, the president wanted her served first, even before the ranking guest. Nixon also banned the soup course from state dinners after he spilled a savory liquid down his vest while entertaining Prime Minister

Pierre Trudeau of Canada. Nixon rationalized his antiepicurean edict to aide Robert Haldeman by saying "Men don't really like soup."[21]

At a little after 10 o'clock, the president toasted the emperor with eloquent words reflecting Nixon's long continual friendship with Haile Selassie:

> He has wisdom. He has had a long life, and, I know from personal experience, an understanding heart...I had the great privilege, which some in this room have enjoyed, of visiting his country in 1957. My wife and I were received as royal guests at that time and treated royally. I returned again to his country in 1967, holding no office, having no portfolio whatever. I was received again as a royal guest and treated royally. This is a man with an understanding heart. [Laughter][22]

Haile Selassie's toast to Nixon stressed Ethiopia's determination to safeguard its "territorial integrity" and to continue "without despair" efforts to find a peaceful solution to the war in Nigeria. He noted that a strong defense of his country could be realized only through the accelerated development of his nation.

The evening's entertainment was provided by pianist Eugene List playing the music of Louis Moreau Gottschalk and Alexander Reinagle, American composers who played for presidents Lincoln and Washington, respectively.[23] While performing an encore, "Creole Eyes," List inserted eight bars of the Whittier College "Alma Mater," to the delight of alumnus Nixon. Two years earlier, List had played a recital in Addis Ababa for the benefit of Saint Paul's Hospital under the sponsorship of Emperor Haile Selassie I Foundation. In April the piano playing president had honored another American pianist, Duke Ellington, with a reception at the White House. The event marked the first time that African Americans were predominant on a White House guest list. Most of America's greatest popular musicians attended, and the party went on until after 2:00 A.M.[24] In 1973, Ellington was to perform in Addis Ababa and receive a medal of honor from the emperor.

At the conclusion of the List program there was dancing and champagne in the Grand Hall for the guests. Gentlemen were invited to enjoy coffee, liqueurs, and cigars. At the evening's end, the emperor's motorcade departed from the North Portico rather than the Diplomatic Entrance to avoid the Ethiopian protestors.

The next morning, the emperor held talks with Robert McNamara, president of the World Bank, at Blair House, and later, Melvin Laird, secretary of defense. At 11:45, Haile Selassie returned to the White House to meet again with the president. They discussed the "agony of Nigeria and Biafra."[25] The emperor wanted counterinsurgency weapons, helicopters, and transport aircraft. Of even greater importance, he said, was his country's need for economic assistance. Nixon confided that a primary tenet of his philosophy regarding foreign affairs was that "one doesn't take one's friends for granted." There was no better friend in Africa than Ethiopia, and this should be taken into account in setting up African priorities. The president asked where his leadership "could usefully be used."[26] In reply, the emperor said he wanted the United States to associate itself with Africa in the realizations of the goals set forth in the charter of the OAU. "Strengthening the relationships between the United State and nations of Africa was a matter of utmost import if Africa was to be protected from the ambitions of communist states to subvert Africa's freedom and independence."

In a brief speech on the White House lawn, Nixon described his talks with HIM as "very worthwhile discussions" on bilateral questions and worldwide problems. "We had an opportunity to discuss on the highest level" all outstanding problems of the world but especially the questions affecting Africa and the Middle East. Haile Selassie extended an invitation to the president to visit Ethiopia again and assured him he would be an honored guest. "The discussions have been most rewarding to me," said the emperor. "May God bless you, your family, and the American people."[27]

In the afternoon, the monarch met with executives of USAID and the Peace Corps, and at 6:30 he gave a reception for the African diplomatic corps in the Regency Ballroom of the Shoreham Hotel. On Thursday morning, the emperor attended a prayer breakfast hosted by U.S. congressmen at the Capitol, repeating an early ritual that he had enjoyed during his 1967 visit. From the Washington Monument, he traveled by U.S. Marine helicopter to the Agricultural Experiment Station at Beltsville, Maryland, where he inspected the U.S. Department of Agriculture's programs in cattle nutrition, sheep feeding, and poultry and egg production. The royal party then helicoptered to Andrews Air Force base, where they departed for Atlanta on a presidential jet.

The emperor was met at Dobbins Air Force Base in Marietta, Georgia, by Atlanta Mayor Ivan Allen and Morehouse College President Dr. Hugh Gloster. They went to the grave of the late Dr. Martin Luther King Jr., in South View Cemetery, where Haile Selassie laid a wreath of red and yellow carnations on the tomb. The emperor paid tribute to the slain civil rights leader as "an example from which all men stand to gain and profit."[28] He met King's father, Reverend Martin Luther King Sr., and his wife, at the cemetery. The emperor told the elder King, "This is one of the greatest honors of my life." King told the emperor it was a great honor to have HIM in Atlanta. "I found it quite necessary to lay a wreath on Dr. King's grave so that we may remember his deeds and contributions to history, and his triumphs—and to honor his father and his wife," the emperor replied.

At a special convocation at King's alma mater, Morehouse College, Haile Selassie was given a standing ovation by the crowd that filled the college gym. The monarch gave a 10-minute speech praising King and the college. "I'm proud that I have the privilege of laying a wreath on the tomb of Martin Luther King Jr., a man who believed in justice and equality for all men," Haile Selassie said.[29] "He was not solely a citizen of these great United States. We prefer to regard him as a citizen of the world." The honorary doctor of laws degree then was conferred upon HIM by President Gloster. Having concluded its business in Atlanta in three hours, the royal party left for Cape Kennedy, for a tour of the space center there.

At the Kennedy Space Center, the emperor, who had been unable to visit Florida because of inclement weather during his 1963 state visit, fulfilled his dream of touring the center and meeting his heroes, the astronauts.[30] He observed preparations for the launch of Apollo 11 that would result in the first manned spacecraft landing on the moon. Using a telephone hookup from the launch control center, HIM spoke to the Apollo 11 crew, Neil Armstrong, Edwin Aldrin, and Michael Collins, who were aboard the lunar module landing craft sitting atop the Saturn Rocket. The monarch extended best wishes to the astronauts as they worked on minor problems in preparation for blasting into space on July 16 (coincidentally, the emperor's birthday). The emperor, who was a keen fan of the space program, encountered astronaut Gordon Cooper, whom he had met at the White House in 1967. A broad smile formed on his resolute mouth, and the sovereign used both hands in shaking the hand of Cooper, who had made two orbital trips into space. President Nixon later was to send the emperor a rock from the moon.

In the afternoon, the royals departed from Patrick Air Force Base near Cocoa Beach, Florida, for a return flight to Andrews to return the president's plane before leaving the United States on a special Ethiopian Airlines flight. En route home, Haile Selassie stopped in Lausanne, Switzerland, to visit a granddaughter, who was convalescing there.

* * *

The Ethiopia that Haile Selassie returned to for his 77th birthday in 1969 was a troubled land. The Eritrean Liberation Front (ELF), after a lull in action caused by dwindling fortunes of its patron Arab nations, was active again. Closer to home, or rather palace, the genie of student unrest had been loosed, and protests by university and occasionally high school demonstrators were now a potential threat to the ruling elite's tranquility. Even the popular and apolitical Peace Corps was targeted for being a part of U.S. support for the reactionary regime. Vehemently anti-American political pamphlets were circulated, and Molotov cocktails were thrown at the Ethiopian headquarters of the Peace Corps. Some Peace Corp Volunteer teachers were beaten, and in the winter of 1969–1970, twenty Peace Corp Volunteers had to abandon their posts, threatened by attack from their own students. On September 9, the American Consul General Murray Jackson was kidnapped by the ELF while driving near his home in Asmara and held for two hours before being released unharmed. These actions started rumor mills grinding away and sparked fears that dissidents might even attack Kagnew. The number of personnel at the listening post was being reduced, and the IEG was concerned that this might be interpreted as abandonment by the United States.

Next door, a military coup d'état, the bane of modern African history, brought an end to the Republic of Somalia in October. Major General Siad Barre took control of the nation, terminated the democratic efforts of Egal, who had enjoyed détente with Ethiopia, and pursued a policy of "scientific socialism," an oxymoronic combination of Somali nationalism, Islam, and Marxist/Leninism. The newly renamed Somali Democratic Republic adopted an anti–United States foreign policy and accused Washington of imperialism. Once again, tensions on the Ethiopian-Somalia border were exacerbated by soviet-supplied arms in Somalia.[31] The emperor thought the obvious solution to these mounting problems was more arms from the United States, so he requested another meeting with Nixon on October 25, 1970.

Four months after the emperor's 1969 state visit, Nixon's secretary of state William Rogers gave HIM good news, from the American perspective, about his requests for additional military aid. Ethiopia was to receive more in FY 1970 than the average of the prior years, somewhat less than FY 1969 and less than anticipated because of severe congressional cuts in the USAID appropriation. U.S. military aid to Ethiopia averaged $12 million to $13 million per year, which was over half of American military assistance for all of Africa. Cutting through the stilted bureaucratese of the State Department, this meant the IEG was getting four UH-1 Iroquois helicopters, C-119K Flying Boxcar transport planes, and arms for the Territorial Army. In addition, there would be increased ammunition and aircraft ordinance and petroleum products for counterinsurgency operations in Eritrea.

NIXON II, 1970

In October 1970, the emperor paid his second state visit to Nixon, attending a White House dinner marking the 25th anniversary of the United Nations. Even in the august company of a host of other heads of state, Haile Selassie continued seeking more U.S. military aid. The emperor saw the growth of soviet and Cuban military activities in Somalia combined with a growing insurgency in Eritrea as posing real threats to his country's security. Nixon reassured Haile Selassie that he would study the military situation, giving full weight to the emperor's proposals. By this time, however, the facilities at Kagnew were being made obsolete by satellite technology, and the Nixon administration was reviewing the value of the listening post in a more technically sophisticated military establishment. At 78 years of age, Haile Selassie was beginning to lose control over the country, and he was no longer the international center of attention he once had been.

Early in the new year, the president gave his "First Annual Report to the Congress on Foreign Policy for 1970." His presentation was a significant statement about future U.S. policies on the world scene. He outlined a foreign policy based on three principles: partnership with allies who had the capacity to deal with local disputes which once might have required U.S. intervention; the preservation of a defensive capability sufficient to deter would-be aggressors; and a readiness to negotiate with friend or foe to resolve conflicts or reduce arms. The president said a lasting peace would require "a more responsible participation by our foreign friends in their own defense and progress."[32] In cases of lesser aggression, the United States expected a threatened nation to provide the military power for its defense. The United States would not hesitate to furnish assistance "where it makes a real difference and is considered in our interests." The goal of the new policy was to encourage the self-reliance of all nations. The president "established procedures for the intensive scrutiny of defense issues in the light of overall national priorities." Speaking specifically about Africa, Nixon "pledged nonintervention except to relieve human suffering and promised limited help both for development and for efforts to resist subversion." "It's my best view of where we've been and where we're going," Nixon said. The president had given the emperor and the IEG much to ponder in the new decade.

At the advent of the 1970s the relationship between the United States and Ethiopia was in decline. Even with all the warning signs around him, the captious emperor failed to see the need for significant reform and expected greater American assistance as the quid pro quo for the continued use of Kagnew. Cold war pressures and the emboldening of young intellectuals imbued with antiregime and anti-American ideas exacerbated tensions between the two countries. The predominance of the old aristocracy and the emperor's handpicked intellectual elite was passing to other ranks of the community. University students were talking openly of the need for change and were clamoring for the end of the U.S. military presence at Kagnew.

In Febrary1970, Secretary of State William P. Rogers embarked on the first ever diplomatic tour of the African continent by a secretary of state. He visited 10 African countries, including Ethiopia, on what he thought would be a 15-day goodwill tour. His purpose was to "show a new interest in Africa on the part of the United States."[33] The African leaders he met, however, were less interested in philosophical goals of the Nixon administration than in getting answers to hard questions about U.S. financial assistance to their countries. In Addis Ababa, the emperor and Foreign Minister Ketema pressed Rogers hard for more military aid, and Haile Selassie's two Chihuahuas even barked at him from the foot of the throne.[34] Rogers, reflecting the administration's thinking, said more arms would not solve Ethiopia's problems. What was needed was faster paced change and reform.

The aging emperor, appearing frail and thought-burdened, was slowing down and his grip on the country was far less firm than it had been only a few years before. He had survived by ignoring problems or suppressing them and as a result Ethiopia was becoming a cauldron prepared to boil. His declining years became a protracted, distended humiliation of celebrity-seeking and gross neglect of domestic matters. Increasingly, those who worked closely with HIM noticed *coup de vieux,* or senior moments, interfering with his daily activities. He had become a relic of a previous age, and his way of life had fallen into the sere, the yellow leaf.

Yet Haile Selassie still reveled in his role as senior statesman and leader of African unity. At the Third Nonaligned Conference in Lusaka, Zambia, the emperor, a founder of the movement and still a major voice, presented a five-point proposal for specific measures against Portugal, South Africa, and Rhodesia if they did not conform to UN resolutions on decolonization and racial discrimination. Superpowers are "no longer overwhelming," proclaimed the Ethiopian leader, and the third world had changed from a position of "fear of involvement" to one of taking an "independent approach" on important issues.[35] Observers noticed that Africans were more forceful and dominant in this conference than in previous ones.

In October, after attending Nasser's tumultuous funeral in Cairo, the emperor returned to the United States for his fifth state visit to meet with President Nixon and to take part in the 25th anniversary session of the UN General Assembly. In New York, he sounded familiar themes at a celebration sponsored by the United Nations Association and Rotary International at the ballroom of the Commodore Hotel. The bearded monarch told an audience of 800 that the UN must be strengthened if it is to avoid the fate of League of Nations. He said the League had succumbed because it became impossible to arrest evil forces by appeasement. In his 30-minute address, the emperor urged the UN to strive harder to surmount world economic problems and to find ways that "oppressed peoples" could "exercise their legitimate rights."[36] Later, he renewed his acquaintance with Mayor John Lindsay in Gracie Mansion.

On the following day, Haile Selassie was one of a legion of heads of state who spoke at the historic 25th anniversary session of the UN General Assembly. The emperor, President Nixon, Prime Minister Indira Gandhi, and British Prime Minister Edward Heath took the rostrum in the great blue and gold assembly hall within hours of each other. Haile Selassie gave such a lengthy address that President Nixon's speech before that group was 20 minutes late. The emperor, referring to his bitter experience at the League, said the UN was a vital organization, adequate to its task if the members so willed it. Applause was noticeably shorter and less enthusiastic for Nixon than for the royal speaker preceding him. Nixon urged the soviets to join with the United States in keeping the competition between the two countries peaceful despite "very profound and fundamental differences."[37]

Haile Selassie, along with 17 presidents and 28 prime ministers, attended the next day's closing session that condemned colonialism and racism in southern Africa and adopted a 10-year program for the development of poorer nations. He enthusiastically joined in the General Assembly's unanimous declaration rededicating UN members to the charter and calling for peace, freedom and an end to the arms race.[38] The emperor heard the closing statement by Secretary General U Thant, who greenly prophesized,

As we watch the sun go down evening after evening through the smog across the poisoned waters of our native earth, we must ask

ourselves seriously whether we really wish some future universal historian on another planet to say, "With all their genius and
their skill, they ran out of foresight and air and food and water
and ideas"; or "They went on playing politics until their world
collapsed around them"; or "When they looked up, it was already
too late." If the United Nations does nothing else, it can at least
serve a vital purpose in sounding the alarm.[39]

That evening, the Nixons gave a White House dinner, the UN's silver anniversary party, for 100 friends including 31 chiefs of state and
heads of government. Such a distinguished guest list was unprecedented and marked the first time so many world leaders had dined
together in the Executive Mansion. Impressive regal figures were received by the Nixons in the Blue Room before the guests sat down at
an E-shaped table in the state dining room. Almost the entire Cabinet was present along with Vice President Spiro Agnew; Mamie Eisenhower; Julie Nixon Eisenhower; and her sister, Patricia Nixon.

The evening had been planned with the most meticulous detail from
security to protocol. The timing, however, was thrown off by security precautions around the White House. Arriving guests faced delays at barricades, where Secret Service agents and metropolitan police
checked credentials. The foreign leaders had been given exact times
for arrival, spaced one minute apart, coming in the reverse order of
their rank and precedence. By that ranking, Haile Selassie, the longest reigning ruler present, would be the last to arrive. But there were
gaps and waits in what had been planned as a steady parade of leaders moving through the Blue Room to shake hands with President and
Mrs. Nixon. From time to time, Nixon was kept waiting in the receiving line with no hands to shake. As he waited, Nixon kept looking at
his wrist watch. The delay between the next to last leader and Haile
Selassie was so great that Nixon finally stepped into the adjoining
Red Room to wait for HIM (and probably to get away from the press).
When the emperor entered 18 minutes late, the Nixons rushed back to
their places in the Blue Room, greeted him effusively, and ushered him
into the East Room where the others were waiting to go to dinner.[40]

As the ranking guest, Haile Selassie sat between the President and
Mrs. Nixon. The guests feasted on salmon, squid with rice and peas,
and a lemon soufflé for dessert while the U.S. Army Strolling Strings
wandered among diners playing light melodies. The president expressed friendship on behalf of United States for the peoples whose
representatives were gathered and called on his guests to work together for peace. Nixon called for a response from the emperor, who

spoke in French and urged the world leaders to support the aims of the UN even though it had not fully lived up to its earlier expectations.[41] After dinner entertainment in the East Room was a 30-minute program of songs performed by Metropolitan Opera tenor James Mc-Cracken and his wife Sandra Warfield, mezzo-soprano. They sang French, Italian, and German songs, and one Irish tune especially for Prime Minister John Lynch of Ireland.[42]

The tradition-shattering state dinner was only part of an extraordinary period of personal diplomacy by President Nixon. Starting at 10:00 A.M. on the next day, the President Nixon met with six heads of state at 40-minute intervals until 4:40 P.M. The statesmen swept up to the White House in police-escorted limousines and were ushered into the Oval Office. In order, Nixon met with the president of Cyprus, the president of Pakistan, the president and prime minister of the Republic of China, the emperor of Ethiopia, the chief of state of Cambodia, and the president of Panama. After the last meeting, Nixon helicoptered to Camp David, probably thankful for the quiet of his sylvan retreat.[43]

In his 53-minute meeting with Nixon, Haile Selassie again had pleaded his mendicant case. The little king needed money *passim ad infinitum.* The president reassured HIM that the United States understood who its friends were and promised to study the military situation, giving full weight to the emperor's statements. Nixon noted that Haile Selassie had been an international symbol of the values of freedom and independence long before most of the chiefs of state at dinner on the previous evening had even entered public life. The leaders also discussed soviet expansion of its naval force in the Indian Ocean, the overall situation in East Africa, the crisis in the Middle East, the work of the OAU, and U.S. private investments in Ethiopia.[44]

Despite the pleas and pressure for increased U.S. military assistance, the FY 1971 funds for the IEG were reduced from $12 million to $10.8 million. The Ethiopian military would have to establish priorities for its expenditures. As if to mute U.S. criticism of the slow pace of reform in Ethiopia, the emperor in 1970 had put a good face on modernization by empowering younger men who were rationalizing economic planning and management. He also recruited foreign advisors from Harvard and the World Bank. To attract foreign investment, the IEG updated the investment law and planned to establish an investment center in Addis Ababa. The new cosmetic initiatives could not cover up the country's basic problem. Ethiopia still did not have enough funds from its own taxes to do what needed to be done. The clock was ticking and each minute spent moved the ancient régime nearer to disaster.

In November, Haile Selassie and Nixon were together again in Paris, among 80 world leaders attending the state funeral of Charles de Gaulle at Notre Dame. By that time, the United States had all but completed its 1960 pledge to equip a 40,000-man Ethiopian army. Nevertheless, the emperor was still seeking an agreement to ensure a continued program of assistance to fully maintain the army and leave several million dollars for additional requirements. Around $13 million per year should cover the cost. The emperor's request was triggered by increased aid going to the Eritrean Liberation Front from militant Arab states whose activities had increased drastically. The activities of the recharged ELF caused the IEG to declare martial law throughout Eritrea. At the same time, communist influence was markedly on the rise among Ethiopia's immediate and unfriendly neighbors. Despite the relative increase in strength of its neighbors, Kissinger believed that Ethiopia had by far the strongest and most effective military establishment in the area. Even though the United States had restored $1 million to the Ethiopian MAP program for 1972, which had earlier been cut by the Office of Management and Budget, the emperor feared that the United States intended to terminate its military assistance program for his country. That fear had strongly motivated his request for the 1970 meeting with Nixon.[45]

In 1970, some 3,000 Americans with their dependents were serving at Kagnew. The station published a monthly letterpress newspaper, and ran the first army-operated television station in the world. The emperor was receiving a hefty rent for the station, and the landlord had a long history of inspecting his real estate. A retired U.S. Army NCO remembered Haile Selassie calling on the post almost every time he traveled to Asmara. The emperor and his entourage would enter Kagnew with great pomp and circumstance at which point the Post Exchange would be closed to all except the visitors. HIM always had a fascination with electrical and mechanical instruments and took delight in perusing electronic devises, radios, and cameras. He would select a few items that the State Department would duly pay for, and then the royal party would depart.[46] On some occasions the monarch would be presented with gifts such as photographs taken during the Apollo 8 flight or a model of the Apollo 8 capsule. During one royal visit, the base square dance club put on a demonstration for the emperor.

The U.S. military observed that relations with the local population were good. A noteworthy ambassador of goodwill was 23-year-old Specialist 5 Hugh Downey, who in his spare time while stationed at Kagnew built five schools, two roads, medical and health services, two farm experimental plots, a library, and recreational facility for children, as well as other projects in the Asmara area. This he was able to accomplish with his own money and contributions from Kagnew friends and relatives. When Downey completed his tour of duty, Haile Selassie summoned him to the palace to thank him personally. Meanwhile military personnel continued what was considered vital communications work at the station in the early 1970s.

The Peace Corps in 1970, with 310 PCVs in Ethiopia, was about half the size it had been four years before. Even though the volunteers had a remarkable and enviable record of good works in their communities in addition to their regular duties, continuing anti-American student demonstrations and unhappiness with the situation in Ethiopia led some PCV teachers to leave before their two year assignments were completed. The Director of Peace Corps/Ethiopia Joseph S. Murphy resigned in February 1970 to protest the emperor's brutal suppression of protests against the murder of a student leader at the university. The once-proud organization of "Kennedy's Children," the pride of the New Frontier, was being forced into decline by circumstances beyond its control.

There were changes in the ambassadorships of Ethiopia and the United States in 1971. Former Indiana Congressman E. Ross Adair, who had been a Capitol Prayer Breakfast host for the emperor during his 1967 state visit to the United States, replaced William Hall, a career Foreign Service Officer, as U.S. ambassador. Nixon met with Adair before he departed for Addis Ababa and told him that the emperor "must be brought to recognize the absolute responsibility for providing an orderly and desirable succession."[47] Nixon maintained that Haile Selassie had done "too much good work to permit it all to collapse because of a failure to face up to the necessity of providing for his succession." For the IEG, Ambassador Minassie Haile left Washington to become minister of foreign affairs in Addis Ababa. Late in the year, Kifle Wodajo became the new Ethiopian ambassador.

The emperor's role in international politics was still so esteemed by Nixon that he kept HIM informed about significant changes in U.S. policy. Vice President Spiro Agnew visited Addis Ababa in July 1971 to inform Haile Selassie in advance that the United States was going to recognize the Peoples Republic of China.[48] Morocco was the only other African country to be so informed.

Nixon sought better relations with his Cold War adversaries, the PRC and USSR. He visited China in February 1972 and went to Moscow in May to sign agreements with the soviets to reduce the risk of military confrontations and to promote cooperation in science, technology, health, environmental matters, and space exploration. Nixon signed the Anti-Ballistic Missile Treaty, SALT I, and "Basic Principles of US-Soviet Relations."

The president's trip to China in 1972 signaled a change in America's Asian strategy. Marking an end of the goal of isolating China in the hope of undermining Beijing's communist government, Nixon's visit signaled America's desire for access to new markets to help a sagging U.S. economy. The president also sought Mao Tse-Tung's help in negotiating an end to the Vietnam War. The United States reached an agreement with North Vietnam in January 1973 on the withdrawal of all U.S. combat personnel, but the fighting did not end until Vietnam's unification under communist control in April 1975.

Also in 1972 the Ethiopian-Somali border again became a concern. The soviets continued arming the military forces of dictator Siad Barre with modern equipment, and the Somalis were spoiling for a fight. This set off the emperor's alarm bells, and he wrote Nixon: "At a time when We were expecting an increase in the U.S. military aid to Ethiopia because of our geographical location and the continued critical condition in our part of the world, it is with dismay and deep concern that We have learnt of the envisioned cut in the U.S. military aid program to Our country."[49] Haile Selassie informed Nixon that he had called Ambassador Adair to explain his "preoccupation in this regard." HIM concluded his letter with the hope that "Our observations will reach Your Excellency in time for your reconsideration of this important matter." The emperor's once strong signature had become shaky.

The growth of soviet and Cuban military activities in Somalia combined with a growing insurgency in Eritrea posed real threats to Ethiopia's security.[50] The emperor had repeatedly used a personal visit to Washington as a device by which to increase or maintain military assistance to Ethiopia, so he again sought a meeting with his old friend Nixon. In April 1973, he received a formal invitation for another state visit in May.

More significant than the arms race for Haile Selassie was a disaster under way to the north of his capital. In Wollo Province the scourge of famine, which periodically wasted Ethiopia throughout its history, had spread from the African Sahel region, where it had begun in 1969. Soon it would bring disaster to other northern provinces, but the IEG seemed unconcerned about it. In fact, the emperor journeyed to Iran with Lulu to help the Shah celebrate the 2,500 anniversary of the Persian Empire. Haile Selassie and his retainers failed to see just how strong and widespread opposition to the old order had grown.

Richard Nixon also would be affected by events that seemed of little consequence to him in 1972. In the midst of the president's lively re-election campaign, an office in Washington's Watergate complex was broken into.

NIXON III, 1973

In preparation for Haile Selassie's visit, Kissinger briefed the president about the latest U.S. activities in Ethiopia and the emperor's probable response to them. HIM's main concern was about "the increased soviet presence in and aid to irredentist Somalia, a concern intensified by falling U.S. military assistance levels and reductions in our presence at Kagnew Station."[51] The U.S. navy no longer relied heavily on Kagnew for its Polaris submarine programs and had submitted plans that would have withdrawn most U.S. personnel from the base by June 1974. The president should acknowledge that a continued U.S. presence at Kagnew was under review, an action that the emperor will view "with concern as a break in Ethiopia's strongest link to the United States." Kissinger called the state visit "a fairly critical moment in U.S.-Ethiopian relations." The U.S. aim was to safeguard its use of Ethiopian facilities for as long as they were needed and to guard "access to potentially important petroleum supplies." This aim should be accomplished without destabilizing the region.

In this setting, Haile Selassie met President Nixon on his final state visit to the United States in 1973. When the emperor made his ceremonial entrance to the White House, he established a record for the most state visits by a foreign head of state—six, a record that would last until it was tied in the next century when Britain's Queen Elizabeth was honored by President George W. Bush during her sixth state visit. The emperor's 80 years were evident when the Nixons bade him an informal welcome in the portico of the West Wing. The little king's beard was more grizzled and his once spry movements had slowed. The president ushered HIM into the Oval Office for a picture-taking session and reminded the emperor, "You have been in this room more than any other head of state. You were here in 1954."[52] Then he told assembled reporters, "The emperor had probably made more visits to Washington than any other head of government."

In the ensuing talks, Nixon and Haile Selassie discussed the threat posed to Ethiopia by the growth of soviet and Cuban military activities in Somalia combined, with a growing insurgency in Eritrea. The emperor presented Nixon with a $450 million shopping list that included F-4 Phantoms, M-60 tanks, surface-to air missiles, and air-to-ground missiles. His timing was abysmal because of U.S. plans to withdraw from Kagnew, although this was not discussed in the Oval Office meeting. In nonmilitary assistance, Nixon announced the approval by USAID of a new U.S. loan of $4.8 million to combat malaria. The president noted that Haile Selassie was accompanied by his foreign affairs minister, Dr. Menassie Haile. "He was the highest-paid interpreter we've ever had in this room," Nixon told HIM and added, "Your Majesty speaks very good English."[53] Considering how much time the two leaders had spent together over the years, the president's evaluation of the emperor's spoken English ability was an informed one. Haile Selassie subsequently told Dr. Minassie that he highly respected Nixon who always was properly correct in their meetings and correspondence.[54]

At the conclusion of his meeting with the president, the emperor was the luncheon guest of Vice President Agnew at the State Department. At 3:30 in the afternoon at Blair House, Acting Secretary of State Kenneth Rush informed the emperor that the future of Kagnew Station was under review, although this reflected no change in U.S. relations with Ethiopia.[55] Haile Selassie had later afternoon meetings with Secretary of Defense William Clements and Dr. John Hannah, administrator of USAID. At 6:30, the State Department held a reception in honor of HIM prior to a black-tie state dinner at the White House.

Rose Mary Woods, the president's secretary, had prepared two lists of guests: the eight o'clock diners, about 100, and the 10 o'clock audience of 135 for the entertainment in the East Room. Reflecting Nixon's interest in sports, among the guests were Gordie Howe, of the Detroit Redwings; Don Newcombe, pitcher for the Los Angeles Dodgers; Richie Petitbon, of the Washington Redskins; and Bob Richards; Olympic pole-vaulter.

At the White House, Haile Selassie found Nixon "vigorous as always and friendly."[56] The emperor's grandson, then rear admiral Eskinder Desta, had again accompanied HIM to America as a member of the official party. In a gift exchange, the president gave Haile Selassie a Bulova Accutron gilt-bronze clock mounted in a piece of lava stone from America Samoa with the presidential seal and a silver-framed photograph of Mr. and Mrs. Nixon.

Pat Nixon was a warm, gracious first lady who loved people, and this hid her uneasiness in the role of hostess.[57] She had worked to make the White House accessible to as many visitors as possible by arranging special tours for disabled and blind persons, preparing a booklet on the gardens, adding exterior lighting, and changing the guards' uniforms to less imposing blazers.[58] Pat restored authentic antiques to the state rooms (many of Mrs. Kennedy's acquisitions had been copies) and arranged for gifts or loans of several important paintings of presidents and first ladies. During her second year, the number of visitors to the Executive Mansion broke all records.

She also practiced her own style of personal diplomacy, being the most traveled first lady and visiting 83 nations.[59] Pat was the first First Lady to travel to Africa, where she spent eight days and traveled 10,000 miles on the west coast. She met privately with the leaders of Liberia, Ghana, and Ivory Coast. A tribal chief in Ghana said her trip bonded U.S.-Ghana relations in a way "not even a lion could destroy."[60] Presidential Assistant H. R. Haldeman praised Mrs. Nixon's trip as the single event of the administration to receive "universal approval."

The White House dinner guests sought Haile Selassie's autograph. Slowly and patiently, he signed dinner cards in the Blue Room, including that of actress Zsa Zsa Gabor. Asked if he often gets requests for his autograph, the emperor replied, "Yes. It's always a pleasure. I sign as many as I can."[61] During dinner, the Army Strolling Strings played. The monarch toasted Nixon as a statesman who had launched an era of negotiations that brought "a fresh breeze in the relations of big powers." Nixon in turn toasted HIM, who had ruled for 57 years, as the "senior statesman of the world." The evening's entertainment was Metropolitan Opera coloratura soprano Gina La Bianca, wearing a fiery chiffon red dress, singing after-dinner songs in five languages. The U.S. Marine Corps Dance Combo then played for those wishing to dance. The emperor, his limbs with travel tired, did not tarry. He departed at 11:30 P.M. from Andrews Air Force Base on an Ethiopian Airlines special charter for Addis Ababa. It was his last hurrah in America.

In Addis Ababa, two days later, Haile Selassie began the 10th-anniversary celebration of the OAU by declaring that all of Africa would be liberated from foreign domination in the next 10 years.[62] Later, he spoke to 23 African heads of state or their deputies at the 10th anniversary meeting at Africa Hall. The emperor advocated a system for the mutual defense of the 41-member nations and the creation of a permanent Africa peacekeeping force.[63] In a subsequent session, there were heated verbal clashes between the Ethiopian delegation and representatives of Libya and Somali. The Libyan spokesman accused the IEG leadership of supporting Zionists and colonialists. Major General Siad Barre accused Ethiopia of preparing for war against Somalia.[64] The latter accusation caused such rancor that the OAU set up a commission to mediate the dispute. The 10th anniversary found the OAU strained, but not torn, by bitter disputes.

Much more worrisome, or it should have been to the emperor, was the spreading famine in Ethiopia's northern provinces. At the very time Haile Selassie's attention appeared riveted on international affairs, his domestic scene, a cauldron of cooling melt, was deteriorating badly. By the spring of 1973, the famine was claiming the lives of hundreds of thousands of peasants of Tigray and Wollo, and thousands more had sought relief in Ethiopian towns and villages. This was reported by university faculty and students, and a British filmmaker made a video program of the suffering that was shown in the UK. Yet, the IEG refused to act and engaged in a cover-up operation and a conspiracy of silence that would not be forgotten by the Ethiopian masses when the truth was revealed.

Meanwhile in the United States, in August 1973, it was announced that most U.S. operations at Kagnew Station would cease by the end of FY 1974. Nixon was demonstrating his belief that the way to govern was by surprise.[65] The emperor no longer held the trump card, and a new era of U.S.-Ethiopian relations would begin. Foreign Minister Menassie made a face-saving request that the press release about the Kagnew withdrawal be simultaneously released in Washington and Addis Ababa and that it treat the decision as a joint one arrived at by mutual agreement. Neither country wanted to give the impression that the United States was abandoning Ethiopia.[66] Menassie then led a strong lobbying effort to increase what the IEG considered far too small a military assistance program.

Kissinger was aware of the consequences of the U.S. action. Ethiopia would be free to seek alternate sources to supplement what the United States could do within the clear limitations on U.S. military aid. The only realistic choices, according to Kissinger, were the USSR or PRC. Questions about the extent of U.S. strategic requirements and future interests, as well as the degree to which the United States should put major resources into a vulnerable regime ruled by an aging emperor vis-à-vis the loss of Ethiopia to radical influences, would affect the total American position in the Red Sea area and be one more case of a U.S.-backed country, Ethiopia, appearing to lose out to a soviet-backed country, Somalia.[67]

Nixon-Kissinger foreign policy involved geopolitical considerations largely unrelated to economic realities or the interests of the peoples involved. The Nixon administration was more concerned with Vietnam and Watergate than the plight of the ancient emperor and gave a basically unfavorable response to the IEG's requests for arms. The United States did agree to continue to grant military aid and training at agreed-upon levels and to supplement the program with credits for military sales, but this was far less than what had been requested. The rebuff by the United States made Haile Selassie's last attempt at personal diplomacy at the White House "an unqualified disaster."[68] The field marshal uniform had become too heavy.

Minutes of the secretary of state's staff meetings under newly designated Secretary Kissinger shed light on American thinking about Ethiopia during this time. Starting in October 1973, the Horn of Africa came up more frequently on the secretary's agenda, but it was still only a small piece of the worldwide puzzle that State struggled to understand. Ethiopia's reaction to the closing of Kagnew and the reduction of U.S. military assistance sparked a discussion in an October 25 meeting. The emperor scheduled an official visit to Moscow at the end of the month, probably with the intention, in part, to press the United States to increase its MAP. Kissinger's advisors noted that the IEG usually wanted more military assistance because of Kagnew, and now that there was no Kagnew, "they want more military assistance because they no longer had it."[69] Verbatim reactions of the State Department leaders to Haile Selassie's again playing his Cold War card are revealing:

> MR. PORTER: Will he do another hundred million dollar stunt this time in Moscow? You remember that famous credit? That scared everybody to death here. And not a damned thing happened.
>
> MR. NEWSOM: They still haven't drawn down about $11 million of that $100 million.
>
> MR. PORTER: He is a great old boy for just that kind of thing.
>
> SECRETARY KISSINGER: He is the world's greatest.[70]

On another occasion, Kissinger said, "My experience is that Haile Selassie does nothing unless it is that he makes the most boring toasts of anybody I have ever heard."[71] A scathing comment, but not as cutting as Korry's 1964 jibe that "veracity is not one of his [HIM's] stronger attributes."[72] Official esteem for the Emperor was not what it had been a few years before. By January 1974, State was paying more attention to the Ethiopian famine and the way the IEG was handling it. Concerns about the stability of the emperor's government precluded any increase in MAP or beginning an escalation in weapons systems.

While reviewing the confused state of affairs in Ethiopia, Kissinger admitted that "I was never in favor of giving up Kagnew. I always thought it would have serious political consequences."[73]

Three months later, Kissinger had forgotten the name of the listening post and had to be reminded that it was Kagnew, not "Catina," as he called it. So much for Kagnew being the center of the American universe that Ethiopians ascribed to it during the 1960s and 1970s.[74] Still worrying about a prospective invasion of Ethiopia by Somali, in April 1974, the IEG made another appeal for $150 million in military assistance. Kissinger was willing to give them $25 million to demonstrate U.S. support of the government, but the social and political situation in Ethiopia was so confusing by that time that top American officials, lacking meaningful intelligence reports, were reluctant to act until they could be sure the emperor would survive the turmoil that was developing.[75] The days of monarchical supremacy were numbered.

Haile Selassie's return home from America with little to show for the effort and the shutdown of Kagnew were contributing factors to the emperor's removal in the creeping coup or revolution that was underway by the end of 1973. Ethiopia's frustrated intellectuals, armed forces, farmers, and emerging business sector were all alienated and objected to the government's botched handling of the famine, a stagnant economy, and the lack of reform in Ethiopia. The gathered strands of the spiders' web could tie up a lion—even the Lion of Judah. The sins of the nation's defender of the faith combined, as all the best of scandals do, allegations of graft, egregious grandiosity, and the seasoning salt of greed—all grist for the revolutionaries' mill. The emperor's achievements were buried under the avalanche of tragic flaws that brought him down. And the accomplishments were many but irrelevant to the mob. University students eventually articulated their demands and "radicalized" the military, whose leadership became anti-American. This led to the September 1974 revolution that overthrew the emperor and brought the autocratic military Derg to power. The United States underscored its rejection of HIM by not having an ambassador at the court of a rapidly failing sovereign after Ross Adair retired from the post in 1974. At the time Haile Selassie was overthrown, the Nixon administration was mired in its own political scandal and was not in a position to pay much attention to Ethiopia. The emperor was forced out of the palace only a month after Nixon was forced out of the White House and resigned from the presidency in light of the Watergate debacle. It was a *Götterdämmerung*, the twilight of the Gods who had reigned so powerfully only months before.

Epilogue

Now my charms are all o'erthrown, And what strength I have's mine
own, Which is most faint; now, 'tis true, I must be here confin'd by you.
—*The Tempest*

The revolution ended the feudal system of Ethiopia headed by its
long-lived monarch. The new rulers, the Coordinating Committee of
the Armed Forces, Police, and Territorial Army, known as the *Derg*,
detained government officials and the emperor. The Derg government
focused on internal issues and declared it would follow a nonaligned
foreign policy. U.S. officials looked to moderate military officers, many
of whom had trained in the United States, to counter the Marxist-
Leninist ideology espoused by extremists of the revolution, but the
Derg evolved into an anti-United States, communist dictatorship
headed by Mengistu Haile Mariam. His regime unleashed a Red Terror that slaughtered thousands of Ethiopians, including Haile Selassie
and many of the nation's leaders. The emperor in his smashed grandeur, rejected even by his most loyal supporters and officially referred
to as the ex-king, was unceremoniously driven in a Volkswagen from
his palace to his place of imprisonment. Haile Selassie died in deten-
tion 11 months later, probably murdered on August 27, 1975.

The emperor's death brought an end to the longevity of an autocratic
feudal state, a whole mythology of social cohesion around anointed
authority and mystery. That such an imperium had survived far after

similar systems of rule had disappeared can be attributed to Haile Se-lassie's petulant refusal to relinquish the leadership (which was the de-spair of his dedicated, educated courtiers). HIM's death also concluded a remarkable record of an African nation's obtaining inordinate finan-cial aid from the United States. Dating back to the early agreements between the two nations in the 1950s, Ethiopia had received about 80 percent of all U.S. military aid for Africa and one-fifth of American economic assistance. As impressive as those figures appear, they were but a small portion of the total U.S. assistance worldwide. In the per-spective of the global picture, Ethiopia's share of U.S. military assis-tance under HIM was only about one-half of one percent.[1]

Mengistu went about ridding his country of the American presence. On short notice, Kagnew was ordered closed, as were MAAG, all USIS offices and libraries in the country, the consulate in Asmara, and several other American programs. The 1953 military assistance agreement was unilaterally abrogated, and even the U.S. embassy staff was ordered cut in half. The United States immediately suspended military assis-tance and stopped delivery of arms previously promised. The Peace Corps endured under trying conditions until its last program was ter-minated in 1977, accused by the Derg of acting as an agent of cultural imperialism. Two years later, USAID closed its operations. The Soviet Union, Eastern Bloc nations, and Cuba became the dominant backers of the new regime.

Armed by the Soviet Union, Somalia went to war with Ethiopia in the Ogaden in 1977 at a time when Ethiopia's military dictatorship was in disarray, seeking to consolidate its power and struggling with a rebellion in Eritrea. The Somali army was repulsed by Ethiopian forces supported by military assistance from the soviets and their cli-ent states, and Cuban and Yemeni troops.[2] This melee of communist cronies induced an unlikely Cold War switch of principal supporters of Horn of Africa nations, with the United States becoming the ally of Somalia and Ethiopia becoming a client state of the Soviet Union.

During its 17-year reign, the Derg was a ruthless ally of the Soviet Bloc in the Cold War and was notorious for its abuse of human rights and its problems in dealing with a major famine in 1984. When the Derg was overthrown in 1991, there was hope that democracy might take root in Ethiopia, but a new cast of Marxist rulers who mastered "capitalist-speak," the Ethiopian People's Revolutionary Front (EPRDF) have maintained "the snares of watchful tyranny" in the troubled land. Today, in comparison with what followed, the reign of Haile Selassie appears far better than it did at the time of his fall.

The decline in the fortunes of the Horn nations might have been foreseen by Henry Kissinger, who in 1972, as head of the National Security Council, known under his direction as the "committee in charge of running the world," wrote a confidential report on the future of Ethiopia. He purportedly recommended that U.S. policy should be to keep that nation in perennial internal conflict, using such vulnerabilities as ethnic, religious, and other divisions to destabilize the country. Kissinger's recommendation appears to have been followed successfully, for not only Ethiopia but the Horn of Africa have been in turmoil ever since.

* * *

The state visits of Haile Selassie to the United States strongly influenced the views of Americans about Africa and Africans during the latter half of the 20th century. But who was the real Haile Selassie, and why were the American people so enamored of him? The image of the emperor was in the eye of the beholder. The image of the international celebrity is projected through our own political, cultural, intellectual, professional, and psychological lenses. Such images reflect substance. "The way we respond to public figures, the feelings they invoke, the interpretations they invite, the meanings they embody"—all are part and parcel of our political experience, the way we understand reality.[3]

Multiple perspectives on HIM have existed ever since he came to power and have depended upon the person or group viewing him and when. Revered by some, reviled by others, Haile Selassie's accomplishments were meaningful and exciting in their time and place. They had great significance then, but they tend to lose their context now, especially in Ethiopia, where his name and character have been vituperated for over 30 years. To the Derg that helped overthrow him and to the present EPRDF rulers, the emperor was a demagogue intent on preserving his power at all costs, a perpetuator of a corrupt arcane system of rule that had evolved under his autocratic direction from feudal fragments that had endured into the second half of the 20th century. While the rest of the world passed it by, the ancient kingdom, adamant for drift, remained mired in debilitating poverty, ignorance, and disease. A national elite, fostered at HIM's court, contributed to the entropy of life. Liege lords, the king's men, were due servility from loyal subjects. If any star among the new rulers began to shine brightly, however, he was *shum-shered*, promoted-demoted to dullness (and probably to ungentle rustication) by the ever watchful emperor. A historical age and one generation with a distinct political and cultural character gave way to another age, another generation, yet the features of the government had frozen into a rictus of stasis. The old order failed to work, and the need for some new machinery was painfully obvious. The young revolutionaries challenged the emperor and the IEG with new difficulties of adjustment.

To opponents of the regime, Haile Selassie was viewed as a tyrant over conquered peoples, a heavy-handed crusher of dissent, and a moss-backed opponent of modernity. To the nations, nationalities, and peoples in the hinterlands, he was a conqueror who divided up their lands as payment to soldier-settlers, the hated *nefteganas* from faraway places, who prospered at the expense of indigenous vassals. With a face as hard and unyielding as quarried stone, the emperor dominated politics, the press, the military and police, and the flow of cash. He indulged sycophants, rewarded cronies, and punished rebels. The Haile Selassie style was one of drama, flattery, purposeful contradiction, and mystery. In the 1960s and 1970s, young radicals interpreted HIM as a dark conspirator who could not tolerate even the slightest challenges, because his existence depended for its survival on unanimity. The emperor endured "by a combination of skillful diplomacy abroad, ruthless political repression at home, and good luck in terms of a passive population" who venerated the throne.[4] To critics, he was a flawed and guilty man who had chances for redemption but passed them by.[5]

Yet, earlier generations admired Haile Selassie for the social and economic advances that he brought his backward country, before Mussolini's fascists interrupted the process, and for his leadership that expelled the conquerors and started anew programs for its development. His governing methods worked brilliantly in the 1930s and 1940s and extended into the 1950s. To many Ethiopians, he was indeed the king of kings and the sacred connection to the people's Old Testament past. He was the stern paterfamilias who respected the faith while seeking to have Ethiopia play an important role in the modern world. It was the emperor who unified its disparate ethnic groups, and then, through terror, diplomacy, theatrics, and his own charismatic persona, kept the cause before the world's wandering attention.

Outside Ethiopia, the marmoreal-featured king was a storied figure, with a reputation for courage that he earned in a dramatic appeal for help. Friends abroad saw him as a moderate reformer of an anachronistic feudal system and an astute user of political power. In his travels, Haile Selassie was bathed in an aura of aloof dignity that came to be regarded as characteristic. He personified a bewitching blend of the ancient and modern. In public, Haile Selassie was never off. He was obsessed with maintaining a correct public image, and his sepulchral face was stubbornly affectless. Always well-dressed and insouciant, the monarch handled himself calmly in the presence of his foreign audiences. Because his authority was absolute, he could speak softly. In the company of inveterate and literate talkers (and some politicians who were not all that literate), he didn't need to raise his voice. Preferring to speak through an interpreter, he replied to questions in short, crisp terms and seemed forceful. He held all the cards. He would move slowly to imprint on his watcher's memory the moment at hand. In a *cordon de célébrité* he received an avalanche of adoration from the public. To American diplomats he was a venerated Cold War ally who was a friend of the West and Israel and appropriately wary, most of the time, of the influence in Africa of the soviets, Egypt, the Arab League, and, later, the PRC.

Which perspective is correct? They both are. By many he was loved. By many he was hated. Haile Selassie emerged as a perplexing figure, a chameleon of an actor playing many roles in different settings. His protean, volatile character had allowed him to escape one unaddressed domestic crisis after another. His contemporaries expressed mixed feelings about the emperor—including his personality, his accomplishments, and his talent—while they acknowledged his power. Even those enthralled by him were often repelled by his autocratic style and by the content of his messages.

Haile Selassie's character is elusive. The inner man is almost totally inaccessible. One of the best efforts to find out about "the private universe of Haile Selassie" was the 1973 interview of HIM in French by Italian journalist Oriana Fallaci. The emperor revealed himself to be locked in another time. When Fallaci asked him if he felt lonely in a world so different from the one he grew up in, he replied, "It is our opinion that the world hasn't changed at all. We believe that such changes have modified nothing. We don't even notice any difference between monarchies and republics." Asked if he ever regretted his kingly fate, HIM said, "We were born of royal blood, authority is Ours by right. Since it is Ours by right and since our Lord the Creator has deemed We might serve Our people as a father serves his son, being a monarch is a great joy to Us. It's what We were born for and what We have always lived for."[6] It was as though an Old Testament prophet had spoken—an anomaly at a time when astronauts were walking on the moon. Haile Selassie was eminently and emphatically of his age and his country, and therein lies the secret of much of his success—and ultimately his fall.

The emperor was not lacking in self-esteem. Having ruled for over half a century, he saw himself as a towering figure of modern history. After he helped in the creation of the OAU, foreign policy hands promoted his image as Africa's elder statesman. He assumed also a stature and wisdom in world affairs that was politely condoned by many world leaders. His attitudes were shaped by the lessons of the invasions of Ethiopia. The Italians twice came out of Eritrea and in 1935 from the Somalilands too; and Gran, the 16th century Muslim invader, from what is now Somalia. Haile Selassie saw himself like the fabled Prester John, holding a Christian island in the midst of a Muslim sea. He sought to control Eritrea, and was paranoid about Somalia, which he anathematized. He also worried about Djibouti as the only port connected by rail to Ethiopia.

The world still awaits a psychobiography of Haile Selassie written by an Ethiopian, preferably a psychiatrist whose first tongue is Amharic and who has a sharp appreciation of the wax and gold inherent in the Semitic languages of Ethiopia. It will be challenging to apply psychological theory and research to the life of the emperor in the tradition of Eric Erikson and Jerrold M. Post, among others, who have combined psychoanalysis and social theory in controversial but engrossing studies of charismatic world leaders.[7] Critics of these studies, such as Richard Nixon, "think that most of the so-called new 'science' of psychobiography is pure baloney."[8] Nevertheless, attempts at analyzing the psychological makeup, character, or motivations of Haile Selassie lack clarity and validity when compared to analyses of other significant historical figures.

Many theorize that the emperor possessed a narcissistic and paranoid personality. His grandiose majesty convinced HIM of his moral and sovereign superiority, which entitled him to use ruthless power at any costs. His esurient self trapped HIM in a paranoid distrust of others and finally rendered him incapable of adapting himself to changing circumstances. His reconciling self attempted to integrate his grandiose majesty with his esurient self, bringing about mediation among feuding African nations, Cold War rivals, and unaligned and neutral camp followers. He even offered to moderate a settlement of the Vietnam conflict. His driving force, his idée fixe, was collective security, especially if it could be managed by the UN. He was also obsessive-compulsive in repeatedly seeking military aid from America to alleviate his persistent fears of Muslim or communist-allied invaders. These foibles of the king only touch the surface of the inner makeup of the complicated, mesmeric ruler of the *Habesha*. More and deeper studies

of Haile Selassie's psychology of political behavior are needed to enhance our understanding of this puzzling potentate.

* * *

Each of the emperor's state visits to the United States, each a great
drama and great history, served as a trail mark along Americans' way
of knowing more about the former dark continent and its peoples. This
ranged from little acquaintance with Africa at the time of the emperor's
first state visit in 1954 to an explosion of media coverage and knowledge about the continent during the Decade of Africa in the 1960s with
its end of colonialism and the creation of the Organization of African
Unity to the realpolitik of the Cold War and public indifference to the
general abandonment of African nations that did not offer some imme-
diate advantage to the United States in its struggle against communism
in the early 1970s. Throughout this period of 20 years, as technology
facilitated communication and made knowledge of other lands and
peoples easier to come by, Haile Selassie was the one constant figure
representing sub-Saharan Africa in the minds of most Americans.

He established his status as a celebrity by simple familiarity, induced
and reinforced by carefully planned and well-executed public performances.[9] His celebrity grew over generations as more people found
new virtues in HIM. He possessed considerable personal charm that
only increased with age and experience. He radiated success and authority, and many Americans were eager to be impressed. At the time
of the emperor's first state visits, the nation was gripped by a kind of
patriotic emotion seldom evoked in the doubting cynical midcentury.
In those years, appreciation of a cultivated African somehow raised the
stature of Americans, and Haile Selassie was a person known for some
serious achievements. As his valor during World War II receded into
the misty past, Haile Selassie became more, and not less, heroic. He
had stood at or near center stage for 50 years from the time of World
War I, to the Great Depression, to World War II, and through the era of
the Cold War. He had stood the test of time. If Ethiopian critics of the
emperor at home or abroad complained bitterly about governance of
the kingdom or about the mendacity of the monarch, most Americans
paid little heed to their jeremiads. There were no truth in advertising
laws in the celebrity industry, and iconoclasts were not welcome. A celebrity need not be admirable, merely spectacular.[10]

The image of the nattily uniformed emperor was a positive one,
even as his exotic veneer eroded and he came to represent just one of

many (probably too many for an individual's attention span) African nations. Through his periodic appearances in the United States, the emperor, "the mirror of all courtesy," remained an international celebrity in the eyes of the public long after he no longer beguiled the State Department. His grave persona, conveyed in his adroit use of public relations, had a long-lasting benign impact on Americans' view of Africa. Without him, the collective "picture in the head" of Africans might have been far different in light of the distressing conditions and perplexing leaders that emerged during the postcolonial era. Renowned rulers such as Nasser, the "leader of the Arabs"; Nkrumah, the "Osagyefo"; Nyerere, the "Mwalimu;" and Kenyatta, "the flaming spear" all flashed on the consciousness of Americans and had their admirers and detractors, but only the Ethiopian king of kings provided permanence in a continuously changing mise-en-scène of the dark continent. While other African leaders disappointed us, we could count on HIM to be steady, consistent, and unshakable—a pillar of rectitude. The beneficent feelings created by Haile Selassie during his journeys to the United States influenced America's thinking about Africa and its people, an influence that continues today.

The State Department, entrusted with the task of making the powerful and famous look good, filled official events with spectacular moments.[11] In the well-scripted visits of Haile Selassie, State choreographed the ceremonial magnificence of the United States and the renown of its president while it also helped shape how the emperor was perceived and understood. History is not only what important people did and said but also what they symbolized. For most of his admirers, Haile Selassie was the embodiment of the idea of the underdog, the little guy who stood up to the bully, but the world didn't have the gumption to come to his help. This image of the worthy hero/victim emerged from a dialectical or collaborative process between the celebrity emperor and his audience that grew with time. The emotions generated by this worthy and controversial figure were run through cultural filters that gave meaning to what he represented.

The emperor and his handsome entourage of Ethiopians, free of group static, speaking Oxbridge English and interacting with an adoring public embossed a more meaningful imprimatur on the visits than that of official agreements and joint statements. While the poignancy of Haile Selassie's speaking at the United Nations, being the first African leader to spend the night in the White House, and traveling in a still racially segregated South is historic, many Americans will remember instead the ticker-tape parades honoring the emperor in New York

City, his attending a baseball game at Yankee Stadium, and his gifts to Jacqueline Kennedy and her children at Camelot. The pomp and circumstance enhanced the public image of the Ethiopian ruler: He was honored at elaborate White House dinners, staged spectacular arrivals by ocean liner in New York and by train in Washington's Union Station, and laid wreaths before the honored memorials in stirring and somber ceremonies throughout the continent. On another grave occasion, Haile Selassie was the most colorful figure in the largest gathering of heads of state in the 20th century who attended President Kennedy's funeral.

In addition to ruffles and flourishes in the nation's governmental and financial capitals, the formally august emperor was an unprecedented center of attention in enthusiastic provincial venues. People from all walks of life were captivated by the little king, magnetized by his quiet Olympian personality while he constantly performed rituals that are remembered to this day. The presence of royalty, about which most Americans knew but little, inspired exquisitist urges in welcoming officials as well as the general public. Everyone seemed to go all out to honor the emperor and to show their communities at their best. Those who took part in ceremonies involving the emperor rhapsodized about the events. Association with an emperor—even the idea of an emperor—guided one's behavior. It was not just what Haile Selassie did but what he meant that imprinted Haile Selassie on Americans' emotional memory. Grande dames of the hinterlands who attended the dinner or the reception in honor of HIM were written up in the local press and the glow of their proximity to celebrity radiated into their communities. Likewise, the men who were ceremoniously inducted into the Order of the Star of Ethiopia felt singularly honored, even though the order's membership was far from exclusive and swelled almost anywhere Haile Selassie received a public encomium. Even the often-decorated Richard Nixon bragged about receiving "a high honor" from HIM during his first state visit. At every stop on the emperor's itinerary, the media expressed admiration for the little king and what he stood for.

In other parts of the Americas, Haile Selassie was deified by the Ras Tefarians in Jamaica, cheered as he drove down boulevards lined with 10,000 troops in Mexico City, and given the royal treatment by the Canadians who were quite proficient at it. There also were gripping behind-the-scenes tales, the compost of secret treacheries that are an integral part of diplomatic relations, stories of state secrets and contradictions—stories that reveal the human complexities behind the mythic African character and his influence on America.

Although the emperor primarily sought military assistance from the United States, he was adept in acquiring economic and educational aid from Point Four, USAID, and the Peace Corps, and even from the American private sector. He also was valued as a moderate influence in postcolonial Africa, where the actions of a new generation of rulers frequently diverged from American interests. At the same time Haile Selassie was criticized for being a wily rug merchant who could not be "out-Byzantined"[12] and a blackmailer in demanding exorbitant rent for Kagnew. His furnishing troops for UN operations in Korea and the Congo demonstrated his staunch support for the collective security of that international body, where he was a long-time friend of the United States. To many observers, the little king was like an actor who played so many roles that his fans wondered if he existed when he was not acting. To them, Haile Selassie seemed to lack substance when he was not on stage. He was the sum of his parts, but who among his critics and admirers could make a meaningful addition of all the segments?

In a simpler time, a less-sophisticated yesteryear, when there were only four independent nations in Africa, when the United States was still finding its way in a post–World War II era, and when right and wrong perhaps were more easily discernable, millions of Americans identified deeply with Haile Selassie. They couldn't get enough of him because they so desperately needed to be reminded of the noble effort of World War II. The petite ruler was a larger-than-life projection of everything Americans wanted to believe about themselves. Then, the United States was on the side of right, and the emperor was there with us. For the generation that remembered the war, Haile Selassie, the small, picturesque figure with his famous cape and beard addressing the League of Nations, as seen repeatedly in newsreels and Allied propaganda films, was a living icon, a hero of the United Nations' success in crushing fascism and Nazism. American hearts were full of sympathy as the emperor courageously exposed Mussolini's evil, shedding the light of truth on the enveloping darkness. He made people feel good about themselves in having been a part of the great crusade. In the less certain times that followed, of police actions and undeclared wars in Korea and Vietnam, Americans so desperately needed to be reminded of the noble effort of World War II. For African Americans in their struggle for civil rights, Haile Selassie led a nation that was a beacon of hope for oppressed people everywhere. For a younger generation of Americans, he personified the optimism of a new era of progress for independent nations freed from the shackles of colonialism. And he was a Christian ruler—a denominational affiliation admired by many in the Americas.

For better or for worse, most Americans tended to like the emperor because of his past accomplishments. Perhaps Haile Selassie's greatest achievement was reigning so long. His longevity and prominence in postwar life underscored his valuable contributions to the 20th century. His image remained indelible and ubiquitous in American culture, and he was superb at maintaining being well-known. By just being periodically, joyfully received in the United States—a great talent in itself—he continued his charismatic appeal and ability to inspire. Few were aware of the emperor's problems back home or of his nation's significance in U.S. communications technology and in its geopolitical importance, especially in the Middle East. For most Americans, fascinated by royalty, there was magic in his majesty—to the point that Haile Selassie was part of popular culture. The emperor seemed to hold many Americans in an inexplicable fascination, what psychiatrists call a "psychic thrall." This gave HIM an aura of awesome authority and celebrity.

The image that the American people developed during Haile Selassie's prominence played a significant role in the election of Barack Obama as president in 2008. The election was a noteworthy milestone for race relations in the nation. With a few exceptions, conscious or explicit racism was not part of the campaign.[13] Social psychologists argue, however, that unconscious or implicit biases have a powerful effect on how people evaluate candidates. As a result, Obama's party spent much money and time creating positive images of the presidential candidate to combat negative racial associations that carry over from an earlier era. The Democrats ran a campaign well suited to combating such unconscious bias. The nature of the campaign demonstrated that race continues to play a complex and profound role in how Americans judge each other politically. In addition to negative factors, there also can be positive images in unconscious biases. When many Americans saw the son of a Kenyan seeking higher office, the remembrance of Emperor Haile Selassie was a part of the subconscious, influencing their affirmative thinking about Africans and people of African descent. In North America, the Lion of Judah was considered great, and his visits to the New World created a positive image of the best from Africa—an image that is still evolving in the United States today.

Notes

PREFACE

1. *Henry V,* Act V, Scene II.
2. George Lakoff and Mark Johnson, *Metaphors We Live By* (Chicago: University of Chicago Press, 2003), 5.
3. e. e. cummings, "XXXV," in e. e. cummings, *Complete Poems 1904–1962,* ed. George J. Firmage (New York: Liveright, 1991), 345.

CHAPTER 1

1. Murray Schumach, "Visiting Emperor Hailed in Parade," *New York Times,* June 2, 1954, 33.
2. White House Social Office, H. B. Tolley: Records, 1952–61, Box 34 "5–26–54, Emp. of Et, H.I.M. HIS—Dinner (1)," June 2, 1954; Prince Sahle Selassie to President & Mrs. Eisenhower, Dwight D. Eisenhower Library, Abilene, KS (hereafter EL).
3. "Selassie Honored at UN," *New York Times,* June 2, 1954, 33.
4. Haile Selassie, *My Life and Ethiopia's Progress, 1892–1937,* vol. 2, ed. Harold G. Marcus (East Lansing: Michigan State University Press, 1994), 2.
5. Ibid.
6. Robert S. Bird, "City Welcomes Selassie in Ticker-Tape Shower," *New York Herald Tribune,* June 2, 1954, 3; Ras Nathaniel, *50th Anniversary of His Imperial Majesty Haile Selassie I: First Visit to the United States (1954–2004)* (Bloomington, IN: Trafford, 2006), 46.
7. Jack Bennett, "Inside Ethiopia: Its Emperor, Who Will Soon Visit U.S., is Gradually Changing its Ancient Ways," *Wall Street Journal,* May 11, 1954, 12.
8. 347 U.S. 483 (1954).

9. Spencer began work for the Emperor in 1936 and was with him in Geneva at the League of Nations; after serving in the U.S. Navy in World War II, he resumed work in Ethiopia in October 1943 and continued until 1960, when he returned to the United States.

10. Kebede Mikael, director of the National Library; Fantaye Wolde Yohannes, director general of the Ministry of Finance; Tafarra Work Kidane Wold, private secretary to the emperor; Captain Workeneh, assistant to the aide-de-camp; and two valets, Mangasha Woldemarian and Lantideru Kelklas. Albert H. Garretson represented the Ethiopian Embassy in Washington, DC, "Official Party," Presidents' Papers Box 48, folder 20 (Coll. No. 70-005), OSU Library, Stillwater, OK; Kenneth Ricker to Ed Morrison, June 15, 1954, Ibid.; William S. Abbott to Kenneth Ricker, memorandum, "Names to be marked off the Official Party list," June 10, 1954, OSU Library, Stillwater, OK (hereafter OSUL).

11. John E. Utter, director of the Office of African Affairs; Katherine McCormick, United States Information Agency; Vincent Wilber, press officer; and John F. McDermott, security officer.

12. Gebru Tareke, *The Ethiopian Revolution: War in the Horn of Africa* (New Haven, CT: Yale University Press, 2009), 16.

13. Theodore M. Vestal, *Ethiopia: A Post-Cold War African State* (Westport, CT: Praeger, 1999), xii.

14. Virginia Morell, *Blue Nile: Ethiopia's River of Magic* (Washington, DC: National Geographic, 2001), 3.

15. Edward Ullendorff, *The Ethiopians: An Introduction to Country and People* (London: Oxford University Press, 1960), 33.

16. Harold G. Marcus, *A History of Ethiopia*, up. ed. (Berkeley, University of California Press, 2002), 1–3.

17. Richard Pankhurst, *The Ethiopians: A History* (Oxford: Blackwell, 2002), 1–6.

18. Marcus, *History*, 3–4.

19. Pankhurst, 7–8.

20. Pankhurst, 24–26.

21. Marcus, *History*, 5–12.

22. Pankhurst, 22–24, 28–39.

23. Pankhurst, 48–53.

24. Pankhurst, 53–60.

25. Pankhurst, 76–80.

26. Marcus, *History*, 14.

27. Pankhurst, 82–84.

28. Marcus, *History*, 31–34.

29. Pankhurst, 84–93.

30. Pankhurst, 93–95.

31. Pankhurst, 96–97, 102–3, 124–26.

32. Marcus, *History*, 34–38.

33. Pankhurst, 109–24.

34. Pankhurst, 131–43.

35. Marcus, *History*, 59–62.

36. Pankhurst, 143–56.

37. Henry Morton Stanley, *Coomassie and Magdala* (New York: Harper & Brothers, 1874).

38. Pankhurst, 173–76.

39. Theodore M. Vestal, "Reflections on the Battle of Adwa and Its Significance for Today," in eds. Paulos Milkias and Getachew Metaferia, *The Battle of Adwa— Reflections on Ethiopia's Historic Victory Against European Colonialism* (New York: Algora, 2005), 21–35.

40. Pankhurst, 176–202.

41. David H. Shinn, "Introduction," in Robert P. Skinner, Aurelia E. Brazeal, and David H. Shinn, *The 1903 Skinner Mission to Ethiopia and a Century of American-Ethiopian Relations* (Hollywood, CA: Tsehai, 2004), 8–9 (hereafter Shinn).

CHAPTER 2

1. Anthony Mockler, *Haile Selassie's War: The Italian-Ethiopian Campaign, 1935–1941* (New York: Random House, 1984), 4.

2. Negussay Ayele, *Ethiopia and the United States* (Santa Clara, CA: Ocopy.com, 2003), 63.

3. Haile Selassie, *My Life and Ethiopia's Progress, 1892–1937,* vol. 1, ed. and trans. Edward Ullendorff, (Oxford: Oxford University Press, 1976), 60.

4. Haile Selassie, vol. 1, 78–81.

5. Leonard Mosley, *Haile Selassie: The Conquering Lion* (London: Weidenfeld & Nicolson, 1964), 129.

6. Haile Selassie, vol. 1, 77.

7. Haile Selassie, vol. 1, 83–84.

8. Weapons Control Edict of April 9, 1924.

9. "Regulations for the Emancipation of Slaves and Their Conditions of Life," issued on March 31, 1924; Harold G. Marcus, *Haile Selassie I: The Formative Years, 1892–1936* (Lawrenceville, NJ: 1987), 59.

10. Mosley, *Haile Selassie,* 130–31.

11. Marcus, *Haile Selassie I,* 68.

12. Haile Selassie, Vol. I, 110.

13. Mosley, 131.

14. Marcus, *Haile Selassie I,* 64.

15. Mosley, 129–31.

16. Richard Pankhurst, *The Ethiopians: A History* (Oxford: Blackwell, 2002), 211.

17. Harold G. Marcus, *A History of Ethiopia,* updated ed. (Berkeley: University of California Press, 2002), 127–29.

18. Haile Selassie, Vol. I, 172–74.

19. Marcus, *Haile Selassie I,* 108.

20. Marcus, *Haile Selassie I,* 111.

21. Evelyn Waugh, "Ethiopia To-Day, Romance and Reality," *The Times*, December 22, 1930; Michael B. Salwen, *Evelyn Waugh in Ethiopia, The Story Behind Scoop* (Lewiston, UK: Edwin Mellen, 2001), iii; Mosley, 170.

22. Waugh, "Ethiopia To-Day," 13; quoted in Phillip Knightley, *The First Casualty, From the Crimea to Vietnam: The War Correspondent as Hero, Propagandist, and Myth Maker* (San Diego, CA: Harcourt Brace, 1975), 173.

23. Waugh, *Remote People* (London: Duckworth, 1985).

24. Waugh, *Black Mischief* (New York: Back Bay Books, 2002).

25. Waugh, *Scoop* (New York: Back Bay Books, 1977).

26. Leonard E. Barrett, *The Rastafarians* (Boston: Beacon Press, 1997), 1,104, 254.

27. Christopher Clapham, *Haile-Selassie's Government* (London: Longmans, 1969), 48.

28. Gebru , 16 (see ch. 1, n. 12).

29. Haile Selassie, Vol. I, 181–85.

CHAPTER 3

1. Evelyn Waugh, *Waugh in Abyssinia (From Our Own Correspondent)* (Baton Rouge: Louisiana State University Press, 2007), 51.

2. Ibid.

3. Ibid.

4. Richard Pankhurst, *The Ethiopians: A History* (Oxford: Blackwell, 2002), 223–26.

5. Harold G. Marcus, *A History of Ethiopia,* up. ed. (Berkeley: University of California Press, 2002), 138–41.

6. Waugh, *Waugh in Abyssinia,* 57.

7. John Hope Franklin and Alfred A. Moss, Jr., *From Slavery to Freedom* (New York: McGraw Hill, 1994), 433–34.

8. Kellog-Briand Pact, 1928.

9. Marcus, *Haile Selassie I,* 165.

10. Haile Selassie, vol. 1, 263.

11. Marcus, *History,* 142–46; Zaude Hailemariam, *Ethiopian Introspection* (Stockholm: n.p., 2008), 134–54.

12. Haile Selassie, vol. 1, 290.

13. Pankhurst, 226–36.

14. Haile Selassie, vol. 1, 296–97; Mockler, 150.

15. Haile Selassie, vol. 1, 297.

16. Haile Selassie, vol. 1, 298–312.

17. Pankhurst, 237–38.

18. Haile Selassie, vol. 2, 36.

19. Alan Moorehead, *Mediterranean Front* (London: Hamish Hamilton, 1941), 37.

20. Haile Selassie, vol. 2, 40–42.

CHAPTER 4

1. Mockler, 263.

2. Mockler, 420.

3. Pankhurst, 251–56.

4. Negussay, 169.

5. Harold G. Marcus, *Politics of Empire: Ethiopia, Great Britain, and the United States, 1941–1974* (Lawrenceville, NJ: Red Sea, 1995), 21.

6. Wm. Roger Louis, *Imperialism at Bay* (Oxford: Oxford University Press, 1977), 7.

7. Marcus, *Politics,* 39.

8. Negussay, 176–77.

9. Ethiopia's foreign policy goals included (1) Ethiopian ownership over the railway to Djibouti; (2) free and unfettered access to the sea; (3) recovery of Eritrea; (4) war reparation from Italy; (5) military assistance to develop a small modern army; and (6) U.S. investments in development projects; John H. Spencer, *Ethiopia at Bay: A Personal Account of the Haile Selassie Year* (Hollywood, CA: Tsehai, 2006), 159; Negussay, 174–75.

10. IEG Ministry of P.T.&T., *Ethiopian Stamp Catalogue,* n.d.

11. Negussay, 177.

12. Negussay, 178; *St. Petersburg Times,* Sept. 7, 1945.

13. David McCullough, *Truman* (New York: Simon & Schuster, 1992), 731.

14. *Oklahoma State University in Ethiopia: Terminal Report 1952–1968* (Stillwater: OSU Press, 1969), 4–5; Jerry L. Gill, *A History of International Programs at Oklahoma State University* (Stillwater: OSU Press, 1991), 7–9.

15. Shinn, 45.

16. Foreign Relations of the U.S. (hereafter FRUS) 1952–1954, vol. 11, Africa and S. Asia, Part 1 (Washington, DC: U.S. Government Printing Office, 1983); Ambassador J. Rives Childs, telegram, Amb J. Rives Childs to State, January 30, 1952, 418.

CHAPTER 5

1. Jeffrey A. Lefebvre, *Arms for the Horn: U.S. Security Policy in Ethiopia and Somalia, 1953–1991* (Pittsburg: University of Pittsburg Press, 1992), 65; John R. Rasmuson, *History of Kagnew Station and American Forces in Eritrea* (Asmara: Il Poligrafico, 1973), 39.

2. John H. Spencer, *Ethiopia, the Horn of Africa, and U.S. Policy* (Cambridge, MA: Institute for Foreign Policy Analysis, 1977), 23.

3. Lefebvre, 65.

4. David Kahn, *The Code Breakers* (New York: Simon & Schuster, 1996), 508.

5. FRUS 1952–1954, vol. 11, Africa and S. Asia, Part 1, Meeting of Ambassador Childs and Duncan Cumming, Chief Administrator of Eritrea, 420; Shinn, 31. By the end of 1948, Ethiopia gave assurances to the United States concerning use of the communications facilities outside Asmara.

6. Spencer, *Ethiopia, the Horn,* 22.

7. S.L.A. Marshall, *Pork Chop Hill* (New York: Berkley, 2000).

8. Marcus, *Politics,* 78, 85–86; Daniel Kendie, *The Five Dimensions of the Eritrean Conflict, 1941–2004: Deciphering the Political Puzzle* (Gaithersburg, MD: Signature, 2005), 94–107.

9. Wm. Roger Louis, *The British Empire in the Middle East, 1945–1951* (Oxford: Clarendon Press, 1984), 290; Shumet Sishagne, *Unionists & Separatists: The Vagaries of Ethio-Eritrean relations, 1941–1991* (Hollywood, CA: Tsehai, 2007), 51–90.

10. Defence Committee DO (48), 14th Meeting, Top Secret, July 30, 1948, CAB 131/5. Quoted in Louis, *The British Empire in the Middle East, 1945–1951,* 294; Negussay Ayele, *In Search of the DNA of the Ethiopia-Eritrea Problem* (San Diego, CA: MediaETHIOPIA, 2003), 31–35.

11. Haggai Erlich, *Ethiopia and the Challenge of Independence* (Boulder, CO: Lynne Rienner, 1986), 212.

12. Marcus, *Politics,* 77.

13. FRUS, 1952–1954, vol. 11, Africa and S. Asia, Part 1, Sec of State to Embassy in Ethiopia, Mar 20, 1952, 419–20.

14. Lefebvre, 56.

15. FRUS, 1952–1954, vol. 11, Africa and S. Asia, Part 1, Secretary of State to Embassy in Ethiopia, Mar 20, 1952, 419–20.

16. Marcus, *Politics,* 89–90.

17. Shinn, 32.

18. Lefebvre, 72; FRUS, 1952–1954, 11: 419–20.

19. Dick Lilienthal, e-mail message to author, January 21, 2004. Lilienthal was stationed at Kagnew in 1952–1953.

20. Spencer, *At Bay,* 277.

21. Spencer, *At Bay,* 268.

22. Marcus, *Politics,* 89–90; Spencer, *At Bay,* 263, 270–77.

23. John Foster Dulles to Pres, memo, October 9, 1953, Box 860, Office File, EL.

24. Spencer, *At Bay,* 268.

25. John Foster Dulles to Pres, memorandum, October 9, 1953, Box 860, Office File, EL.

26. FRUS, 1952–1954, vol. 11, Africa and S. Asia, Part 1, Editorial Note, October 14, 1953, 451.

27. Haile Selassie, letter to Eisenhower, February 26, 1954, Ann Whitman File, Int'l Series, Box 9, "Ethiopia (1)," EL.

28. Spencer, *At Bay,* 269.

29. Patrick McGeehan, "A Push to Bring the S.S. *United States* Back Home," *New York Times,* January 11, 2010, http://cityroom.blogs.nytimes.com.

30. Spencer, *At Bay,* 269.

31. Peter Kihss, "Ethiopia's Emperor Lands here amid Noisy Welcome," *New York Times,* May 26, 1954, 1.

32. Richard Pankhurst, "Shakespeare in Ethiopia," *Research in African Literatures* 17 (2) (Summer 1986): 169–96.

33. Spencer, *At Bay,* 269.

CHAPTER 6

1. For state visit arrival ceremonies, see http://en.wikipedia.org/wiki/State_Arrival_Ceremony.

2. Ball to Amembassy AA, airgram, April 30, 1963, National Security Files, Box 69A, Ethiopia, Haile Selassie Visit, 10/63, John F. Kennedy Presidential Library, Boston, MA (hereafter JFKL). Ball lays out the ground rules for state visits to the United States.

3. "It Took 10 Years: U.S. Hails Selassie," *Christian Science Monitor,* May 26, 1954, 6.

4. "Selassie Endorses Collective Security," *Christian Science Monitor,* May 27, 1954, 10.

5. Robert S. Bird, "City Greets Haile Selassie on First Visit," *New York Herald Tribune,* May 26, 1954, 1.

6. Spencer, *At Bay,* 133.

7. "Lion," *New Yorker,* June 5, 1954, 30–31.

8. "Selassie in Washington, May Lease U.S. a Base," *New York Herald Tribune,* May 27, 1954, 3.

9. "Lion," *New Yorker,* June 5, 1954, 30–31.

10. "Selassie in Washington, May Lease U.S. a Base," *New York Herald Tribune,* May 27, 1954, 3.

11. Robert S. Bird, "Haile Selassie to Arrive Tuesday: First U.S. Visit," *New York Herald Tribune,* May 22, 1954, 5.

12. James L. Hicks, "Haile Here," *The Afro-American,* June 5, 1954, 8.

13. "President Greets Ruler of Ethiopia," *New York Times,* May 27, 1954, 24.

14. The American Presidency Project, Dwight D. Eisenhower, XXXIV President of the United States, 1953–1961, 124. Toasts of the President and Emperor Haile Selassie of Ethiopia, May 26, 1954.

15. Evelyn Peyton Gordon, "The White House was Pruned and Polished," *Washington News,* May 27, 1954; Bob Colacello, "The White House Dinner Theater," *Vanity Fair,* June 2010, 162–78.

16. Editorial, "Lion of Judah," *Washington Post,* May 28, 1954, 16.

17. Joseph Jasper, "2,500 Lunch with Haile," *The Afro-American,* June 5, 1954, 1.

18. "Selassie Seeking $100,000,000 Loan," *New York Times,* May 28, 1954, 5.

19. James L. Hicks, "Haile Selassie Reminds United States Congress of Its Place in Sun," *The Afro-American,* June 5, 1954, 2.

20. William S. White, "Selassie Asks Unity to Balk Aggression," *New York Times,* May 29, 1954, 1.

21. "U.S. Hears Selassie," *Christian Science Monitor,* May 28, 1954, 5.

22. "Text of Haile Selassie's Address to U.S. Congress," *New York Times,* May 29, 1954, 4.

23. James L. Hicks, "People of African Origin Helped U.S.," *The Afro-American,* June 5, 1954, 1.

24. FRUS, 1952–1954, vol. 11, Africa and S. Asia, Part 1, Memorandum of Conversation, by the Director, Foreign Operations Administration (Stassen), May 29, 1954, 454–55.

25. FRUS, 1952–1954, vol. 11, Africa and S. Asia, Part 1, 455.

26. The contents of the memo that Haile Selassie left with Eisenhower are contained in FRUS, 1952–1954, vol. 11, Africa and S. Asia, Part 1, Memorandum of Conversation, by the Officer in Charge, North African Affairs (Wellons), June 29, 1954, 456–58.

27. Spencer, *At Bay,* 24.

28. Spencer, *At Bay,* 269–70.

29. "Ethiopia's Haile Selassie Visits Princeton Campus," *The Daily Princetonian,* May 31, 1954, 1.

30. "Selassie Returns for 5 Days in City," *New York Times,* May 30, 1954, 34.

31. "Selassie Keeps Ten-Year Date with Late President," *The Afro-American,* June 12, 1954, 8.

32. Murray Schumach, "Selassie Tours Harlem amid Cheers," *New York Times,* May 31, 1954, 1.

33. David M. Manshel, e-mail message to author, October 13, 2009.

34. Murray Schumach, "Selassie at Ballpark Gets Diplomats Upset," *New York Times,* June 1, 1954, 1.

35. John F. Simmons, Chief of Protocol, to Gov. Adams, memorandum, May 14, 1954, Central Files Official Files, OF 177, Box 860, EL.

CHAPTER 7

1. Joan McPartlin, "Boston Greets Selassie," *Boston Daily Globe*, June 3, 1954, 1.

2. Spencer, *At Bay*, 270.

3. "Haile Selassie Crams 4 Visits into Hub Stop," *Boston Daily Globe*, June 4, 1954, 1.

4. James L. Hicks, "Haile Visits Boston in Route to Canada," *The Afro-American*, June 12, 1954, 9.

5. "Desk-Thumping Acclamation for Ethiopian King in House," *Ottawa Citizen*, June 4, 1954, 1; *Toronto Globe and Mail*, June 4, 1954, 9.

6. Pierre Vigeant, "L'empereur d'Ethiopie dans la capital Canadienne," *La Devoir*, Montréal, June 5, 1954, 1.

7. Spencer, *At Bay*, 270.

8. Frank Swanson, "Selassie Pays Tribute to Archibald, Patten," *Ottawa Citizen*, June 4, 1954, 12.

9. "Sidelights on the Emperor's Visit," *Ottawa Citizen*, June 4, 1954, 12.

10. See, Armour Landry, "Réception en l'honneur d' Hailé Sélassié (Empereur d'Éthiopie) à l'hôtel Windsor de Montréal," June 4, 1954.

11. "Les Canadiens font une oeuvre utile en Ethiopia," *La Devoir* (Montreal), June 5, 1954, 1.

12. Charles J. Wartman, "School Decision Will Win World Praise—Selassie," *The Afro-American*, June 19, 1954, 2.

13. Mather Eakes, "Terminal Building Getting New Look," *Daily Oklahoman*, June 20, 1954, 12A.

14. "Greet Emperor Haile Selassie Here Tonight," Chicago *Daily Tribune*, June 7, 1954, 12; "25,000 Watch Selassie Trip from Airport," *Chicago Tribune*, June 8, 1954, 1.

15. "Selassie Spry as He Ends Whirlwind Visit," *Chicago Tribune*, June 9, 1954, 6.

16. "Selassie Admires Silos in Farm Country Trip," *Daytona Beach Morning Journal*, June 10, 1954, 20.

17. "Emperor Selassie Whirls through Crowded Schedule," *Austin Daily Herald*, June 9, 1954, 1; Editorial, "Pot Pourri," *Austin Daily Herald*, June 9, 1954, 4.

18. Ed Blackwell, "American Farm Methods Impress Haile Selassie," *The Afro-American*, June 26, 1954, 8.

19. Editorial, "Selassie has Proved Loyal and Courageous," *The Spokesman-Review*, June 6, 1954, 4.

20. "Haile Selassie to Visit Coulee Dam Thursday," *Spokane Daily Chronicle*, June 7, 1954, 8; "Haile Selassie of Spokane to Greet Emperor Selassie," *The Spokesman-Review*, June 9, 1954, 20; Editorial, "A Distinguished Guest is Here," *Spokane Daily Chronicle*, June 10, 1954, 4.

21. AP, "Emperor Says Ethiopia has Stymied Reds," *Walla Walla Union-Bulletin*, June 12, 1954, 1.

22. Editorial, "California Welcomes Emperor as Symbol of Fight for Freedom," *Oakland Tribune*, June 14, 1954, 38.

23. "Bay Area Gives Haile Selassie Warm Welcome," *Oakland Tribune*, June 14, 1954, 1.

24. Edd Johnson, "S. F. Gives Haile Selassie a Royal—and Busy Day," *San Francisco Chronicle,* June 15, 1954, 1; "Selassie Ends Whirlwind Bay Tour, Heads for L.A.," *Oakland Tribune,* June 15, 1954, 2.

25. FRUS, 1952–1954, Memorandum of Conversation, by the Officer in Charge, North African Affairs (Wellons), June 30, 1954. Subject: Ethiopian Proposals for Further Discussions with the United States Government, 465.

26. Spencer, *At Bay,* 270.

27. "Selassie Arrives with Entourage," *Los Angeles Times,* June 16, 1954, 1.

28. Herbert M. and Della Hanson, *For God and Emperor* (Nampa, ID: Pacific Press Publishing Assoc., 1958), 183.

29. AP, "Movie Fan Selassie Visits Filmland Set, Meets Stars," *Pacific Stars and Stripes,* June 21, 1954, 9. The emperor had a collection of 160 different medals that he wore on various occasions; 101 were from foreign governments and 22 were of his own design. Berihun Kebede, *Ye Asie Haile Selassie Tarik* [*Haile Selassie and His Time* (Amharic)] (Addis Ababa: Artistic Publishing, 2000), 879–1081.

30. Kenneth C. Field, "Los Angeles 'Captured' by Haile Selassie," *Washington Afro-American,* June 22, 1954, 7.

31. "Haile Selassie Sees L.A. Area, Likes It," *Los Angeles Times,* June 18, 1954, 1.

32. Don Brackenbury, "L.B. Tour Impresses Emperor," *Long Beach Independent,* June 18, 1954, 1.

33. Woodson Harris, Stillwater Airport, telephone interview with author, March 2, 2006.

34. Troy Gordon, "Selassie Thanks A&M for Aid, Receives Indian War Bonnets, Other Mementos," *Tulsa Daily World,* June 19, 1954, 1. Blue Eagle presented war bonnets, a piece of pottery with native cornmeal inside, representing the sustenance of life, and a branch of evergreen representing eternal life, to the emperor, Prince Sahle, and Princess Seble. He named Sahle "Thunder Eagle" and gave the name "Princess Morning Star" to Seble. Later in the evening, Blue Eagle received a gold medal commemorating the Emperor's visit. Blue Eagle founded the art department at Bacone College and served as its head from 1935 to 1938. His paintings are acclaimed for the use of natural colors and exquisite detailing. Blue Eagle traveled extensively and did much to popularize Native American painting. "Oklahoma Indian Art," label copy, Thomas Gilcrease Museum, Tulsa, Oklahoma.

35. "Emperor Will Land in Stillwater this Afternoon," *The Daily Oklahoman,* June 18, 1954, 25.

36. Roy P. Stewart, "Ethiopia Monarch Lauds State, A&M," *The Daily Oklahoman,* June 19, 1954, 1.

37. Gordon, "Selassie Thanks A&M." Chaplin Bills, A&M college architect, designed the Alemaya campus that included five college structures connected by covered passages and 10 staff houses built of native limestone found near the college site.

38. Abe Hesser, Stillwater, OK, interview with author, February 17, 1999.

39. Bill Harmon, "Prince Stows 3 Hot Dogs, Plus Sundaes," *The Daily Oklahoman,* June 20, 1954, 1.

40. Banquet Invitation List, Presidents' Papers Box 48, folder 20 (Coll. No. 70-005), OSU Library, Stillwater, OK.

41. "Emperor Haile Selassie Greeted by City," *Stillwater Daily News-Press,* June 18, 1954, 1.

42.   William S. Abbott, Claremore, OK, telephone interview with author, February 25, 1999.

43.   "Hundreds are Disappointed, Miss Glimpse of Emperor," *Stillwater Daily News-Press*, June 20, 1954, 1.

44.   Gordon, "Selassie Thanks A&M."

45.   Roger V. Devlin, "The Rambler," *Tulsa Tribune*, June 19, 1954, 11.

46.   William S. Abbott to Vesta Etchison, memorandum, June 10, 1954, Presidents' Papers Box 48, folder 20 (Coll. No. 70-005), OSU Library, Stillwater, OK.

47.   Gordon, "Selassie Thanks A&M."

48.   "Oklahoma A&M Sees an Emperor Stern and Dignified," *The Daily Oklahoman*, 20 June 1954, 17; Gordon, "Emperor Leaves Pleasant Memories with Sooners Who Shook Royal Hand," *Tulsa Daily World*, 20 June 1954, 1; Devlin, "The Rambler."

49.   "Haile Selassie is a Master of Diplomacy," *The Daily Oklahoman*, June 20, 1954, 17.

50.   "Emperor Will Land in Stillwater this Afternoon."

51.   William S. Abbott, Claremore, OK, telephone interview with author, February 25,1999; Bill Harmon, "Selassie Calls for a Doctor," *The Daily Oklahoman*, June 22, 1954, 3.

52.   "City is Ready for Visit of Emperor," *Stillwater Daily News-Press*, June 17, 1954, 1.

53.   "State's Going 'Formal' for Selassie Visit," *Tulsa Daily-World*, June 18, 1954, 1; "Protocol Will Prevail during Emperor's Stay," *The O'Collegian*, June 15, 1954, 1; Devlin, "The Rambler."

54.   UP, "Haile Selassie is in Mexico," *Galveston News*, June 20, 1954, 8.

55.   *New York Times*, June 20, 1954, 32.

56.   "El Senor Presidente Recibira hoy al Emperador de Etiopia," *Excelsior*, Mexico, D.F., June 19, 1954, 1; Pedro Gringoire, "Haile Selassie y la Nueva Etiopia," *Excelsior*, June 20, 1954, 6A; Raul Horta, "El Emperador de Etiopia es Huesped de Honor de Mexico," *Excelsior*, June 21, 1954, 1.

57.   Pablo Sanchez, "El emperador de Etiopia Rindio Homenaje a los Heroes de Mexico," *Excelsior*, June 21, 1954, 1.

58.   "Homenaje de Mexico a S.M. Haile Selassie," *Excelsior*, June 22, 1954, 1; *Excelsior*, June 23, 1954, 1.

59.   Daniel Dickinson, "The Last of the Ethiopian Emperors," *BBC News*, May 13, 2005, 2.

60.   "Small of Stature," *New Orleans Times Picayune*, June 25, 1954, 9.

61.   Charles Nutter, "New Orleans Warmly Greets Haile Selassie," *The Christian Science Monitor*, June 28, 1954, 1.

62.   UP, "Haile Selassie Assailed by Rep. Burdick," *Los Angeles Times*, June 24, 1954.

63.   Podine Schoenberger, "Crowd at Airport, Parade Welcome Haile Selassie," *New Orleans Times Picayune*, June 26, 1954, 9.

64.   "New Orleans Gives Haile Key to City," *The Afro-American*, July 3, 1954, 14.

65.   Doris Anderson, Stillwater, OK, interview with author, March 30, 2009.

66.   Nutter, "New Orleans Warmly Greets."

67.   "Selassie Hails Magnificent Demonstration Here," *The Bayonet*, July 1, 1954, 3.

68.   "Selassie Is Here After Tour," *New York Times*, June 27, 1954, 30.

69. "Ruler in Hospital Here," *New York Times*, June 29, 1954, 29.

70. "Tiger Cub and Baby Jaguars Amuse Citizens and Emperor at Bronx Zoo," *New York Times*, July 3, 1954, 4.

71. FRUS, 1952–1954, Memo of Conversation, by the Director, Office of African Affairs (Utter), July, 2 1954; Subject: Ethiopian Requests for Aid, 470–71.

72. "Planetarium Display put on for Selassie," *New York Times*, July 8, 1954, 19.

73. FRUS, 1952–1954, Memorandum of Conversation, by John Root, Office of African Affairs, Subject: Ethiopian Proposals for Further Discussions with the United States Government, July 7, 1954, 472–73.

74. "Police Host to Royalty," *New York Times*, July 9, 1954, 19.

75. "Selassie Back in New York," *Washington Afro-American*, July 13, 1954, 20.

76. AP, "Royal Visit," *The New London, CT, Evening Day*, July 12, 1954, 3.

77. "Regretful Selassie Leaves U.S. for Home," *New York Times*, July 13, 1954, 13.

78. Editorial, "Lion of Judah," *New York Times*, July 13, 1954, 22.

79. Rabbi Harry J. Stern, "At a Dinner with the Emperor of Ethiopia," *Canadian Jewish Chronicle*, July 9, 1954, 7.

80. UP, "Selassie Praises U.S. Hospitality," *New York Herald Tribune*, August 8, 1954.

81. Martin Haars, "Eine blonde Locke für den Kaiser," Kaiser Haile Selassie I. in Hamburg (12.–14.11.1954), Unpublished paper, University of Hamburg, June 25, 2009.

82. FRUS, 1955–1957, vol. 18, Africa, Letter from Dep. Under Sec. of State for Pol. Affairs (Murphy) to Asst. Sec. of Defense (Gray), July 5, 1956, 327–29.

83. FRUS, 1955–1957, vol. 18, Africa, NSC 304th meeting, November 15, 1956, 332.

84. FRUS, 1955–1957, vol. 18, Africa, Aide-Memoire from IEG to Embassy in Ethiopia, March 12, 1957, 339–43. Vice President Nixon visited Haile Selassie on March 12, 1957, 340.

85. Lefebvre, 105.

86. Earl H. Voss, "U.S. Seems Unruffled by Red Aid to Ethiopia," *Washington Star*, July 1, 1959, 1.

87. FRUS, 1952–1954, vol. 11, Africa and S. Asia, Part 1, Editorial Note, 46.

88. FRUS, 1958–1960, vol. 14, Africa, memorandum of Conference with Pres. Eisenhower, NY, Sep 27, 1960, 195.

89. Quoted in Richard Reeves, "How Eisenhower Really Felt about War," *Tulsa World*, June 19, 2004, A21.

90. The Farewell Speech of President Dwight D. Eisenhower, January 17, 1961.

91. Thomas J. Hamilton, "Appeal to the World," *New York Times*, September 23, 1960, 1; FRUS, 1958–1960, vol. 14, Africa, Editorial Note, July 23, 1960, 185–86.

CHAPTER 8

1. FRUS, 1958–1960, vol. 14, Africa, 45. Discussion at the 397th meeting of the National Security Council, memorandum, February 26, 1959, 181–85.

2. Ibid.

3. Ibid.

4. General Andrew J. Goodpaster, Staff Secretary and Defense Liaison Officer to President Oral History Interview OH-477, 10, EL; Getachew Metaferia, *Ethiopia*

and the United States: History, Diplomacy, and Analysis (New York: Algora, 2009), 45–52.

5. Dennis FitzGerald, Oral History Interview OH-387, 15, EL; see Eugene Burdick and William J. Lederer, *The Ugly American* (New York: W. W. Norton, 1999); Getachew Metaferia, 53–58.

6. See generally, Robert A. Dahl, *Who Governs?: Democracy and Power in the American City* (New Haven, CT: Yale University Press, 1961), 1–10.

7. Joseph S. Nye Jr., *Understanding International Conflicts* (New York: Pearson/Longman, 2005), 59–62.

8. Joseph S. Nye Jr., *Soft Power: The Means to Success in World Politics* (New York: Public Affairs, 2004), 5–8.

9. G. John Ikenberry, *After Victory: Institutions, Strategic Restraint, and the Rebuilding of Order after Major Wars* (Princeton, NJ: Princeton University Press, 2000), 163–214.

10. Theodore M. Vestal, "Public Diplomacy in the U.S. Supreme Court: The Warren Years—Part 1," *Journal of Supreme Court History* 33, no. 3 (2008): 371–93; "Public Diplomacy in the U.S. Supreme Court: The Warren Years—Part 2," *Journal of Supreme Court History* 34, no. 1 (2009): 98–124.

11. X (George F. Kennan), "The Sources of Soviet Conduct," *Foreign Affairs* 25, no. 4 (July 1947), 566–82.

12. *National Geographic,* April 1965, 576–77.

CHAPTER 9

1. FRUS 1955–1957, vol. 18, Africa, 120; Embassy in Ethiopia to the Department of State, telegram, April 18, 1957, 353–54.

2. Shinn, 34.

3. Lefebvre, 103.

4. Lefebvre, 94–95.

5. See generally, Abdi Sheik Abdi, *Divine Madness: Mohammed Abdulle Hassan* (London: Zed Books, 1993).

6. Wm. Roger Louis, *The British Empire in the Middle East, 1945–1951* (Oxford: Clarendon Press, 1984), 274–75.

7. Lefebvre, 79.

8. Louis, 281–82.

9. "Somaliland Protectorate and the Horn of Africa," Cabinet memorandum by Mr. Lennox-Boyd advocating the creation of a Greater Somalia, CP (56) 180, July 25, 1956, CAB 129/82.

10. Robert D. Kaplan, *Surrender or Starve, Travels in Ethiopia, Sudan, Somalia, and Eritrea* (New York: Vintage Books, 2003), 3–47.

11. Richard Greenfield, *Ethiopia: A New Political* History (London, Pall Mall, 1965), 397–98.

12. Shinn, 36.

13. Lefebvre, 123.

14. Richards cable to SecState, December 17, 1960, Ann Whitman File, Int'l Series, Box 9, "Ethiopia (1)," EL.

15. Tirfe Mammo, *The Paradox of Africa's Poverty: The Role of Indigenous Knowledge* (Trenton, NJ: Red Sea Press, 1999), 100.

16. FRUS, 1961–1963, vol. 21, Africa, 271. Special National Intelligence Estimate, January 24, 1961, 425–28.

17. Theodore Roosevelt, *Life Histories of African Game Animals,* vol. 1 (New York: Scribners, 1914), 173.

CHAPTER 10

1. Members of the official party, limited to 10 by U.S. protocol, in addition to HIM included the following: Princess Hirut (Ruth) Desta, granddaughter of the emperor; Ras Imru Haile Selassie, cousin of the emperor; Ketema Yifru, acting Minister for Foreign Affairs; Yilma Deressa, minister of finance; Teferra-Work Kidane-Wold, minister of the imperial court; Dr. Menassie Haile, chief of the political section of HIM's private cabinet; Major General Wolde-Selassie Bereka; Brigadier General Assefa Demissi; Berhanu Dinke, ambassador of Ethiopia to the United States; and Yohannes Kidane-Mariam, private secretary to HIM.

2. Nan Robertson, "Kennedy Greets Selassie as Man History Will Recall," *New York Times,* October 2, 1963, 1; see also David Brinkley, "A State Visit," in *Brinkley's Beat* (New York: Random House, 2003).

3. Sterling Seagrave, "Ethiopian Emperor Haile Selassie Greeted by President at Start of Visit," *Washington Post,* October 2, 1963, A4.

4. Dorothy McCardle, "Leopard Coat is Gift to First Lady," *Washington Post,* October 2, 1963, C3.

5. Benjamin Reed to McGeorge Bundy, memorandum, October 2, 1963, National Security Files Ethiopia, General, 8/63–11/63, JFKL.

6. Betty Beale, *Power at Play* (Washington, DC: Regnery Gateway, 1993), 80.

7. Dorothy McCardle, "Town Looks up to Visiting Giant," *Washington Post,* October 2, 1963, C1. Jacqueline Kennedy and party while in Greece used the yacht *Christina* offered by Aristotle Onassis.

8. Arthur M. Schlesinger Jr., *A Thousand Days: JFK in the White House* (Boston: Houghton Mifflin, 1965), 557.

9. Winzola McLendon, "Selassie Places Solid Silver Wreath Made from Coins at Lincoln Shrine," *Washington Post,* October 3, 1963, 1.

10. "Selassie, Kennedy Join Views on Free Africans," *Washington Post,* October 3, 1963, A5.

11. Ibid.

12. *Washington Post,* October 3, 1963, A20.

13. Arch Parsons, "Selassie Denied Full U.S. Aid in Somali Dispute," *Washington Post,* October 4, 1963, A8.

14. Theodore M. Vestal, "Emperor Haile Selassie's First State Visit to the United States in 1954: The Oklahoma Interlude," *International Journal of Ethiopian Studies* 1 (2003), 133–52.

15. Rusk to Amembassy AA, telegram, August 23, 1961, National Security Files, Box 69, Ethiopia General 2/61–2/62, JFKL.

16. Richards to Sec of State, telegram, January 19, 1962, JFK National Security Files, Box 69, Ethiopia General 2/61–2/62, JFKL.

17. Schlesinger, 509.

18. Richard Reeves, *President Kennedy: Profile of Power* (New York: Simon & Schuster, 1994), 441.

19. Reeves, *Kennedy,* 455.

20. JFK President's Office Files, Box 116, Ethiopia, General, 1961, JFKL.

21. "Emperor Selassie Greets Peace Corps," *New York Times,* September 22, 1962, 8.

22. Theodore M. Vestal, "Consequences of the British Occupation of Ethiopia during World War II," *Horn of Africa* 18 (2000), 60–69.

23. UPI, "Selassie's Gift Yacht Runs into Heavy Seas of Protest in Congress," *Philadelphia Inquirer,* August 27, 1962.

24. Haile Selassie to JFK, cable, October 30, 1962, JFK President's Office Files, Box 116, Ethiopia, General, 1961, JFKL.

25. Vance to Dept State, airgram, Country Team Analysis of Situation and Recommendations on Possible U.S. Actions to Speed Reforms in Ethiopia, December 19, 1962, JFK President's Office Files, Box 116, Ethiopia, General, 1961, JFKL.

26. Ball to Amembassy AA, airgram, April 30, 1963, National Security Files, Box 69A, Ethiopia, Haile Selassie Visit, 10/63, JFKL.

27. Korry to JKF, June 28, 1963, National Security Files, Box 69, Ethiopia, General, 6/63–7/63, JFKL.

28. Korry to Sec State, telegram, July 25, 1963, National Security Files, Box 69, Ethiopia, General, 6/63–7/63, JFKL.

29. Reeves, *Kennedy,* 37–8.

30. Korry to Sec State, telegram, August 21, 1963, National Security Files, Box 69, Ethiopia, General, 8/63–11/63, JFKL.

31. Hedrick Smith, "Selassie Is Still Unconvinced by U.S. Reason for Somali Aid," *New York Times,* October 4, 1963, 3.

32. "Selassie Strolls amid Ticker Tape," *New York Times,* October 5, 1963, 3. Two-time ticker-tape parade recipients, in addition to New York sports teams, include Eisenhower, de Gaulle, aviators Amelia Earhart and Wiley Post, Astronaut John Glenn, Admiral Richard Byrd, and golfer Bobby Jones.

33. Ibid.

34. Sam Pope Brewer, "Selassie at UN, Recalls 1936 Plea to League," *New York Times,* October 5, 1963, 1; Darius S. Jhabvala, "Once More He Prods the Conscience of the World," *New York Herald Tribune,* October 5, 1963, 1; Louis B. Fleming, "Selassie Addresses UN Assembly, Praises Kennedy's Racial Policies," *Washington Post,* October 5, 1963, A9.

35. "End Colonialism, Selassie Urges," *New York Times,* October 7, 1963, 3.

36. "Selassie Cancels Trip to Florida," *New York Times,* October 6, 1963, 81.

37. Russell Elman, "Ashbury Visited by Lion of Judah," *Ottawa Citizen,* October 9, 1963, 12.

38. Benjamin Reed to McGeorge Bundy, memorandum, October 2, 1963, National Security Files, Box 69, Ethiopia, General, 6/63–7/63, JFKL.

39. Korry to JKF, June 28, 1963, National Security Files, Box 69, Ethiopia, General, 6/63–7/63, JFKL.

40. Shinn, 39; Lefebvre, 112–13, citing the McNamara-Merid memo in 1962 and subsequent agreement signed in 1963.

41. Dr. Minassie Haile, telephone interview with author, February 15, 2000.

42. Korry to Sec State, telegram, December 11, 1963, National Security Files, Box 69, Ethiopia, General, 8/63–11/63, JFKL.

CHAPTER 11

1. "Obituary, Rose Fitzgerald Kennedy," *The Boston Globe,* January 23, 1995.

2. Tom Wicker, "A Hero's Burial," *New York Times,* November 26, 1963, 1.

3. Julius Duscha, "Kings, Presidents and Premiers Here," *Washington Post,* November 25, 1963, 1.

4. "Emperor Says Tragic Death Loss to Entire World," *Voice of Ethiopia,* November 25, 1963, 1.

5. *Voice of Ethiopia,* November 26, 1963, 1.

6. Laurence Barrett, "Face to Face, Johnson and World Leaders," *New York Herald Tribune,* November 26, 1963, 6.

7. Scott Stossel, *Sarge: The Life and Times of Sargent Shriver* (Washington, DC: Smithsonian Books, 2004), 321.

8. Korry to Warren, telegram, July 4, 1963, Box 116, Luncheon for Emperor of Ethiopia; Address Haile Selassie I University, Addis Ababa, Ethiopia, July 29, 1963, Box 811, Earl Warren Papers, Manuscript Division, Library of Congress, Washington, DC.

9. *John Fitzgerald Kennedy. Eulogies to the Late President Delivered in the Rotunda of the United States Capitol, November 24, 1963 by Mike Mansfield, Earl Warren, and John W. McCormack,* United States Congress, Senate, U.S. Government Printing Office: Washington, DC, 1963.

10. Korry to SecState, telegram, Nov 30, 1963, National Security Files, Box 69, Ethiopia, General, 8/63–11/63, JFKL.

11. Anthony Lewis, "Mrs. Kennedy Maintains a Stoic Dignity throughout Final Hours of Public Grief," *New York Times,* November 26, 1963, 5; *Voice of Ethiopia,* November 27, 1963, 1.

12. Memorandum of conversation, Dept. of State, November 26, 1963, NSF Country File, Africa, Ethiopia, vol. 1, 11/63–2/65, Box 88, Lyndon Baines Johnson Library, Austin, TX (hereafter LBJL).

13. "World Leaders Confer with Johnson after Paying Tribute to Kennedy at the Grave," *New York Times,* November 26, 1963, 6.

14. Max Frankel, "Johnson Meets with Visitors," *New York Times,* November 26, 1963, 1.

15. *Voice of Ethiopia,* November 27, 1963, 1.

16. *Voice of Ethiopia,* November 28, 1963, 1.

17. Memorandum of conversation, Dept. of State, November 26, 1963, NSF Country File, Africa, Ethiopia, vol. 1, 11/63–2/65, Box 88, LBJL.

18. Johnson to Haile Selassie, June 18, 1964, NSF Country File, Africa, Ethiopia, vol. 1, 11/63–2/65, Box 88, LBJL.

CHAPTER 12

1. Langston Hughes, *The Collected Poems of Langston Hughes,* edited by Arnold Rampersad with David Roessel, Associate Editor, © 1994 by the Estate of Langston Hughes. Used by permission of Alfred A. Knopf, a division of Random House, Inc.

2. Lady Bird Johnson, *A White House Diary [by] Lady Bird Johnson* (New York: Holt, Rinehart and Winston, 1970), 47, 110–11.

3. Ibid.

4. Betty Boyd Caroli, *First Ladies* (Oxford: Oxford University Press, 1995), 230.

5. Lady Bird Johnson, *A White House Diary*, 47, 110–11.

6. Charles S. Gillispie, Richmond, VA, telephone interview with author, July 16, 2003.

7. Dorothy McCardle, "LBJ Brings History Up to Date," *Washington Post*, February 15, 1967, C1. LBJ's use of the phrase "our native mountains" might have been hyperbole coming from a native of the Hill Country of Texas.

8. James R. Jones to W. Marvin Watson, memorandum, February 14, 1967, NSF Country File, Africa, General, vol. 5, 6/66–1/69, Box 77, LBJL.

9. Betty Beale, *Power at Play: A Memoir of Parties, Politicians and the Presidents in My Bedroom* (Houston: Regency, 1993), 174.

10. "Ethiopia's Needs Told by Selassie," *Washington Post*, February 15, 1965, A2.

11. Dr. Minassie Haile, telephone interview with author, February 15, 2000.

12. Vaughn Davis Bornet, *The Presidency of Lyndon B. Johnson* (Lawrence: University of Kansas Press, 1984), 181.

13. Joseph Palmer II, oral history, AC 78–14 (Asst. Sec. for Af. Affairs, 1966–1969), 3, LBJL.

14. Palmer, 33.

15. Palmer, 34.

16. Jack Valenti to Amb. Tashoma Haile-Mariam, August, 31, 1965, NSF Country File, Africa, General, vol. 3, 5/65–3/66, Box 76, LBJL.

17. Shinn, 46.

18. "Text of Johnson's Address to AP on Nuclear Cuts and U.S. Foreign Policy," *New York Times*, April 21, 1964, 14.

19. Remarks to a Joint Session of the Congress, Announcing the passage of and his signing the Voting Rights Act of 1965, March 15, 1965, *Public Papers of the Presidents of the United States: Lyndon B. Johnson, 1965* vol. I, entry 107: 281–287. Washington, DC: Government Printing Office, 1966.

20. Letters from the President to African Leaders (39 in all), enclosing "The American Promise": Voting Rights Act, May 8, 1965, NSF Country File, Africa, General, Box 77, LBJL.

21. *Public Papers of the Presidents of the United States: Lyndon B. Johnson, 1965*, vol. 2, entry 301: 635–640. Washington, DC: Government Printing Office, 1966.

22. David Wise and Thomas B. Ross, *The Invisible Government* (New York: Random House, 1965).

23. Bornet, 182.

24. Remarks by President Lyndon B. Johnson on U.S. Africa Policy at a Reception Marking the Third Anniversary of the Organization of African Unity, the White House, May 26, 1966.

25. Richard Eder, "President Terms White Supremacy in Africa Odious," *New York Times*, May 27, 1966, 1.

26. NSAM 356: Implementation of Korry Report on Development Policies and Programs in Africa, October 5, 1966; [Review of African Development Policies and Program as Directed by the President, Edward M. Korry], NSF Country File, Africa, General, Box 77, LBJL.

27. Robert J. Berg and Jennifer Seymour Whitaker, eds., *Strategies for African Development* (Berkeley: University of California Press, 1986), 266–67.

28. Bornet, 182.

29. Ibid.

30. Hamilton to W. W. Rostow, memorandum, November 29, 1966, NSF Country File, Africa, General, vol. 5, 6/66–1/69, Box 77, LBJL.

31. Harry C. McPherson Jr. to LBJ, memorandum, January 11, 1966, NSF Country File, Africa, General, vol. 3, 5/65–3/66, Box 76, LBJL.

32. Korry to SecState, telegram, December 11, 1963, NSF Country File, Africa, Ethiopia, vol. 1, 11/63–2/65, Box 88, LBJL.

33. Lefebvre, 118.

34. Shinn, 40.

35. Baffour Agyeman-Duah, *The United States and Ethiopia: Military Assistance and the Quest for Security, 1953–1993* (Lanham, MD: University Press of America, 1994), 68.

36. FRUS, 1964–1968, vol. 24, Africa, memorandum from the Assistant Secretary of Defense for International Security Affairs (McNaughton) to Secretary of Defense McNamara, SUBJECT, Visit of Emperor Haile Selassie of Ethiopia, February 4, 1967, 558–59.

37. "Johnson Hails Selassie as an Ignored Prophet," *Washington Post,* February 14, 1967, 2.

38. Editorial, "Haile Selassie," *Washington Post,* February 14, 1967, 16.

39. Editorial, "Royal Visitor from Ethiopia," *Christian Science Monitor,* February 16, 1967.

40. "Johnson and Haile Selassie Confer," *New York Times,* February 15, 1967, 2.

41. *New York Times,* February 16, 1967, 41

42. "Ethiopia's Needs Told by Selassie," *Washington Post,* February 15, 1965, A2; "Johnson Greets Selassie on Visit," *New York Times,* February 14, 1967, 2.

43. Charles S. Gillispie, Richmond, VA., telephone interview with author, July 16, 2003.

44. John Buché to Margaret K. McHugh, February 10, 1967, Box 116, "Luncheon for Emperor of Ethiopia," February 14, 1967, Earl Warren Papers, Manuscript Division, Library of Congress, Washington, DC.

45. Dorothy McCardle, "LBJ Brings History Up to Date," *Washington Post,* February 15, 1969, C1.

46. Sam Pope Brewster, "Ethiopia Willing to be Mediator," *New York Times,* February 17, 1967, 2.

47. Sylvan Fox, "Emperor, 74, and Boy, 6 1/2, Meet with a Grin and a Proper Bow," *New York Times,* February 15, 1967, 41.

48. Brewer, "Ethiopia Willing."

49. Sam Pope Brewer, "Selassie Seeking More Private Investment," *New York Times,* February 18, 1967, 37.

50. Haile Selassie to LBJ, February 18, 1967, LBJL.

51. W. W. Rostow to LBJ, Mar 9, 1967, LBJL.

52. Duah, 56.

53. Benjamin H. Read, Exec. Sec of Dept of State, to Walt W. Rostow, memorandum, April 13, 1967, LBJL.

54. "Talks with Robert Kennedy put U.S. Commitment in Spotlight," *Christian Science Monitor,* June 16, 1966, 11.

55. Benjamin Welles, "Cooperative Aid to Africa Backed," *New York Times,* May 27, 1967, 11.

56. "The Vice President's Report to the President on his Nine African Nation visit—1/12/68," NSF Country File, Africa, General, Box 77, LBJL.

57. Ibid.

58. Ibid.

59. Langston Hughes, *The Collected Poems of Langston Hughes*, eds. Arnold Rampersad and David Roessel (New York: Knopf, 1994), 551; "A Chronology of the Life of Langston Hughes," 19; "Notes to the Poems," Appendix 3, 682. A hand-written copy of the poem is in Yale University's Beinecke Rare Book and Manuscript Library. The poem was first published in *Negro Digest* (November 1966), 48. The author was present at the Liberation Day ceremony.

60. AP. "Selassie Applauded at UCLA," *Independent*, April 25, 1967, 3; John E. Lenker, "Emperor of Ethiopia Distinguished in History," *Redlands Daily Facts*, April 22, 1967, 16.

61. Wendy Belcher, "Priests Identify UCLA Library's Sacred Treasures," *UCLA Today*, April 12, 2005.

62. "Selassie in L. B., Inspects Off-shore Drilling Projects," *Independent*, April 26, 1967, 3; UPI, "Emperor of Ethiopia Likes Sunday Disneyland Visit," *Redlands Daily Facts*, April 24, 1967, 6.

63. Ryszard Kapuściński, *The Emperor: Downfall of an Autocrat* (New York: Vintage, 1983), 5.

64. "In Ottawa, Emperor Appeals for More Aid," *Montreal Gazette*, May 2, 1967, 21.

65. Henry Heald, "Selassie Praises Canada," *Winnipeg Free Press*, May 5, 1967, 1.

66. CP, "Lulu Steals Act Again," *Winnipeg Free Press*, May 4, 1967, 1.

67. Paulos Milkias, *Haile Selassie, Western Education and Political Revolution in Ethiopia* (Youngstown, NY: Cambria, 2006), 229–30.

68. Roy Kervin, "Haile Selassie: Expo's First State Visitor," *Montreal Gazette*, May 2, 1967, 21.

69. Terry Haig, "Very Private Affair Was Emperor's Lunch," *Montreal Gazette*, May 4, 1967, 18.

70. Jan Wright, "Ethiopian Folkloric Troupe," *Montreal Gazette*, May 3, 1967, 20.

71. Claude Henault, "Premiere Johnson Breaks Protocol in Welcoming Ethiopian Emperor," *Montreal Gazette*, May 4, 1967, 4.

72. "Haile Selassie Leaves Canada after Last Talk with Pearson," *Montreal Gazette*, May 5, 1967, 15.

73. FRUS, 1964–1968, vol. 24, Africa, Special, National Intelligence Estimate, "The Outlook for Internal Security in Ethiopia," April 11, 1968, 598–99.

74. See, John G. Stewart and Sam Proctor, "Report to the Vice President, Youth and Peace Corps," NSF Country File, Africa, General, vol. 5, Box 77, 6/66–1/69, The Vice President's Report to the President on his nine African nation visit, 1/12/68," LBJL.

75. Shinn, 47.

76. Robert D. Kaplan, *Surrender or Starve, Travels in Ethiopia, Sudan, Somalia, and Eritrea* (New York: Vintage, 2003), 16.

CHAPTER 13

1. *New York Times*, March 30, 1969, 14.

2. Henry Kissinger to President, memorandum, July 7, 1969, NSC: Country Files: Africa, Box 736, Nixon Presidential Library, Yorba Linda, CA (hereafter NPL).

3. "Selassie Foes Hit Chancery, 14 Arrested," *Washington Post,* July 8, 1969, 1; UPI, "Ethiopians Protest Arrival of Selassie in Washington," *New York Times,* July 8, 1969, 2.

4. William J. Robbins, "U.S. Concerned over Violence at Embassies in Washington," *New York Times,* July 9, 1969, 6.

5. UPI, "Ethiopians Protest Arrival of Selassie in Washington," *New York Times,* July 8, 1969, 2.

6. For example, Editorial, "He Made It," *The Progress-Index* (Petersburg, VA), July 10 ,1969, 4.

7. For example, *Albuquerque Journal,* July 15, 1969, A-4.

8. "Inside the News—Briefly," *The Christian Science Monitor,* May 16, 1973, 8.

9. Conrad Black, *Richard M. Nixon: A Life in Full* (New York: PublicAffairs, 2007) 277, 359–63; Rick Perlstein, *Nixonland: The Rise of a President and the Fracturing of America* (New York: Scribner, 2008), 44–49.

10. Spencer, *At Bay,* 290; LaFebvre, 77; Thomas F. Brady, "Nixon Pays Visit to Haile Selassie," *New York Times,* March 12, 1957, 10; Thomas F. Brady, "Nixon Requests Base in Ethiopia," *New York Times,* March 13, 1957, 3; FRUS, 1955–1957, vol. 28, Africa, Aide-Memoire from IEG to Embassy in Et, March 12, 1957, 339–43.

11. Dennis FitzGerald, oral history interview OH-387, 17, EL.

12. Black, 349.

13. "Nixon to See Pope Today," *New York Times,* August 1, 1966, 2; Perlstein, 62.

14. "Nixon Confers with Selassie," *New York Times,* June 13, 1967, 14.

15. Black, 497.

16. Richard Reeves, *President Nixon, Alone in the White House* (New York: Simon & Schuster, 2002), 33, 710.

17. WH Central File CO (Countries) [EX] CO 48 Ethiopia, Box 26, July 7, 1969, NPL.

18. William Borders, "Redoubtable Ethiopian Emperor," *New York Times,* July 9, 1969, 6.

19. Henry Kissinger to President, memorandum, "Purpose of Visit on 8 July 69," July 6, 1969, NSC: Country Files: Africa, Box 914, VIP Visits, NPL.

20. FRUS, 1969–1976, vol. E-5, part 1, Documents on Sub-Saharan Africa, 1969–1972, memorandum of conversation, Washington, July 8, 1969, 1–6.

21. Reeves, *Nixon,* 62.

22. The American Presidency Project, Richard Nixon, 259, Toasts of the President and Emperor Haile Selassie I of Ethiopia. July 8, 1969.

23. Early in his administration, Nixon required that the musical selections planned for state dinners be submitted to him for approval. Reeves, *Nixon,* 96.

24. April, 29 1969; see A. H. Lawrence, *Duke Ellington and His World* (London: Routledge, 2001), 393–96.

25. UPI, "Nixon & Selassie Discuss Nigerian War and Mideast," *New York Times,* July 10, 1969, 4.

26. Memorandum of Conversation (Palmer), July 9, 1969, NSC: Country Files: Africa, Box 736, NPL.

27. Reuters, "Selassie Winds Up 5-Day Visit," *Washington Post,* July 10, 1969, A23.

28. AP, "Emperor Will Visit King Grave," *Wellsville Daily Reporter,* July 15, 1969, 5.

29. AP, "Ethiopian Leader Honors King," *San Antonio Express,* July 11, 1969, 13A.

30. AP, "Apollo 11 Countdown Continuing," *Cumberland News*, July 12, 1969, 1.

31. David D. Laitin, "Scientific Socialism, 1970–75," in *Somalia: A Country Study*, ed. Helen Chapin Metz (Washington, DC: Library of Congress, 1993).

32. Robert B. Semple Jr., "Nixon Gives 'Durable Peace' Plan with Greater Reliance on Allies; Cautions Russians on Middle East," *New York Times*, February 19, 1970, 1.

33. Charles Mohr, "Rogers, In Rabat, Opens 15-Day Trip to African Lands," *New York Times*, February 8, 1970, 1.

34. Charles Mohr, "An African Critic Exhorts Rogers," *New York Times*, February 13, 1970, 7.

35. Marvine Howe, "Nonaligned Parley Ends; Liberation Groups Backed," *New York Times*, September 11, 1970, 5.

36. Kathleen Teltsch, "Selassie Says UN Must Be Bolstered," *New York Times*, October 23, 1970, 3.

37. Henry Tanner, "Nixon, at the UN, Bids Moscow Keep Rivalry Peaceful," *New York Times*, October 24, 1970, 1.

38. AP, "UN Anniversary Session Reaffirms Peaceful Aims," *Arizona Republic*, October 25, 1970, 2A.

39. Henry Tanner, "UN Condemns Racism as Special Session Ends," *New York Times*, October 25, 1970, 1.

40. Dorothy McCardle, "Heads of State Dine Together in White House," *News Journal* (Mansfield, OH), October 26, 1970, 15.

41. Philip Shabecoff, "Trade Talks Set by Nixon and Sato," *New York Times*, October 25, 1970, 1.

42. Los Angeles Times–Washington Post News Service, "White House Entertains UN Visitors," *The Victoria Advocate*, October 25, 1970, 9A.

43. Tad Szulc, "Foreign Leaders Meet with Nixon," *New York Times*, October 26, 1970, 1; UPI, "Nixon Readies for Last Week of Campaign," *Delta Democrat-Times*, October 26, 1970, 1.

44. FRUS, 1969–1976, vol. E-5, part 1, Documents on Sub-Saharan Africa, 1969–1972, memorandum of conversation, Washington, October 25, 1970, 2:00 P.M., 1–3.

45. FRUS, 1969–1976, vol. E-5, part 1, Documents on Sub-Saharan Africa, 1969–1972, President's Assistant for National Security Affairs (Kissinger) to President Nixon, memorandum, January 20, 1971, 1–6.

46. Lt. Col. T. Edward Vestal, e-mail message to author, November 15, 2002.

47. Marshall Wright for the president's File, memorandum, June 21, 1971, re Meeting of RN with Ambassador E. Ross Adair, June 16, 1971, NSC: Country File: Africa, Box 736, NPL.

48. Spiro T. Agnew, *Go Quietly...or Else* (New York: Morrow, 1980), 34.

49. Haile Selassie to Richard Nixon, March 15, 1972, NSC: Country Files: Africa, Box 751, Ethiopia, NPL.

50. FRUS, 1969–1976, vol. E-6, Foreign Relations, 1969–1976, Documents on Africa, 1973–1976, memorandum of conversation, Washington, May 15, 1973, 11:03–12:13 P.M., 1–6.

51. Henry Kissinger to Richard Nixon, memorandum, Re May 15, 1973, May 12, 1973, NSC: Country Files: Africa, Box 915, NPL.

52. FRUS, 1969–1976, vol. E-6, Foreign Relations, 1969–1976, Documents on Africa, 1973–1976, memorandum of conversation, Washington, May 15, 1973, 11:03–12:13 P.M., 1–6.

53. Ibid.; "Callaway is Sworn in as Secretary of Army," *New York Times,* May 16, 1973, 53.

54. Dr. Minassie Haile, telephone interview with author, February 15, 2000.

55. Memorandum of conversation, Washington, May 15, 1973, Note 1.

56. "Nixon Talks at Selassie Fete," *Long Beach Press-Telegram,* May 16, 1973, A2.

57. Beale, 67.

58. Caroli, *1st Ladies,* 250.

59. Caroli, 251–52.

60. Carl Sferrazza Anthony, *First Ladies: The Saga of the Presidents' Wives and Their Power, 1961–1990* (New York: Morrow, 1991), 2: 195–96.

61. "Nixon Talks at Selassie Fete," *Long Beach Press-Telegram,* May 16, 1973, A2.

62. "Selassie Sees Free Africa by '83," *New York Times,* May 18, 1973, 45.

63. Thomas A. Johnson, "Selassie Calls for Africa Force," *New York Times,* May 25, 1973, 7.

64. Thomas A. Johnson, "African Nations Clash at Parley," *New York Times,* May 27, 1973, 8.

65. Reeves, *Nixon,* 15.

66. FRUS, 1969–1976, vol. E-6, Foreign Relations, 1969–1976, Documents on Africa, 1973–1976, telegram, Embassy in Ethiopia to Department of State, September 17, 1973, 1–4.

67. Embassy in Ethiopia to Department of State, telegram, November 10, 1973, NSC: Country Files: Africa, Box 736, NPL.

68. Spencer, *At Bay,* 323; Paulos Milkias, 194–213.

69. Department of State, Secretary's Staff Meeting, October 19, 1973.

70. Department of State, Secretary's Staff Meeting, January 7, 1974.

71. Washington Special Actions Group Meeting, April 24, 1974.

72. Korry to Secretary of State, memorandum, March 31, 1964, NSF Country File, Africa, General, vol. 1, 2/64–6/64, LBJL.

73. Department of State, Secretary's Staff Meeting, January 7, 1974.

74. Department of State, the Secretary's Principals and Regionals Staff Meeting, April 22, 1974.

75. Washington Special Actions Group Meeting, April 24, 1974.

EPILOGUE

1. Shinn, 43–44.

2. Said S. Samatar, "Somalia's Difficult Decade, 1980–90," *Somalia: A Country Study,* Helen Chapin Metz, (Washington, DC: Library of Congress, 1993).

3. David Greenberg, *Nixon's Shadow* (New York: Norton, 2003), xxv.

4. Newsweek Feature Service, "Haile Selassie Rules 19th Century Empire," *Arizona Republic,* July 6, 1969, B9.

5. See the thoughtful articles of Berihun Assfaw, mainly in Amharic; For example, "*Ase Haile Selassie ena Geizachew*" (Haile Selassie and his Time), 2003; "Emperor Haile Selassie, Sylvia E. Pankhurst and the Ethiopian Independence," 2004, http://www.ethiosun.com/sylviapank.pdf.

6. Oriana Fallaci, "Journey into the Private Universe of Haile Selassie," *Chicago Tribune,* June 24, 1973, sec. 2, 1.

7. See, for example, Erik H. Erikson and Robert Coles, *The Erik Erikson Reader* (New York: Norton, 2001); Jerrold M. Post, *Leaders and Their Followers in a Dangerous*

World: The Psychology of Political Behavior (Ithaca, NY: Cornell University Press, 2004).

8. Vamik D. Volkan, Norman Itzkowitz, and Andrew W. Dod, *Richard Nixon: a Psychobiography* (New York: Columbia University Press, 1997), 143.

9. Daniel Boorstin, *The Image: A Guide to Pseudo-Events in America* (New York: Vintage, 1987), 61–62.

10. See Joseph Epstein, "The Culture of Celebrity," in *In a Cardboard Belt!: Essays Personal, Literary, and Savage* (New York: Houghton-Mifflin, 2007), 356–72.

11. George Lakoff and Mark Johnson, *Metaphors We Live By* (Chicago: University of Chicago Press, 2003), 5.

12. Korry to JKF, June 28, 1963, National Security Files, Box 69, Ethiopia, General, 6/63–7/63, JFKL.

13. Gregory S. Parks and Jeffrey J. Rachlinski, "Opening Statement—Barack Obama, Implicit Bias, and the 2008 Election," Implicit Race Bias and the 2008 Presidential Election: *Much Ado About Nothing?*, *PENNumbra*, Philadelphia: University of Pennsylvania Law Review, 2010, http://www.pennumbra.com/debates/.

Selected Bibliography

Abbink, Jan. *Ethiopian Society & History: A Bibliography of Ethiopian Studies, 1957–1990.* Den Haag: CIP-Gegevens Koninklijke, 1990.

Abdi Sheik Abdi. *Divine Madness: Mohammed Abdulle Hassan.* London: Zed Books, 1993.

Agyeman-Duah, Baffour. *The United States and Ethiopia: Military Assistance and the Quest for Security, 1953–1993.* Lanham, MD: University Press of America, 1994.

Anthony, Carl Sferrazza. *First Ladies: The Saga of the Presidents' Wives and Their Power, 1961–1990,* vol. 2. New York: Morrow, 1991.

Bahru Zewde, *A History of Modern Ethiopia, 1855–1974.* Athens: Ohio University Press, 1991.

Barrett, Leonard E. *The Rastafarians.* Boston: Beacon Press, 1997.

Beale, Betty. *Power at Play.* Houston: Regency, 1993.

Bereket Habte Selassie. *The Crown and the Pen: The Memoirs of a Lawyer Turned Rebel.* Lawrenceville, NJ: Red Sea Press, 2007.

Berg, Robert J. and Jennifer Seymour Whitaker, eds. *Strategies for African Development.* Berkeley: University of California Press, 1986.

Black, Conrad. *Richard M. Nixon: A Life in Full.* New York: Public Affairs, 2007.

Boorstin, Daniel. *The Image: A Guide to Pseudo-Events in America.* New York: Vintage, 1987.

Bornet, Vaughn Davis. *The Presidency of Lyndon B. Johnson.* Lawrence: University of Kansas Press, 1984.

Brinkley, David. *Brinkley's Beat: People, Places, and Events that Shaped My Time.* New York: Random House, 2003.

Brown, Pamela S. and Fassil Yirgu. eds. *One House: The Battle of Adwa 1896—100 Years.* Chicago: Nyala, 1996.

Burdick, Eugene and William J. Lederer. *The Ugly American*. New York: Norton, 1999.

Caroli, Betty Boyd. *First Ladies*. Oxford: Oxford University Press, 1995.

Clapham, Christopher. *Haile-Selassie's Government*. London: Longmans, 1969.

Daniel Kendie. *The Five Dimensions of the Eritrean Conflict, 1941–2004: Deciphering the Political Puzzle*. Gaithersburg, MD: Signature, 2005.

Daniel Teferra. *Economic Development and Nation Building in Ethiopia*. Lanham, MD: University Press of America, 2005.

Daniel Teferra. *Lessons of Peace and Development: Gurage Entrepreneurship in Ethiopia*. Lanham, MD: University Press of America, 2008.

Erlich, Haggai. *Ethiopia and the Challenge of Independence*. Boulder, CO: Lynne Rienner, 1986.

Gebru Tareke. *The Ethiopian Revolution: War in the Horn of Africa*. New Haven, CT: Yale University Press, 2009.

Getachew Metaferia. *Ethiopia and the United States: History, Diplomacy, and Analysis*. New York: Algora, 2009.

Greenberg, David. *Nixon's Shadow*. New York: Norton, 2003.

Greenfield, Richard. *Ethiopia: A New Political History*. London: Pall Mall, 1965.

Haile Selassie. *My Life and Ethiopia's Progress, 1892–1937*, vol. 2. Edited by Harold G. Marcus. East Lansing: Michigan State University Press, 1994.

Haile Selassie. *My Life and Ethiopia's Progress, 1892–1937*, vol. 1. Edited and translated by Edward Ullendorff. Oxford: Oxford University Press, 1976.

Hanson, Herbert M. and Della Hanson. *For God and Emperor*. Nampa, ID: Pacific Press Publishing Association, 1958.

Ikenberry, G. John. *After Victory: Institutions, Strategic Restraint, and the Rebuilding of Order after Major Wars*. Princeton, NJ: Princeton University Press, 2000.

Indrias Getachew. *Beyond the Throne: The Enduring Legacy of Emperor Haile Selassie I*. Addis Ababa: Shama, 2001.

Jerry L. Gill. *A History of International Programs at Oklahoma State University*. Stillwater: Oklahoma State University Press, 1991.

Johnson, Lady Bird. *A White House Diary [by] Lady Bird Johnson*. New York: Holt, Rinehart and Winston, 1970.

Keller, Edmund J. *Revolutionary Ethiopia: From Empire to People's Republic*. Bloomington: Indiana University Press, 1991.

Kahn, David. *The Code Breakers*. New York: Simon & Schuster, 1996.

Kaplan, Robert D. *Surrender or Starve: Travels in Ethiopia, Sudan, Somalia, and Eritrea*. New York: Vintage, 2003.

Kapuściński, Ryszard. *The Emperor: Downfall of an Autocrat*. New York: Vintage, 1983.

Lefebvre, Jeffrey A. *Arms for the Horn: U.S. Security Policy in Ethiopia and Somalia, 1953–1991*. Pittsburg: University of Pittsburg Press, 1992.

Levine, Donald N. *Wax & Gold: Tradition and Innovation in Ethiopian Culture*. Chicago: University of Chicago Press, 1965.

Lewis, Herbert S. *Jimma Abba Jifar, an Oromo Monarchy: Ethiopia, 1830–1932*. Lawrenceville, NJ: Red Sea Press, 2001.

Lockot, Hans Wilhelm. *The Mission: The Life, Reign, and Character of Haile Selassie I*. New York: Palgrave Macmillan, 1990.

Louis, Wm. Roger. *The British Empire in the Middle East, 1945–1951*. Oxford: Clarendon Press, 1984.

Louis, Wm. Roger. *Imperialism at Bay*. Oxford: Oxford University Press, 1977.

Marcus, Harold G. *Haile Selassie I: The Formative Years, 1892–1936*. Lawrenceville, NJ: Red Sea Press, 1987.

Marcus, Harold G. *A History of Ethiopia*. Berkeley: University of California Press, 2002.

Marcus, Harold G. *The Life and Times of Menelik II: Ethiopia, 1844–1913*. Lawrenceville, NJ: Red Sea Press, 1995.

Marcus, Harold G. *Politics of Empire: Ethiopia, Great Britain, and the United States, 1941–1974*. Lawrenceville, NJ: Red Sea, 1995.

Marshall, S.L.A. *Pork Chop Hill*. New York: Berkley, 2000.

McCann, James C. *People of the Plow: An Agricultural History of Ethiopia, 1800–1990*. Madison: University of Wisconsin Press, 1995.

Messay Kebede. *Survival and Modernization, Ethiopia's Enigmatic Present: A Philosophical Discourse*. Lawrenceville, NJ: Red Sea Press, 1999.

Mockler, Anthony. *Haile Selassie's War: The Italian-Ethiopian Campaign, 1935–1941*. New York: Random House, 1984.

Moorehead, Alan. *The Blue Nile*. New York: Harper Perennial, 2000.

Moorehead, Alan. *Mediterranean Front*. London: Hamish Hamilton, 1941.

Morell, Virginia. *Blue Nile: Ethiopia's River of Magic*. Washington, DC: National Geographic, 2001.

Mosley, Leonard. *Haile Selassie: The Conquering Lion*. London: Weidenfeld & Nicolson, 1964.

Munro-Hay, Stuart and Richard Pankhurst. *World Bibliographical Series,* vol. 179: Ethiopia. Oxford: ABC-Clio, 1995.

Negussay Ayele. *Ethiopia and the United States*. Santa Clara, CA: Ocopy.com, 2003.

Negussay Ayele. *In Search of the DNA of the Ethiopia-Eritrea Problem*. San Diego: MediaETHIOPIA, 2003.

Nye, Joseph S. Jr. *Soft Power: The Means to Success in World Politics*. New York: Public Affairs, 2004.

Nye, Joseph S. Jr. *Understanding International Conflicts*. New York: Pearson/Longman, 2005.

Ofeansky, Thomas P. and LaVerle Berry, eds. *Ethiopia: A Country Study*. Washington DC: Federal Research Division of the U.S. Library of Congress, 1993.

Oklahoma State University in Ethiopia: Terminal Report 1952–1968. Stillwater: Oklahoma State University Press, 1969.

Ottaway, David and Marina Ottaway. *Ethiopia: Empire in Revolution*. New York: Africana Publishing, 1978.

Pankhurst, Richard. *The Ethiopians: A History*. Oxford: Blackwell, 2002.

Pankhurst, Richard. *A Social History of Ethiopia*. Trenton, NJ: Red Sea Press, 1992.

Paulos Milkias. *Ethiopia: A Comprehensive Bibliography*. Boston: G. K. Hall, 1989.

Paulos Milkias. *Haile Selassie, Western Education and Political Revolution in Ethiopia*. Youngstown, NY: Cambria, 2006.

Paulos Milkias and Getachew Metaferia, eds. *The Battle of Adwa—Reflections on Ethiopia's Historic Victory Against European Colonialism*. New York: Algora, 2005.

Perlstein, Rick. *Nixonland: The Rise of a President and the Fracturing of America*. New York: Scribner, 2008.

Prouty, Chris and Eugene Rosenfield. *Historical Dictionary of Ethiopia*. London: Scarecrow Press, 1982.

Ras Nathaniel. *50th Anniversary of His Imperial Majesty Haile Selassie I: First Visit to the United States, 1954–2004*. Bloomington, IN: Trafford, 2006.

Rasmuson, John R. *History of Kagnew Station and American Forces in Eritrea*. Asmara: Il Poligrafico, 1973.

Reeves, Richard. *President Kennedy: Profile of Power*. New York: Simon & Schuster, 1994.

Reeves, Richard. *President Nixon, Alone in the White House*. New York: Simon & Schuster, 2002.

Sandford, Christine. *The Lion of Judah Hath Prevailed*. London: Frontline Books, 1999.

Schlesinger, Arthur M. Jr. *A Thousand Days: JFK in the White House*. Boston: Houghton Mifflin, 1965.

Schwab, Peter, ed. *Ethiopia and Haile Selassie*. New York: Facts on File, 1972.

Shirreff, David. *Barefeet and Bandoliers: Wingate, Sandford, the Patriots and the Part They Played in the Liberation of Ethiopia*. New York: Palgrave Macmillan, 1995.

Shumet Sishagne. *Unionists & Separatists: The Vagaries of Ethio-Eritrean relation, 1941–1991*. Hollywood, CA: Tsehai, 2007.

Skinner, Robert P., Aurelia E. Brazeal, and David H. Shinn. *The 1903 Skinner Mission to Ethiopia and a Century of American-Ethiopian Relations*. Hollywood, CA: Tsehai, 2004.

Spencer, John H. *Ethiopia at Bay: A Personal Account of the Haile Selassie Years*. Hollywood, CA: Tsehai, 2006.

Spencer, John H. *Ethiopia, the Horn of Africa, and U.S. Policy*. Cambridge, MA: Institute for Foreign Policy Analysis, 1977.

Stossel, Scott. *Sarge, the Life and Times of Sargent Shriver*. Washington, DC: Smithsonian Books, 2004.

Teshale Tibebu. *The Making of Modern Ethiopia, 1896–1974*. Trenton, NJ: Red Sea Press, 1995.

Tirfe Mammo. *The Paradox of Africa's Poverty: The Role of Indigenous Knowledge*. Lawrenceville, NJ: Red Sea Press, 1999.

Ullendorff, Edward. *The Ethiopians: An Introduction to Country and People*. London: Oxford University Press, 1960.

Vestal, Theodore M. *Ethiopia: A Post-Cold War African State*. Westport, CT: Praeger, 1999.

Volkan, Vamik D., Norman Itzkowitz, and Andrew W. Dod. *Richard Nixon: a Psychobiography*. New York: Columbia University Press, 1997.

Waugh, Evelyn. *Waugh in Abyssinia (From Our Own Correspondent)*. Baton Rouge: Louisiana State University Press, 2007.

Wrong, Michela. *I Didn't Do It for You*. New York: HarperCollins, 2005.

Index